Avoiding Emotions, L

Avoiding Emotions, Living Emotions explores the psychoanalytic encounter and examines how emotions are formed and experienced by both the patient and analyst. The author narrates key theoretical concepts through the presentation of clinical material from adult and child analysis and emphasizes the importance of being able to foster these narrations.

Offering new insights into how the mind works, topics of discussion include:

- Bion's thinking and its fertilization: clinical implications
- variations on transference and countertransference
- image and narration.

Providing the reader with clinical exercises and case reports, this book will be of great interest to psychoanalysts, psychotherapists and psychiatrists, as well as being a helpful tool in psychoanalytic and psychotherapeutic work on a day-to-day basis.

Antonino Ferro is a Training and Supervising Analyst in the Italian Psychoanalytic Society, the American Psychoanalytic Association and the International Psychoanalytical Association. He has been a visiting professor of psychoanalysis in various institutions in Europe, North America, South America and Australia. He received the Sigourney Award in 2007.

THE NEW LIBRARY OF PSYCHOANALYSIS
General Editor: Alessandra Lemma

The New Library of Psychoanalysis was launched in 1987 in association with the Institute of Psychoanalysis, London. It took over from the International Psychoanalytical Library which published many of the early translations of the works of Freud and the writings of most of the leading British and Continental psychoanalysts.

The purpose of the New Library of Psychoanalysis is to facilitate a greater and more widespread appreciation of psychoanalysis and to provide a forum for increasing mutual understanding between psychoanalysts and those working in other disciplines such as the social sciences, medicine, philosophy, history, linguistics, literature and the arts. It aims to represent different trends both in British psychoanalysis and in psychoanalysis generally. The New Library of Psychoanalysis is well placed to make available to the English-speaking world psychoanalytic writings from other European countries and to increase the interchange of ideas between British and American psychoanalysts. Through the *Teaching Series*, the New Library of Psychoanalysis now also publishes books that provide comprehensive, yet accessible, overviews of selected subject areas aimed at those studying psychoanalysis and related fields such as the social sciences, philosophy, literature and the arts.

The Institute, together with the British Psychoanalytical Society, runs a low-fee psychoanalytic clinic, organizes lectures and scientific events concerned with psychoanalysis and publishes the *International Journal of Psychoanalysis*. It also runs the only UK training course in psychoanalysis which leads to membership of the International Psychoanalytical Association – the body which preserves internationally agreed standards of training, of professional entry, and of professional ethics and practice for psychoanalysis as initiated and developed by Sigmund Freud. Distinguished members of the Institute have included Michael Balint, Wilfred Bion, Ronald Fairbairn, Anna Freud, Ernest Jones, Melanie Klein, John Rickman and Donald Winnicott.

Previous general editors have included David Tuckett, who played a very active role in the establishment of the New Library. He was followed as general editor by Elizabeth Bott Spillius, who was in turn followed by Susan Budd and then by Dana Birksted-Breen.

Current Members of the Advisory Board include Liz Allison, Giovanna di Ceglie, Rosemary Davies and Richard Rusbridger.

Previous Members of the Advisory Board include Christopher Bollas, Ronald Britton, Catalina Bronstein, Donald Campbell, Sara Flanders, Stephen Grosz, John Keene, Eglé Laufer, Alessandra Lemma, Juliet Mitchell, Michael Parsons, Rosine Jozef Perelberg, Mary Target and David Taylor.

The current General Editor of the New Library of Psychoanalysis is Alessandra Lemma, but this book was initiated and edited by Dana Birksted-Breen, former General Editor.

ALSO IN THIS SERIES

TITLES IN THE NEW LIBRARY OF PSYCHOANALYSIS TEACHING SERIES

Avoiding Emotions, Living Emotions

Antonino Ferro

Translated by Ian Harvey

The translation of this work has been partly funded by SEPS
Segretariato Europeo per le Pubblicazioni Scientifiche

Via Val d'Aposa 7 – 40123 Bologna – Italy
seps@seps.it – www.seps.it

LONDON AND NEW YORK

Title of the original Italian edition: Evitare le emozioni, vivere le emozioni
© 2007 Raffaello Cortina Editore, Milan

First published 2011
by Routledge
27 Church Road, Hove, East Sussex BN3 2FA

Simultaneously published in the USA and Canada
by Routledge
711 Third Avenue, New York NY 10017

Routledge is an imprint of the Taylor & Francis Group, an Informa Business

© 2011 Antonino Ferro

English translation © 2011 Ian Harvey

British Library Cataloguing in Publication Data
A catalogue record for this book is available from the British Library

Library of Congress Cataloging in Publication Data
Ferro, Antonino, 1947–
[Evitare le emozioni, vivere le emozioni. English]
Avoiding emotions, living emotions/Antonino Ferro; translated by Ian Harvey.
  p. cm.
Original Italian edition published as: Evitare le emozioni, vivere le emozioni,
©2007 Raffaello Cortina Editore, Milan.
Includes bibliographical references.
ISBN 978–0–415–55502–9 (hbk.) — ISBN 978–0–415–55503–6 (pbk.)
1. Transference (Psychology)   2. Emotions.   3. Psychoanalysis.
4. Psychotherapist and patient. I. Title.
RC489.T73F47 2011
616.89'17—dc22

2010048786

ISBN: 978–0–415–55502–9 (hbk)
ISBN: 978–0–415–55503–6 (pbk)

Typeset in Bembo by RefineCatch Limited, Bungay, Suffolk
Paperback cover design by Sandra Heath
Printed by TJ International Ltd, Padstow, Cornwall

Contents

1

Avoiding emotions, living emotions

One of our greatest difficulties as a species concerns our ability to experience emotions, a difficulty caused by defects in our mental development. The experiencing of emotions depends on a great deal of constant work, which in turn presupposes the integrity of the apparatus that allows them to be assimilated, managed and contained (Ferro 1999c, 2002h, 2006a).

Avoidance

We can compare protoemotions to 'stocks of pinheads' (I am referring to the sensoriality of which they are made) that have undergone various degrees of processing. Even in the best of situations (in the case of well-functioning minds) there is a superabundance of them, and extraordinary demonstrations of this can be found in group phenomena.

Without for the moment wanting to describe the various possible degrees of 'cooking', or of amalgability and containability, of protoemotional states, I would like to offer some reflections on how the AVOIDANCE of emotions is one of the main activities of our mind.

When one modality clearly prevails over the others, it becomes a symptom.

Generally we can say that we have evacuative mechanisms, the projection outwards of these 'stocks of pinheads', phenomena such as paranoia, schizophrenia, hallucinations, delusions, and then in some ways also different forms of autism.

We can evacuate into the body of the individual in the form of psychosomatic illnesses or into the social body in such forms as character disorders, criminality and collective stupidity.

Protoemotional states can be contained in spaces in the mind. Aggregates of compressed protoemotions form phobias if the strategy deployed is one of avoidance; obsessiveness, if the strategy is control; hypochondria, if the strategy involves confining it to one organ of the body; and so on.

It must be repeated that avoidance is at all events an attitude to be found in any mind. Certainly we need to reflect further on Bleger's concept of the agglutinated nucleus and Ogden's concept of the autistic-contiguous nucleus.

To exemplify this point further, let us look at some operating strategies deployed to avoid emotions (or rather their non-metabolized precursors) in various clinical situations.

One central modality is *narcissism*.

A patient with an extremely narcissistic structure who works as the manager of a finance group has two dreams.

In the first he covers the whole distance from his home to my studio, a mile or so, in a straight line following a rope stretched out along the road. He sees and watches everyone from above (his intelligence has always been his strong point).

However, the real reason he does this, he explains to me, is to avoid the cars that speed along the road and which could run him over. In other words, emotions have such a kinetic force that they could run him over. Keeping a safe distance from every protoemotion saves him from being hit and from losing the power of thought (keeping the thread).

The second dream is even more telling. He is the captain of a galleon where everything has to work perfectly. A team made up of members of the crew constantly does the rounds to make sure that the sails are immaculate, that there are absolutely no leaks, and so on.

In these conditions the ship sails on happily.

If even the slightest thing is found out of place, catastrophe will ensue. The sails will rip, a small leak will lead to the ship sinking. He would come up for court martial, followed by dishonourable discharge, and perhaps even a death sentence.

In Gigi's life everything must be perfect: work, his children's marks at school, invitations to dinner parties with friends. Even the slightest flaw forebodes catastrophe. But why?

Because – this is the reply we construct together – imperfection activates emotions and these are difficult to manage; that is to say, there is no team on board to manage and deal with emergencies and the emotional winds or waves they generate. The effort Gigi makes to ensure that everything is perfect is truly enormous, but it is nothing compared to what he would have to do if new and unpredictable emotions were activated.

I think that autistic behaviour often also has the same root: the constancy of every detail, the repetition of every gesture in exactly the same way, the miniaturization of emotions (bonsai emotions, as one patient put it) all serve the avoidance of emotional impacts which would otherwise be impossible to manage.

More in general, why is it that often we do not live burning passions but we extinguish them in routine, weariness, repetition, boredom, the intellectualization of emotional lava? Simply to keep circulating emotions ticking over. Carmelo prefers the tired routine with a wife he has not been in love with for a long time rather than venturing past the Pillars of Hercules which appear in a dream at the moment he meets a female colleague who might interest him. Basically he prefers the known familiarity of domesticated aspects of himself rather than setting off in search of possible new emotional dimensions.

The strategies people invent are extremely diverse. One need only think of anorexia, in which the split-off and intolerable parts (or protoemotions) are projected backwards, but are 'seen' with a kind of scanner that enables the anorexic to see behind her back 'the weight' of the split-off protoemotional states that present themselves as heavy and enormous (and the anorexic sees herself as fat because, considering the split-off functions she perceives, she is!).

I have always maintained that analysts, or psychoanalytic thinking, can only exist if there is a patient and a setting. However, allow me to contradict myself with allowance from Manzoni (who speaks generously of 'that jumble of the human heart'): I believe that macro-social phenomena have the same function of 'stopping' intolerable emotional states.

One need only think of fanaticism, of all the guarantors of truth and certainty, and of the function of every religion: to think of ourselves as 'ludus naturae' without a why, without a before and without a where is too frightening, it activates too many emotions. Religion really is the opium of the people – but in the medical sense that opium is an antidote to intolerable pain, the realization namely that the meaning of life is just living it and nothing more, and that there is nothing in life that transcends it.

3

I could carry on talking about collective defences against emotions triggered by anything that disturbs the 'minimal emotional regime', and in this context one need only think of racism, dogmatism, the delusion of faith-based constructions, wars, and general stupidity, but I can only return to myself and to my specific situation: the consulting room.

A patient has not left the house for ten years and spends his time alone at his computer. He has a phobia of showing his face which is covered with hideous pimples and he avoids any contact or meeting anyone other than his parents.

Several attempts at therapy have been unsuccessful because of his immediate denial or perhaps because of the inability of some of the psychiatrists and psychoanalysts he has consulted to recognize the scale of the problem.

Then Fausto has the good fortune to meet a new analyst who reports the case to me in supervision. He addresses the problem in the right way, both with Fausto and with me: he gives no importance to the 'fact'. Then, near the end of our meeting, he also gives me the telling piece of information:

Fausto doesn't have a face covered with pimples; in fact, he has a particularly smooth skin. I immediately think of the poster for the film *Lord of War*, where the protagonist's face is partly made up of bullets, shells, cartridges. I imagine their tips 'pressing' under Fausto's skin giving the impressions of pimples.

It would be easy to think of these 'bullets' in terms of aggressiveness, whereas to me they are explosive protoemotional states on the point of being evacuated, awaiting only the mental readiness of the other to find a place where they can be contained and transformed.

Some time later, during a second supervision of this case, Fausto is relieved to tell me that he had started to leave the house after his father had taken him rifle shooting in the woods. The mental apparatus of the analyst is the rifle which allows for the modulated explosion of emotions in a way that is all in all contained in a reliable 'combustion chamber'.

Let me digress slightly here: transference can be understood as the opening of a channel of communication for the passage of bullets into the mind of the other, where the transformation process, the alphabetization of those 'bullets' and, if we want, also a contained explosion can be set off.

Needless to say, in this case the mind of the analyst will tend to boycott this infection, since it involves dealing with a more intense protoemotional level.

This boycott is mostly staged using inadequate theories that filter the reception and timing of what the patient wants to communicate: this I think is one of the reasons behind a certain inertia in psychoanalytic theories which Bion in the last seminars he held at Tavistock (Bion 2005) did not hesitate to describe as paraphrenia. The whole point of such theories is to allow us to hold on to something out of a fear that our knowledge is inadequate: they are a kind of raft that keeps us from drowning in anxiety.

Some simplifications are possible: one is the view present in many schools of thought that psychoanalysis is a therapy that is only suitable in cases of neurosis (the corollary being its alleged ineffectiveness in more severe pathologies); another is the fear that the 'monster beneath' many psychosomatic diseases might jump out and require the 'face to face' approach suggested by the otherwise brilliant school of French psychosomaticists, who seem not to realize that continuing to photograph Loch Ness (face to face) is the best way to avoid (or to ensure?) Nessie emerging from the depths of the loch and in fact the best way to secure protection from this fear.

But also the extreme use of theory in sessions, analysis as a package tour – as can often be seen at the point when an analyst becomes a member of the association – where everything is already known (the primal scene, castration anxieties, fantasies of exclusion, (weekend) separation anxiety interpreted *ad nauseum*, filler reconstructions made in order to make ends meet, etc.) or bringing the patient back to the model clearly present in the mind of the analyst (whatever model it is) – these are all just various ways of staying this side of the Pillars of Hercules I mentioned earlier.

The rumen

Another central assertion for me is that if it is true that one of our mind's activities (working downhill) is to protect ourselves from the emotions, it is also true that there is another function (working uphill) that tries to re-establish contact with what has been expelled or segregated or at any rate placed at a distance.

Often career choices, choices in love, sometimes entire threads of life have this rumen-like function, that is, their purpose is to restore contact with protoemotions, with the 'stock of pinheads' that have been evacuated, split off, made lethargic, isolated, or whatever.

A patient who has been suffering from serious constipation asks for an analysis. Her condition has also meant that she has been hospitalized repeatedly for 'intestinal blockage'.

She also describes a family situation made up of 'emotional tsunamis', of violent accusations and quarrels. She has a depressed sister who hardly ever speaks, except during periods of manic verbosity.

The father seems to have led a double life: an irreproachable family man, he was discovered to have been a regular participant at orgies involving high-class call-girls and drugs.

It seems clear that Laura's world is split between two modes: on the one hand, hypercontinence that paralyzes all emotion, and on the other, total evacuative incontinence of all kinds of emotion.

When Laura began planning her analysis she gave up her idea of following in her grandfather's footsteps as a notary, choosing instead to become a criminal lawyer.

This career choice becomes the 'rumen' which allows her to come closer to discrete quanta of protoemotions through her profession: her job brings her into constant contact with young offenders, drug addicts, immigrants, thieves, blackmailers, all of whom share a basic sense of desperation that is acted out in various ways. The work carried out in the analysis – containing, judging, condemning, understanding and defending these 'characters' – is narrated through her career choice, which becomes a way of taking back through the window what had been driven out through the door.

Although Martha could have had a satisfactory relationship with her husband, sexual frigidity was her way of freezing primitive states of wild protoemotions. She froze them in the same way as she froze her 'sexual' relationship with that area of her mind. The alternative would have been to be abused and 'raped' by these uncontrollable emotions.

At some point during her analysis Martha decides, after years away from the subject, to put her degree in psychology to proper use and to work with abused children who were the victims of all kinds of violence. Again, for Martha the 'professional' choice becomes 'the rumen' which enables her to re-appropriate her frozen sensory stocks.

A point I shall never tire of making is that the violence, the explosiveness, the uncontainability of emotions should never be confused with aggression. Aggression is a normal faculty of the species which in my view can as such never be in excess. What is in excess is the pressure coming from protoemotional states that plead to be collected, contained and transformed.

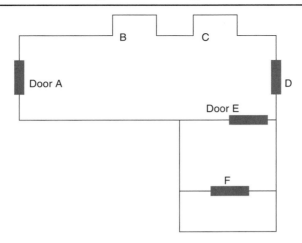

Figure 1.1 Diagram of a small flat.

One day a patient told me a story which I think expresses this notion very well. He even provided me with a drawing of the location to make it easier to understand.

He was on holiday in Spain with a couple of friends and his girlfriend. The only place they had found to stay was beside a beach some distance from the nearest town in a large farmhouse that was being developed into a hotel complex. They were taken to a small flat in one wing of the complex. There was a door (A) leading to a long corridor off which were the doors to a kitchen (B) and a bathroom (C). There was also a door (D) which no one told them about and then door (E), which gave access to a room with two beds, and then a door (F) to another room with two beds (Figure 1.1).

Tired out after a long day and an evening in a nearby country inn, they went back to spend the night in the flat. They closed door A, securing it with a metal bar because they were aware they were in a very isolated spot.

In the middle of the night they are awakened by screams, shouts and banging on door A. They are very scared; they approach the door, which is evidently on the point of giving way under the pressure of what appears to be a rowdy horde of people. Frightened, they try to say something, but their words are met with more screaming; various incomprehensible languages resound. In panic they lock themselves in the bedroom and barricade door E, moments before door A is broken down by the howling mass. This 'mass' bursts in furiously like a river in flood that sweeps away everything in its path. Screaming and shouting, they try to break down the second door but eventually give up.

7

Only the next morning do they learn that door D was the entrance to the home of the last farmers still living on the farm who had left their children asleep at home while they went to a party in the nearby village. On finding door A closed they were seized by panic, fearing that someone wanted to harm their children. Terrified, they had broken down every obstacle that stood between them and their children.

Independently of how the story was worked through in the session, it seems to show how emotional urgency lies behind much behaviour that may on the surface appear aggressive.

Protoemotional or emotional forces are often like tsunamis; they cause destruction but are not aggressive, nor I would say are they even destructive. Their effects come from the uncontainability of the forces involved and sometimes because of inadequate embankments or insufficient storm drains or the erosion of coral reefs (defence?).

Transferring emotions

One possible way of working is to ask oneself the question, after a patient has spoken: to which internal object projected on to the analyst is he talking. A very clear example is provided by Guignard (2006), who tells of one of her Russian supervisees to whom a patient from a different ethnic group said 'Russian cow!' Guignard asked the supervisee what object she thought the patient was talking to. Her reply was: to the mother.

Then it was clear that by talking to the object mother projected on to the analyst and giving the cow milk, the patient was expressing her envy and hatred towards a nourishing mother. Guignard then went on to explain the similarities and differences between objects and people.

That would not be the way I see it; I would ask to look at the previous session to find out why the patient is angry with her analyst, what happened, what happened there, which makes sense of her anger – without any ready answers, simply based on what we know about cows, milk, mothers, and objects.

I would act like Isabella in the fable by Carla Muschio (2005); I wouldn't just go down to the cellar, but would look in the cellar for the door that opens up new and unexpected worlds. I am speaking of an analysis that looks to the future, focusing not on the past and on content, but on the transformation of the patient's apparatus for thinking (I care little about what).

> At the first session after two days missed because of national holidays, Marina recounts a dream in which there was a door or rather two doors that opened and there stood Mr Lanti, who could easily break into her house. She was terrified. But her husband was there, too, and much to her relief he closed two other doors.
>
> She then tells me what an enormous effort it is for her to come to Pavia because her older sister lives here. Her sister tells her things that she finds intolerable; every time it is a bad experience, the sister recounts memories of their childhood, things that should remain unsaid.
>
> I keep to the manifest text and say that she seems to be afraid of her incontinent sister who instead of receiving her and her concerns swamps her with her own.
>
> She says this was her experience of her older sister as a child (the sister performed the role of mother after her real mother had suddenly fallen in love with a wealthy ship-owner and abandoned husband and children) who used to tell her that. . . . But even more it was the experience of her husband, who had been abused by his grandfather, or at least that is what he fears may have happened. (Of course I think of all these communications as relevant to my contributions, which are perceived by various characters in the field as incontinence.)
>
> I tell her that I fully understand the suffering that this adult incontinence produces in her and her husband. It is like putting dirty laundry in a washing machine which rather than cleaning it makes it even dirtier. That's precisely what happens, she adds.
>
> At this point I think I can venture an interpretation. It seem to me that now, unlike in the early days of analysis when the sessions missed were a source of suffering, it is the other way round: the sessions that take place are a source of suffering and I am the 'anti' person who says things against her, things that rob her of her well-being.
>
> A sense of well-being was what I gave her when I closed the door of my studio on official holidays. She confirms this intervention in full, adding however that she still thinks it's worth coming.
>
> I want to say at this point that in my view things are not getting worse. On the contrary, I now feel that I can touch some nodal points. But I make a slip and say: 'Certainly things are not any better . . . no, no, I mean worse!' 'There we are, with your slip you have ruined my day, my week.

I will be tormented thinking that things are getting worse than before, that I am making no progress, that I am going backwards.' I say: 'Here I am, the "anti" person, I've flooded you with anguish, I am a presence that makes you feel bad.'

'It's just that there is always another side that comes out,' Marina replies, 'just like with the "anti" person and her husband.' I say in my turn: 'It is even more true that I feel bad if you say you are even happier when we do not meet, but apart from my regret, it is much better now that you can express this discomfort about the meeting, meeting with me, with another human being.'

'But don't you understand that we are here now?' Marina continues. 'It's as if you now had had the courage to act like a heart surgeon, you took my heart in your hand; or like a pulmonologist who finally manages to drain through a tube a mediastinal or subphrenic abscess which had caused incredibly high fever, seemingly without cause.'

The session continues, touching on different scenes involving parents and children from the present and from the 'past'.

I conclude the session by saying that now the problem of 'influence' seemed clearer. This was the problem that had long haunted her in her life, that is, not knowing to what extent her decisions were hers and to what extent they were induced.

Analytic sessions appear to me to be like a dream of the mind where different stories from different times and places of the field land, are diffracted, overlap. The shared experience is where circular emotional states, feelings and thoughts are allowed to circulate with the analyst (also a place in the field) in the dual polarity described by Riolo (1983), namely guaranteeing and safeguarding the setting and the exchanges, and promoting a dream-like activity on the part of the pair. The session becomes a shared, co-narrated, co-acted dream where stories, transformations, insights come to life – but also above all aptitudes, aptitudes to dream, to transform into reverie, into emotion, into image, into the ability to dream what has taken the pressing form of an abscess of sensoriality to which there was no access.

Each session is a pearl, a bead on the necklace/rosary that paves the way through all the various mysteries not to contents but to the ability to go on the journey back and forth which is the Star Trek of our lives. Or to put it another way, analysis leads to the development of the mind, the ability to dream, to feel, to think. Then content is totally free.

It makes little difference to me whether a patient goes through his entire analysis deploying an infantile scenario or Westerns or science fiction or his 'workplace'. The driving force of the story is the need to find a space–time in which to develop the capacity to think and say that which cannot be said.

In this sense transference is also the transference of these skills from the analyst to the field and from the field to the patient, who in turn brings along the fuel and the equipment for this process.

At the session after the one described above, Marina starts off by talking about a patient of hers who has great emotional outbursts that are like oscillations and are often indistinguishable from incontinent outbursts.

She goes on talking about her patient, about the fact that for him 'the death of his parents' was a traumatic event and that similarly for his wife, 'her sister's death' was like being hit and run over by a train.

Then she continues talking about her own experience of not being understood and the feeling that this is enough to rob her of joy and sometimes even of the will to live. Now I feel I can say that perhaps when she feels not understood, it is precisely there that she feels overwhelmed by emotions she cannot contain, it is there that she is a desperate orphan.

She fully agrees on this point and then tells me that near my studio she had seen posters for a film version of *Oliver Twist* which she decided to go and see because that's how she feels when her husband does not understand her. How can she fix it? How can she cope with these frustrations without being overwhelmed?

I say that with time we will have some larger pots which will enable us to contain the emotional ingredients that are now brimming over. She says: 'There you go again. You've ruined my day! You shouldn't give me culinary examples, I hate culinary examples, only my mother knew how to cook. I cannot cook, I hate cooking.' But maybe, I add, 'the mother who ran away' who we have spoken about so often is saying something not only about the tragic loss of her mother as a child but also about all the feminine aspects of herself she felt she had to abandon because they were connected to her mother. She had had to avoid all rivalry with her because otherwise she would have felt guilty about her mother's flight (in this way I implicitly interpret her difficulty in carrying out her work plans, which she fears set off rivalry with me, by postdating it in history and putting it in a setting different from the current one).

She is touched by this intervention; she says that she may not know how to cook but she can knit, she is a dab hand with a knitting needle. On the other hand, however, it might also be nice to cook.

At this point she tells me that the house next door to hers is being sold and that she and her husband have decided to buy it. It is expensive but worth it: it will allow them to expand their house from 100 to 160 square metres and there will be room for everyone.

It's the working together on the emotions present in the field, weaving and re-weaving them, which fosters the development of the container/contained through reverie, through unison. That is, all the transformative transitions made session after session lead to an enlargement of the house and the ability to knit and weave the protoemotions into pictures, stories, namely the development of a range of skills, not least the ability to contain and to dream. Transference is what continually brings with it protoemotions, the protocontents that will be the raw materials of such transformations.

One thing I would like to stress is that it is not easy to be in a position of PS without persecution, that is, to draw on one's own negative capability before interpreting. Having to wait calmly can be made easier by connecting up with the manifest content, inwardly formulating unspoken trial transference interpretations, making connections with the countertransference and having confidence in one's method.

Living emotions

Experiencing emotions is the culmination of a series of operations. Sometimes the first step is when a story starts to take shape in the mind of the analyst, who begins to create broader scenes in which previously split-off functions can come to life again, at least somewhere in the field. As it happens, the field is always highly contagious; there is nowhere in the field that does not end up infecting all the others.

There's no gazelle without a tiger: shyness and persecution
Louise is a lovely girl with a meek and slightly jaded air about her.

She studies Italian and is very fond of detective stories, especially of the Agatha Christie type where the culprit is found out after a process of investigation.

12

For years she has suffered from agoraphobia and social phobia; she can't appear in a bathing costume, always puts on two pairs of underpants, sweats excessively and has a thrusting jaw. She also suffers from panic attacks. She displays a number of obsessive symptoms, such as repeated checking of doors and windows out of fear of intrusion by strangers.

She has cleaning rituals that involve having repeated baths and showers every day. She washes her hair daily and is always applying deodorant.

She prefers vegetarian food and never eats 'meat on the bone or entrails'.

At night she must always sleep alone 'because she is afraid she opens her mouth in a strange way'.

There are enough indications here to suggest to me the existence of a split-off part, which I think of as a panther, a tiger, a wolf. I am reminded of the film *The Tiger Woman* and then of Verga's short story 'The She-Wolf'.

I think I can already suggest a hypothesis at this point: Louise is persecuted by her split-off part, or rather by the emotions that come together in the split-off part that seems to refer to the image of a wild beast, where emotions are not manageable. Louise is afraid that her 'secret' would be found out; hence the showers, the cleaning habits that purge her of these continually re-forming emotions. They keep these emotions away from the door, emotions which if they were scattered and sprayed outwards would say something about her and pollute an outside world which takes on tiger-like qualities and becomes dangerous, threatening.

The gazelle must keep running to escape the tiger. She does this by trying to appear perfect, but it makes her sweat!

Louise tells me that she has found a man she likes but who causes her many problems. I cannot believe my ears when I learn that his name is 'Leo'.

Poirot might consider himself lucky at this point: the case, at least in terms of knowledge, is resolved. However, this is where further work has to start, which involves untangling the threads that are woven together to form Leo and weaving them with the threads that make up the fabric of Louise.

In Louise's story, Leo has a little dog with sharp teeth that she learns to trust and not be afraid of.

I'll stop here, but the work with Louise went on to become a matter of complementing the genetic heritage of a gazelle with the genetic heritage of a lioness, which was to happen when a 'Darix Togni' function came to life in the field through the introjection of the analytic function capable of metabolizing the jungle emotions that terrorized the patient so much. This allowed her to combine

13

tenderness and passion under the watchful eyes of the 'lion-tamer' – the weaving/narrating function of the mind.

I do not believe in generalizations, but in my view many cases of shyness, pathological shyness, the paranoia of the shy, social and relational phobias (fear of answering the phone, for example) have this common root. There is one part, or rather several split-off functions, that arouse fear and must be continuously monitored, avoided and washed away. And if they are sprayed around they become the root of persecution.

Depending on their degree of alphabetization, these protoemotions may have a defective alpha function or an insufficient container.

Often the less serious cases are the result of children being treated too well, leaving them no way of trying out primitive emotions like anger, jealousy and rivalry. They thus become gazelles, shy and introverted, and the emotions they are not given the opportunity to experience remain split off for a long time, generating fear, insecurity and a sense of persecution.

Often behind this lie parents who have pacified their emotions too much, who have not allowed themselves to inflict that quantity of inevitable frustration which would foster the development of the apparatus for metabolizing and containing emotions. Often these are people with an inadequate alpha function or with an insufficiently robust container. They establish 'pacified' relationships with their children, which I would term of the female homosexual type ♀ ♀, which leave ♂ emotional hypercontents split off outside.

Of course, depending on the intensity of these processes we may face ever more serious disorders, involving ever more primitive defence mechanisms, all the way up to the many possible different ways of evacuation.

The syndromes of children that are treated too well are, accordingly, no less serious than those of overly abused children (Borgogno 1994).

Other times, after a long period of analytic work that has developed the weaving and containing qualities of the mind, the emotions can live vividly in the consulting room and be shared.

Underwear or Red Cross?

After years of analysis, one day Nando begins to talk to me about something when I feel myself slipping into a state of drowsiness from which I later awake, suddenly aware that I have missed part of what he has been saying.

I try to intervene by using something that I had heard earlier, but Nando seems unconvinced. Suddenly he says: 'I felt that your breathing was regular, too regular.' I don't know what to do; the simple fact is that I had fallen asleep. At this point I tell him that perhaps he was afraid of my absence and my inability to recall the important events we were working on and to pick up the threads of all the main themes of the recent period. Nando seems to me absent.

After the session I am unhappy. I feel I wasn't honest. At the same time I realize that I had fallen asleep, as if I had received an injection of thiopental (Pentothal) to cope with something painful, a life-saver in the face of excessive tension.

I had then done the same thing, giving an over-interpretation that caused Nando to withdraw.

I say to myself, 'perhaps the real problem is not the negative quality of the emotions (jealousy, anger, envy) but their intensity'.

The following day Nando is reluctant to talk. He says that at yesterday's session an image had come into his head that had tormented him. He had seen a man with his genitals exposed, an exhibitionist, and he had tried to move away. It is clear, I tell him, that yesterday that is exactly what happened. I had been excessive in the second part of the session; in telling him all the things I had said I had been an exhibitionist. I add that it was true that at the beginning of the session I was a bit drowsy and had briefly fallen asleep, as if I had received an injection of thiopental. Perhaps the same thing had happened to him when I had gone too far in what I said: he had withdrawn. Surely it was an excess of emotion that had caused both of us to withdraw?

Nando is relieved. He tells me that at the moment when he had perceived me as being absent the day before he had been telling me about the intense emotion he had felt at meeting an old girlfriend again (the analysis had been interrupted for a week). He had almost run away, he had turned red . . . this was the part I had not heard. The scene had taken place on an ice rink.

I ask, 'Why didn't you ask me whether I was awake when you heard my breathing becoming regular?' Nando said he had been afraid that he was being boring and that was why I was so distant.

I say it is as if his wife had fallen asleep next to him and instead of getting angry, he had said, 'I must be rather uninteresting'.

During the rest of the session we speak explicitly and directly about what happened to him and to me in the face of strong emotions, when the ice seemed to melt.

The day after, Nando recounts two dreams. In the first he has an experience of utter exclusion, in the second he is with a very attractive woman doctor who speaks to him in a very frank and sincere way. He catches a glimpse of her red panties, she puts him on the couch and gives him a proper check-up.

The red underwear also reminded him of the Red Cross.

Then the doctor came up to him and gave him a very beneficial massage.

Luciana and the speech therapist

Ever since our first meeting Luciana has indicated that closeness and contact cause her great agitation and anxiety. She is seeing a married man, although their relationship is not very close.

The topic she dwells on most is that of her 'niece', who has speech problems and who she is worried may be autistic.

As an adolescent Luciana had a number of 'phobic problems': she felt compelled to clean everywhere, she saw risks and possibilities of infection, she spent hours disinfecting the bathroom, kitchen, door handles, etc. Sometimes she would even wear the kind of protective mask used by hospital staff.

After she began her relationship with Mario, the married man, she often stalked him to check up on him.

She is a nurse and has worked for a long time in the burns department. She also checks the gas all the time, as well as locks on doors and windows, often to the accompaniment of magical thoughts and long-drawn-out rituals.

She says that as a child her biggest problem was with 'colour' rather than form.

Up to this point it seemed to me that more protoemotions were activated in Luciana than she could cope with: contact and closeness are the situations that most ignited protoemotional states that 'burned' if they were not treated and processed.

The long story about her little niece seems to be a way of speaking about her inability to put into words what she feels in sensorial/protoemotional terms.

Essentially, her phobic avoidance issues and her obsessive control issues are a way of defending her alpha function that would otherwise be swamped.

The constant cleaning seems to refer to the way in which she cleanses herself of all protoemotions that are aroused in her which she must then also hypercontrol because she fears they are dangerous, polluting and

16

explosive. After all, unrefined oil pollutes; so too do protoemotions which are not refined and processed.

After a period of therapy, a cat comes to her house who was to become the protagonist of many sessions. Subsequently, Luciana begins to recount long stories of books and films she has seen.

Meanwhile, the 'niece' is going to a new speech therapist who is very good. Luciana also begins to describe her dreams: in one she picks up a lizard, in another she sees a python, and in a third a baby appears in her arms.

It would seem then that our work is making strides: there is the arrival of something more lively (starting with the cat) and the fact that she can now activate a narrator/dreamer function that is freer and less controlling and is expressed in books and films and then finally in dreams. The emotions seem to be getting more accessible, even to the point of becoming children that can be looked after (after moving through the lizard and python stage).

She then adopts – albeit at a distance – an Indian girl and they start up a prolific correspondence.

As a final step she goes to work in the sterilization department of the burns unit whose task it is to ensure that everything is aseptic and safe throughout the hospital.

However aseptic the place is, stories of several male and female colleagues start to come to life. They each have their own specific characteristics, and almost turn into Felliniesque characters. We have the 'insane Nurse', the 'touchy Dwarf', the 'Drunkard', the 'Sex Bomb', the 'Gay', the 'Astrologist', the 'Cripple'. So the film of the analysis truly becomes the shared story of these characters, each of whom embodies aspects of Luciana that at first had been silent and now that she had been to the speech therapist have found expression and words.

The crucial point seems to be not so much a question of which defences the patient adopts (phobic, obsessive), but his or her ability to develop an alpha function that weaves and dreams what had once been silent and inexpressible.

Required evacuation

I trust I have not given the impression that I believe that all sensoriality can be transformed into alpha elements, or into – to put it in one word – creativity. There is a physiological and necessary quota not only of beta elements but I would also say of catabolites of alpha elements which otherwise would become toxic and prevent the cycle of transformations.

There are a number of evacuative or para-evacuative activities of our mind that are vital. These are motor, protoemotional evacuations and discharges of various kinds. They can be seen in the consulting room, even in those dreams that some people call evacuative and which we have all come across in our own psychic life as in those restless nights when our first dreams fail in their task and only those that follow are able at that moment to metabolize and create a fresco of our mental life. I think there is a whole series of small 'manias', rituals and perversions that function precisely in this way.

I have always been struck by an episode described in the biography of Georges Simenon, an author who was able to weave extraordinary plots not only in his Maigret books but even more so in his other novels. After finishing a book he would allow himself hours of pure relief of tension, getting his faithful driver to bring him prostitutes so that he could abreact/celebrate the completed creative act. I remember a colleague at a Congress on Sublimation who quoted Balzac's comment that 'a night of love' costs 'half a volume'. All the same, though, you've got to live!

2

Image and narration: an endless game

A paradox of analysis: narrative derivatives

Given an adequately functioning analyst, a physically present patient and a sufficiently well-functioning setting, there is nothing that can be said, narrated, drawn, played out in the analyst's consulting room that cannot be considered a 'narrative derivative of waking dream thought' or of what remains of it.

It is not a question of there being external communications, and then others that are internal, and yet others that belong to transference: there is nothing in the analysis that does not pertain to the 'consulting room'.

I accept that it is not easy: a frigid wife, an angry husband, a child with problems, an absent mother, and so on, would come in handy to relieve us of responsibility, burdens and accusations. But as Melanie Klein explained, the internal world is as real as the outside world and it is only the former that we as analysts are called upon (and competent) to deal with.

The point I am making would of course not apply if one of the three component parts of analysis were missing.

Shortly after the Christmas holidays, Erminia comes to the session in a state of despair and tells me that her father-in-law has committed suicide with a gunshot to the temple. A few days earlier he had said he could not bear the approach of the festivities, a period when everyone was happy but which for him meant only pain and nostalgia. The day before he had also gone to the cemetery to visit his wife's grave, a clear sign of the depth of his despair and anger. This death has other implications for Erminia: she had been thinking of separating from her husband but now understands that he needs her. What's more, her husband will be coming into a large inheritance which will perhaps boost his self-confidence.

There is no doubt that such a communication can only be accepted on the manifest level of pain, suffering, guilt and anger.

But if we are in analysis, there is more to it. In fact, to put the point radically so as to be absolutely clear: it is only this *more* that belongs specifically to us as analysts.

A surgeon cannot operate on a patient suffering from peritonitis outside the operating theatre, and the same goes for us: we can operate only in the present and 'inside' our consulting room.

If – as in this case – we cannot interpret these emotions explicitly in the transference (because it would be inappropriate and foolish to do so), we can push the boundaries of the room to the point of understanding every narrative, every character, every story, every emotion.

We will think that the patient has found an extremely compelling 'narrative derivative' to signify her mental state to us: she speaks without knowing of her despair, her pain, her loss, her feeling like a 'little match girl' in the face of our absence. She discovers a world of needs that 'someone' has (and there's no harm in calling him the husband). She also understands that this pain can likewise contain a gain, a development.

So certainly we will not be able to interpret it, but we can be in unison with the patient, sharing emotions that, although their official place is in other scenarios, in reality can only be relevant to the analysis.

Without this particular tragic event she would have found other narrative derivatives to act as bearers of the emotions in the field. It could have been the story of a film, a newspaper article, a childhood memory, or even a dream – all of these could have staged the drama that was silently portrayed by her dream thought but was also looking to be shared.

Reverie and the construction of meaning

And . . . where is the tail?

Luciano is a seven-year-old child who for many years has been suffering from an allergic disease that causes him great suffering and restricts his activities. At our first meeting he seems to be relatively at ease and so I ask

Figure 2.1 Luciano's little animal, Lucky ('Ti voglio bene': 'I love you').

him to start talking. 'I'll talk about my Lucky'. He takes a sheet of paper and begins to explain that he has had this little animal for a long time. He explains as he draws that he keeps him in his father's 'study' because if he comes up to the animal and takes him in his arms, he immediately turns red, first at the spot where Lucky touches, and then the redness spreads and then . . . he describes the particular type of disability that he suffers from. As he continues to draw I realize with amazement that there's something striking about the names (Figure 2.1).

He tells me that the creature lives underground, digging deep tunnels where he takes refuge. Luciano is good at making contact with others; he is a very likable boy. He continues to draw and in the meantime I ask him some general questions. Every time his immediate response is to say: 'What did you say?' This happens over and over again. I'm quite impressed by Lucky: he tells me that Lucky belongs to a breed that has no tail, while there is another similar breed that has a tail and is very unruly and aggressive. At this point I gain an overall view: Lucky Luciano, his 'not hearing' (hidden as he is in his den), and especially the two long tails, which transform the drawing in my mind. I see him as consisting of an upper part with Lucky and a lower part with Luciano, with two enormous animals which were unknown until my reverie. The field is thus redefined on the basis of my hypothesis, which of course remains unexpressed to the child but becomes an organizer of thoughts and further 'hypotheses' for me: I can imagine that Luciano is allergic to the unknown parts of himself which must be metabolized, transformed in such a way so as to stop attracting the excess of anti-bodies which his non-self parts continue to produce.

Reverie and dream: a dialogue

Curly-haired girl

I open the door to let in Francesco, a promising young surgeon who is about thirty years old. For a moment I am bemused at the sight of a tall, angelic-looking, curly-haired girl.

I focus on the image and after a few moments I get back my usual Francesco.

I am amazed, I would almost say stunned, by my sensory misperception. I try to persuade myself that it must be a sort of reverie, but I can make no connection.

During the session we had had the day before I had offered some strong interpretations of aspects of Francesco's sex life or rather of fantasies involving his sexuality. In a dream Francesco had found himself at the wheel of an F14, and in another he was Flavio Briatore piloting an offshore racing boat.

Even though these images were a little manic, they prompted in Francesco the feeling that he was making new discoveries. Francesco is a young man who had always seen himself as respectful and even obsequious. He is a genuinely good person, but like everyone he is more than that. The session continues and Francesco recounts a dream which starts with a video game. Then, as part of the same dream, he comes to my studio, which is room 360. I tell him that my impression is that he sees the analysis as a game, where there are no hidden corners, no corners you are not allowed to explore – an all-round, 360-degree game.

He smiles, saying that to his astonishment he has started to realize that there are many things inside him he did not know were there. At this point he adds that he has had another dream: in it a male nurse approached a delicate, young girl, and the nurse appeared to have bad intentions, perhaps he wanted to use violence.

Only at this point do I return to my initial reverie: the sweet, curly-haired girl. I tell him that maybe what I had said about sexual fantasies the day before had in some ways opened up as yet inaccessible corners in him but at the same time had also shocked him a little. He confirms this fully by saying that it is not easy to discover that you are more like Gerard Depardieu than one of the seven dwarfs, as he had always thought.

I reply by saying that conceivably even some of the seven dwarfs had sexual fantasies about Snow White. He bursts out into a loud, liberating laugh.

But if the 'transformational' space that makes use of a conversational style is one of the driving forces of the analysis, it is also true that sometimes direct interpretation is what opens up new horizons.

Immediately prior to this group of sessions there had been one session in which Francesco talked about the sense of satisfaction he felt at his success in the department of endocrinology surgery where he works.

He had talked about this with a good friend of his, Giuseppe, who had undermined, or at least tried to undermine, his joy by suggesting a series of suspicious, disturbing interpretations of his success at work, even going so far as to predict some frankly catastrophic scenarios.

Francesco then changed scene and starting talking about the work he and his father were doing at their country house. There was a pine tree in front of the house which took up a lot of space, cast too much shade and which they had decided to cut down. Although pine trees do not have very deep roots, the task had not been simple. The father had had to cut a wedge in the trunk of the pine tree and at a safe distance Francesco had pulled on a rope attached to the top of the tree, which had then come down with incredible ease. This had freed up new space, light could now enter the house and spaces previously deep in shade were once again filled with light, revealing many details in the hedges and the flowers they had never seen.

Together they had decided to plant a plane tree, just one, a sturdy tree with roots that go straight down, apparently Napoleon's favourite tree.

Only then did I ask him, 'What's a possible short form of Giuseppe?' 'Pino,' he replied, 'but why do you ask?'

'Because,' I explained, 'I think you told me the story of your reactions to your success at work very well; then you went on to tell me about how you managed to eradicate the tree of Giuseppe-Pino's paranoia and this has opened up possibilities for new thoughts.'

The 'rope' and the 'pine' thus entered our personal 'family' lexicon and helped us find a way out of minor persecutory situations that arose from time to time.

In particular, I remember there was one time when Francesco found himself experiencing persecutory anxiety caused by something his professor had told him. The professor's name was Boschi, and all I needed to do was

23

to ask him if it was a forest (in Italian, *bosco*) of pines, to help him see things in the right light.

Taking away to make room is I think one of the activities that analytic work should promote. In my view, however, this applies not only to our patients but also to our theories. An obsolete theory (and I think any theory of the day before is outdated!) takes away space for new points of view.

I was forgetting the second part of my interpretation, namely when I said that where there was a pine tree of persecution there could now be a plane tree of self-awareness and self-worth. After all a Napoleon was also an old coin, and there was no reason he should be afraid of his legitimate aspirations.

The organizing function of the analyst

There are patients who bring along all the ingredients themselves, so that our function is merely to find a link between them and a different light with which to illuminate them.

A very experienced foreign colleague who comes to see me quite frequently tells me in a session that he sees his ex-girlfriend Giovanna, from whom he is separated, as a dangerous tick. Then he tells me that for some time now he thinks he might have a secret brother his father has told him nothing about. He goes on to tell me in great detail about the many women of various ages with whom he has amorous friendships and sometimes something more.

Being a militant Freudian, he asks himself what having spent a long time in his parents' bedroom could have meant to him. He still remembers the disgust he felt for the bed with its smell of semen, and how his dad had embarrassed him by standing around wearing only his pyjama top.

As our sessions were irregular, there was no way to make transference interpretations, so I opted for a sort of construction of the elements he gave me.

There's one element I forgot: he came to the session wearing a huge cowboy hat.

I tell him that in my view he still sees his ex-girlfriend as dangerous, like one of those ticks that give you high fever, and that perhaps this is the unknown brother; that in a certain sense he is very vulnerable with regard to Giovanna, he is still hurt and perhaps he has replaced Giovanna with a string of baby-sitters. This is what happens to those who spend so much time in their parents' bedroom: they find it difficult to gain access to their own space, the fate namely of the main character in the film *Tanguy*. But perhaps, I add, he also smells a 'male' odour, and it is the smell of male genitalia, of virility that has always caused him difficulties, although the cowboy hat opens up a new perspective. He is as it were struck – or perhaps touched – by this perspective.

He tells me about a call he made to Giovanna, during which he talked to her in an aggressive and sarcastic tone that he would otherwise never have expected to use.

I tell him that it is important, however, that the cowboy is not governed by the 'injured brother child'. He acknowledges that this is what he has done and that a real cowboy would not do that.

At the end of the session I ask him for an increase in fee. 'You get dearer all the time!' is his comment. 'It's not such a bad thing to be dear,' I reply.

Transformations

Obviously this section can only be understood if the reader has a full knowledge of what Bion wrote about the subject (Bion 1965) and my own subsequent development of the subject (Ferro 1996a).

Affection: the basis of narrative transformations

Through the appearance on the scene of various characters (the husband who makes fun of her, the mother who does not understand her, a friend who criticizes her) a patient indicates to me that the quality of my interpretation, however appropriate and soft it may be in my eyes, is neither of these in hers.

I take her point of view on board, making it into the key to finding a style of interpretation and a timing that may correspond more closely to her needs.

Towards the end of the session I then find the words to acknowledge to her that something I had said to her – and perhaps even more the way I had said it – may have hurt and annoyed her.

The following day she tells me about seeing a very pretty 'iron pot' at her mother's house which she asked if she could have. Her mother had agreed, and her father had asked her if she knew the history behind it. She hadn't, so he had told her that originally it was an 'iron bullet' that an uncle who had fought on the Russian front had later worked into a pot. He had then brought it back with him from the war and the vessel had been passed on to them. The parents say they are happy it can now belong to her.

25

The patient tells this story to her husband, who talks about it being a 'conversion' from something bad into something beautiful; the patient specifies that it was rather a *transformation*.

This transformation was only the last stage in a series: starting from my welcoming stance in listening to the patient's point of view, passing through the transformation that takes place in my mind with regard to style of interpretation, up to the change I had made to it and, finally, on to the patient's receptivity towards this transformation.

The transformation started from me, and will end up belonging to her as a possibility of a more comfortable way of listening to me and making room for my words in the pot that is now also hers. I do not interpret this to the patient. I simply mention a famous song: 'Mettete dei fiori nei vostri cannoni' ('Put some flowers in your cannons').

'Yes,' replies the patient. 'It was by Equipe 84, one of my favourite groups.'

I reflect on the fact that 84 was also the street number of my previous office. During the session I mention this in passing, by way of response to some statements made by the patient. She had said that even her mother seemed to have changed her way of dealing with her, and only at the end of the session did I comment that it seemed to me that she wanted to show that she had understood my different way of being with her (I forgo explaining to her that the bullet/pot 'of iron' could be two ways of feeling me – and being herself at the same time – so as not to provoke the patient's renewed irritation).

I must stress that this could fall into what Corrao has called 'narrative transformations' and I (Ferro 1996b) have called 'transformative narratives'. I think it is important to emphasize that ultimately what underlies narrative transformations are 'affective transformations'.

One type of transformation: dream work

Stefano has a dream in which he is in a museum; looking down from a landing he sees some Egyptian mummies get up and walk. He thinks he must find a way to 'bring them out'.

That same session he had noticed things he hadn't realized were in my studio (but in fact had always been there); at the same time he says he does not know if he prefers a life à la Depardieu or one 'with the least possible turbulence'.

It is clear that the dream put into visual form de-mummification, the awakening of new feelings and emotions within himself; he is posing himself the problem of bringing out, of manifesting emotions that were once locked up in coffins in the Egyptian Museum.

Here a number of questions arise: what do patients speak about, what time/space do they speak about? How do you interpret a dream?

Needless to say, there are other ways of interpreting these communications, but I suspect they would possibly clash with the criterion of 'economy' that applies across the board to all possible interpretations, as pointed out by Eco (1996). Moreover, we should not forget that according to the vertex taken by Bion the dream is the phenomenon that is richest in alpha elements and somehow the one that is least in need of interpretation unless of the type suggested by Meltzer when he says that a dream can only recall another dream by the analyst. It is a sort of exchange of poetic communications 'between minds', even though sometimes the paraphrase of a poem can be helpful.

Analysis — and the device of analysis — is stronger than the theories we use, and I believe that the psychoanalytic method, which is the greatest legacy that Freud left us (as Tagliacozzo has pointed out), is a kind of *Puss in Boots* (Ferro 2006d) capable even of devouring ogres. Paradoxically, the field can function in a transformative way of which analyst and patient are unaware.

Precursors of transformations: tolerance and narration

After a long period of changing her position in relation to me in the consulting room (first opposite me, then close to the couch, then allowing me to sit with my back to her and finally ending up in my chair while I sit behind her at my desk), a patient tells me about an unbearable female clerk who works for her company who behaves inappropriately, wants to do everything her own way, is always enforcing her rules and cannot stand being in a dependent position.

She then adds that she is fed up with her business partner because he wastes so much time. We talk about these topics for some time before the patient decides to go ahead with sacking the clerk she calls the 'stronzona' (literally 'big turd', something like 'total asshole').

I acknowledge the impossibility of working with such a person, and agree that it looked like she wanted to take her place, perhaps even occupy her 'chair' in the company.

The patient picks up the allusion and snorts loudly. At this point I offer a full interpretation of how she sees her behaviour as inadequate and how she is afraid of wasting time. I add that the problem is not so much the physical places in the room, but what these places become signifiers of: she cannot stand the idea of letting me come closer and taking the place of the patient for fear (this picks up an issue that had come up in previous sessions) that I might see how incapable or ugly she is.

I add that I do not think she is any different from other human beings, but that in any case I am not there to deal with any possible ugliness or failure.

The patient keeps silent for a while, then goes on to say that on the plane back from Paris where she had gone on business she had found herself sitting next to a cute-looking guy she found attractive and likeable but her business partner had begun to speak of the importance of the patient marrying in church, doing things the proper way, and this had embarrassed her so much that she hadn't talked to the cute young man even though he had made several efforts to start up a conversation.

I say that perhaps she is beginning to be attracted by the idea of a new (mental) position with regard to me, the idea of leaving me, that is, putting me in my place (the armchair) and her in hers (the couch), but what I had said, which she had perceived as moralistic and orthodox, had prevented her from opening a dialogue with herself about being confident enough to trust herself with me and going on the couch. 'Now we've got there!' she answers laconically, 'and I promise I'll think about it!'

A few days later, talking about the cost of a new but demanding work project, she comes back to the subject of 'position'. 'There shouldn't always be a desk between us,' she says.

I reply by saying that the desk seems to be a kind of Berlin Wall which keeps her separate from aspects of herself she fears. I add that it reminds me of the film *Good Bye Lenin*. She says she does not know the story so I briefly explain the plot to her: a woman remains in a coma for a long time and by the time she regains consciousness the Wall has fallen and a new world has opened up. Her family is concerned about her reaction to this new situation and uses a thousand expedients to construct a fictitious reality in which they pretend that everything is just as it was before. One day the woman has to go out alone and, now free from surveillance, she experiences what her family thought would be a shocking experience as joyful: change was possible and also beautiful. I add that it seems to me that the time is also ripe for the woman in the room.

28

A further transformation: the superego regulation of the analyst

After several months of analysis Daniele describes a dream: expecting to be sent very detailed e-mails from me, in fact all he receives are some very short e-mails with attachments containing pictures and small stories.

I offer a reading of the dream (which I later thought of as dictated by my superego): I did not provide him with what he expected to receive. 'On the contrary,' he says, 'in this room I feel like a balloon, and the images, the short stories you tell me are like brief shoves given to the balloon as it floats around the room, always discovering new points of view.'

Playing with the patient, playing with meanings, playing with ourselves – all this leads us to a kind of creativity whereby previously unthought-of new meanings are formed by a single member of the analytic couple.

Is there a continuum or a discontinuum between humans and other animals?

On this field you play a big game. Personally I am inclined to think that there is more mind in mammals than we can tolerate. At the same time I think there is more mind in human beings than we are accustomed to assume; likewise, that there is a qualitatively different mind that ends up also implying a quantum leap.

Normally we all think of man as an evolution of earlier states which thanks to the development of the mind is now better able to harness the instincts and drives we share with other primates. I would argue for the coexistence of a point of view that is the mirror image of this, namely that the mentalization present in our species is also a factor of great disturbance with regard to the operation of drives/instincts that as such function well.

Only if the mind has been able to develop in the best way possible can it be maturing and enriching, but for a variety of reasons each time the mind is dysfunctional it becomes a factor of de-regulation also with regard to basic instinctive drives which had functioned well.

The mind is the best but also the worst aspect of our species, a gift of evolution, but also a burdensome and perilous legacy of evolution and for evolution.

How we achieve a well-functioning mind is something I have talked about elsewhere (Ferro 2006b). By making some adjustments to Bion's theories I have already talked about the defects that the mind can have and how these can interfere with its operation (good functioning), with the proper functioning of the body (psychosomatic illnesses) and with the proper functioning of the 'social body' (delinquency, character disorders, collective stupidity).

If it is true that the 'functioning of the mind' is specific to our species, this implies a series of cascading consequences of which we are not clearly aware.

To use different terminology, we could say that if there is a continuum between us and the species that precedes us on the evolutionary ladder, then there are no major problems or major gaps. If, on the other hand, there is a leap, which is the 'lighting up' of the mind, we really have something specific and special, what Catholicism would call 'soul' and what I would more simply call the 'psyche'.

But if that is the case, the mind would not only regulate or de-regulate the rest of the human apparatus but override it.

Take sexuality for example: we've always thought of sexuality in terms of bodies, and in this light it is easy to define what is heterosexual, male homosexual or female homosexual. This stops being the case if we look at sexuality as a mode of coupling between minds (Figure 2.2).

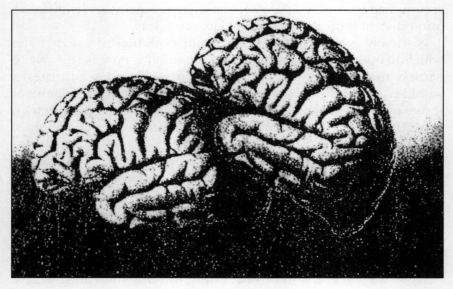

Figure 2.2 Two brains in captivity during an attempt at coupling in order to generate an idea.

From this point of view male homosexual would stand for ♂ content that seeks to mate with ♂ content, to subdue it, or to aid it, while female homosexual would be ♀ ♀, a relationship of peaceful homogeneities with protoemotions that remain split off.

A true heterosexual relationship would only be ♂ ♀, in other words, content that couples in a fertile way with a container that allows its development and develops in its turn. This would mean that homosexual and heterosexual are relevant to the functioning of minds. A couple made up of two men might perform a heterosexual function if their minds mate creatively, or a male or female homosexual functioning (♂ ♂). The same is true for a phenotypically heterosexual couple that could have a homosexual functioning (♂ ♂) of minds, a clash or a continuous ♀ ♀ fusional functioning, and so on.

The more weight we give to the mind, the more what we have just said will be 'cognitively' effective. The existence of the soul (psyche) would imply the lawfulness of phenotypically heterosexual (but in fact homosexual) relations. And we can even pose the question about what type of profound sexuality (between minds) a phenotypically heterosexual couple might have. This applies of course to all other possible levels: having children – it will be perfectly ethical for any kind of couple to have children; if anything, what would have to be established is whether the couple is fertile. I think it would be a useful exercise to apply this premise to any type of behaviour.

Piero and Linda

Piero and Linda are a married couple who ever since our first session have shown me two alternating registers of functioning.

Either they clash violently with each other, each trying to browbeat the other, or one of the two, or more often both, show a false acquiescence that produces a kind of total 'dead calm'. Even their sex life has two registers: one in which one of the two does not feel willing, leading to the explosive frustration of the other; and another where they pretend an involvement they don't really feel. This is what I mean by male homosexuality (♂ ♂) or female homosexuality: essentially, from a mental point of view they are a homosexual couple. And each of them also has a homosexual way of functioning in relation to him/herself. Either they are in perpetual conflict between incompatible functions of self, or they are in a state of autistic estrangement from self. So either they are at odds with self or have no contact with self.

31

Transience

Another consequence of the 'mind' is, as has been pointed out many times, our awareness of our end and often our inability to tolerate it, our not knowing and not being able to receive answers at a point in evolution that only allows us to ask questions; and not being able to cope with the lack of answers leads us towards that form of anaesthesia and if necessary lies that we call religion, fanaticism, faith and so on. When Bion (1970) talks about liars he brings us into contact with this truth in an extraordinary way. Only by allowing our ability to think to mature over a long period of time can we face – without exorcism – the transience of our existence without the need to cling to lies, albeit shared lies.

Delinquency and accountability

This theory of the mind also opens up a range of concerns about evacuative pathologies in the somatic body or the social body. Crime, character disorders, violence have only marginally been considered as arising from a mental dysfunction. Whereas the more archaic level of mental dysfunction, namely the evacuative, would lead to hallucinations/delusions, or diseases in the body or diseases evacuated into the social body.

The case of Mara is brought up during a supervision group. The person presenting the case apologizes, saying that it is not a psychiatric case but only a 'social' one.

Mara suffers from panic attacks and has gastrointestinal symptoms that make her life difficult. She can't digest and frequently suffers from diarrhoea. She knows and has dealings with people on the margins of society: Raul, a small-time fraudster; Anselmo, a drug dealer; Louis, a thief and a robber. She has also had a number of abortions. It seems clear that the graph of Mara's mental functioning might be as follows:

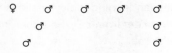

In other words, what we have is a situation of (♂) protoemotional states in superabundance which are not given a transformative reception and are split off and then evacuated into the various characters – Raul, Anselmo, Louis. What is distinctive about them is that they are 'behaviours' with (extremely) low levels of thought.

The evacuation of these aspects could have been carried out using a more apparently psychiatric method (hallucinations, delusions), in more medical forms (such as Crohn's disease, ulcerative colitis, etc.) or through social means (police-judiciary).

Viewed from this perspective, would criminality be the equivalent of a psychosomatic illness in the social body?

Accordingly, any kind of delinquency would fall within the field of psychiatry/psychoanalysis. Also therapy should not only be a question of containment or judgement but should also concern itself with the activation of that halt in mentalization or rather in the transformation of the silent de-mentalization which is crime.

In the case of Mara, when she decided to start therapy, Raul, Anselmo, Luigi became characters in her therapy, characters who could be understood as split-off and evacuated aspects of herself, but which came back to ask for a 'hearing' in the form of that return of the repressed, the split-off, or the never-thought that I have previously called the rumen.

Raul had an affair with his neighbour and began to feel previously unknown emotions: obviously, in the therapy the neighbour was the welcoming and thinking part of the analyst.

This implies a reformulation of a number of legal concepts, starting from criminal liability. Imagine a mother who kills her child in a fit of rage. This is due to a swift *coup de main* (or assault) in which a certain 'split-off and unknown' part of the mother takes possession of the levers of command. The mother acts, troubled by this alien functioning which leads her without her knowledge to commit this murderous act.

Strictly speaking she is not 'in full possession of her faculties', but the question of social danger remains. When she once again picks up the 'reins of government', so to speak, the woman is absolutely normal, but who's to say that this won't happen again? There's no guarantee.

Let us take the case of a father who kills his three-year-old son because he cannot stand his crying at night. What are we to think? That this man cannot stand a depressed part of himself that cries and that he wants to eliminate. He acts accordingly; he could not act differently. What I am saying is that the criminal act is not a choice, it is a behavioural obligation: on that particular occasion the subject could do nothing else.

A husband is exasperated by his wife who cannot stand that the family has relations with others. Constantly in the grip of feelings of persecution, he kills his wife and wants to get rid of the body. But he does not know what to do and is found out as he makes a clumsy attempt to bury her in the garden. This man wants to silence a part of himself which he does not know how to get rid of in any other way. He wants to find some inner peace. He acts out of necessity and for self-therapeutic purposes.

Frequent stupidity is thus also one characteristic of crime because it is often an action based on a thought and we no longer know what that thought was. There is a wonderful book by Ferrandino entitled *Pericles the Black Man* that illustrates this point.

3

Examples and queries

Misperception or hyper-perception?

There are many situations of mental suffering in which there is no consensus as to the perception of oneself or others, or of the world. Often this type of pathology is seen as misperceptive, albeit to varying degrees: ranging from the para-physiological body dysmorphic disorder of adolescence, passing through anorexia and on to hallucinatory phenomena (from visual flashes to proper visual hallucinations) or delusional phenomena.

The model of the mind I am proposing sees all these phenomena as hyper-perceptive, in which the person 'sees' (or hears, or smells, etc.) hidden, projected split-off aspects of self that escape the objective gaze of the other, whilst the 'ultrasound' or 'tomographic' gaze of the same person allows us to see, just as infrared light makes it possible to see in the dark.

So-called body dysmorphic disorder registers non-integrated aspects of the adolescent or non-metabolized aspects of ourselves.

A young patient saw himself as having a huge nose. This caused him great suffering and his skin was so thin it looked as if it were about to rip open: in actual fact he saw parts, or rather elephantine functions, of himself, which threatened him with an explosiveness that frightened him.

The issue of anorexia is no different, as I mentioned before. Here the thread-like image seen by others is less real than that seen by the person with anorexia, who sees behind him the huge and heavy part (function) of himself that he must continually split off by way of a survival strategy. He sees B, whereas B is not perceived by others (Figure 3.1).

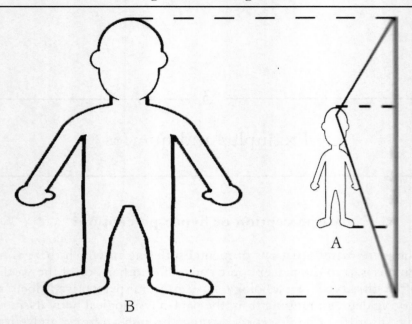

Figure 3.1 How a person with anorexia sees their body.

It is no different in paranoid disorders where intolerable aspects of self are spread over the others who become persecutory custodians of these aspects. Sometimes these custodians are chosen at random and according to chance; at other times they are sought in the same way as a director looks for an actor for a special part by a careful process of casting.

The same happens in hallucinatory phenomena where the patient sees split-off and projected aspects of his self in an outside world that is coloured with these functions or fragments of functions. In all patients there remains an albeit minimal directorial role that lets you 'see' what others miss.

Luca's accusations
Luca is constantly talking about courts because of a minor legal case in which he is involved. The scenario in Luca's stories becomes increasingly Kafkaesque and catastrophic. It becomes possible, however, to find a way out of the situation the analyst had previously trivialized when the analyst realizes how Luca perceives the analysis, and manages to really see it

through his eyes: for him it is a place where he is for ever being examined, disapproved of, criticized. The analyst will not say anything about this but the new 'perception' will allow him to modify his way of being and gradually bring about the progressive disbanding of the court.

The split-off parts should be seen as made up of balls (like balls of wool) of various colours that have been gathered together and which have to be disentangled, separated out into small coloured threads (different emotions) and then slowly woven and harmonized in the patient's emotional structure in a manner and at a speed that he finds tolerable.

We should recall that symptoms or defences are the result of years of hard work to avoid worse trouble, so deconstructing and constructing are processes that, given the patient's thresholds of tolerance of pain, require care and vigilance.

The horse fair

Denise has a relationship with a man who is twenty years her senior.

Denise has always had a symbiotic relationship with her mother, and once while she was on her way to visit her mother in hospital, she had had a serious accident that had necessitated the amputation of three fingers.

A few years later, during a fight with her previous boyfriend, she had another accident that led to the amputation of a foot. She then had reconstructive surgery involving the insertion of implants that were especially successful.

Massimo, the man she has now had a firm relationship with for some time, has become her prosthesis. Although she still has issues of anger, despair, jealousy, every time he goes away, he makes her life worth living.

Periodically she loses control and has terrible outbursts of anger against Massimo, who says he is no longer willing to put up with these emotional earthquakes.

The therapist who has now taken over Denise's case grasps immediately that there is no place in the patient for interpretations of content and simply collects, names and highlights the varying emotions – the disappointment, the anger, the despair, and so on – to which her relationship with Massimo (understood of course as the analyst's 'mask') exposes her. According to Denise's description, this method of elaborative containment work becomes the new habit she and Massimo share – 'going to horse fairs'.

These are described in all their characteristics – irritability, familiarity, impatience – and each fair and each horse corresponds to one of Denise's emotions or group of emotions.

The geometry that makes it possible to switch from the projective example of the patient to the exercise of rewriting in the field is not straight-forward but this is what enables the analyst to find his way around.

After some months of this kind of work, Denise decides to take a horse-riding course so as to be able to mount horses. It is clear that Denise now feels ready to move from a level more descriptive of her emotions to one where she can ride them directly, get in touch with them and begin to keep them in check. Not only that, but in the periods of waiting for Massimo (intervals between one session and another), Denise has started an activity she had previously never practised: she begins to make charcoal drawings in which a recurrent motif is beaches battered by waves (riding the waves?).

Negative transference can be interpreted 'directly' or indirectly (with the awareness that the interpretation takes place 'in' the trans-ference and not 'of' the transference, consciously utilizing the char-acters suggested by the patient (the head physician when his mother . . . his bank . . . his dentist . . . etc.)).

The transference is first accepted (whatever it is), then understood and cooked, and finally 'said'. If a patient starts off a session saying he has 'stomach ache and can't digest heavy food', I would not inter-pret this statement and would just cook light interpretative food that day – easy-to-eat food. If the patient complains about his bank and says that they tend not to act in his interests but are only out to sell him some banking product, I would not make a direct interpretation but would recognize the feeling of 'no confidence' and 'betrayal' that he feels about his bank.

From a field perspective, and when the analyst is aware of how extensive his field of operation is, there are no such things as 'off-field' interpretations if characters present in the field are used. This will give us interpretations of the field that show a particular func-tioning that the whole field has taken on, or in the field if they reflect an affective motion in a locus in the field.

Klute

(translator's note: the Italian title – *Uno squillo per l'ispettore Klute* – contains the Italian word for call-girl)

Martino is an officer in the *carabinieri* who cannot say no. Ever since he started an affair with a police inspector he 'has felt that he is suffocating', but he cannot tell her that he wants to split up with her.

38

His adolescence was very sad and lonely, and becoming an officer in the *carabinieri*, where he made a rapid career thanks to his studies in computers, helped him find a role and way of life.

There is a facet of Martino that is apparently at odds with the rationality that envelops him and with which he envelops everything: he has a keen interest in the primitive peoples of Africa. Alongside his unsatisfactory life with Cristiana – a policewoman who deals with immigrants – he has a secret relationship with a Cuban call-girl he finds sexually extremely satisfying. The young Cuban, who in fact turns out to be the daughter of a diplomat who works in a European city, is actually in Italy to pursue her postgraduate studies. Occasionally, however, despite having attended a boarding school run by nuns in France, she works as a call-girl for the sheer pleasure and excitement she gets from meeting 'unknown' men.

It is clear from the beginning that there are very different forces at work in the field; some are rational defences, whereas others point to protoemotional aspects.

The mixture could be explosive, or indeed very 'tasty', because everything is going to depend on how these aspects will be mixed by the contribution of the analyst. We still do not know which ingredients will be added (or removed) and how they will 'shaken'. Undoubtedly it is a story that looks promising right from the outset as it opens up a wide range of possible events.

Questions to be clarified

Is there such a thing as a non-instinctual mind?

This is an extremely important question. On the one hand, we have Freud, the development of 'French psychoanalysis' and the idea of 'unconscious phantasy' as the 'psychic representative of the drive'. Everything we know about the various levels of drives, their destiny, their genealogy, their entanglement and disentanglement is part of our common psychoanalytic heritage. Then, on the other hand, we have relations with the object and the qualities it possesses. Sexuality understood as the *primum movens* (or prime mover) behind drives is present to a significant degree.

In the model that motivates me and which at the same time I am trying to develop, the category of the mind (thinking–feeling–dreaming) is both different and more complex.

The mind originates in the transformation of sensoriality into alpha elements, in the newborn via the passage of this sensoriality through the alpha function of the mother, then via the passage of sensoriality through its own alpha function, once it has been introjected and is sufficiently functional. The category of sensoriality is not identical with the instinctual area; it is much broader. The sensory area encompasses all sources of stimulation, that is, proprioceptive stimuli (hunger, thirst, etc.) but also exteroceptive stimuli (light, heat, colour), in other words, everything that pertains to the mind as an experience both from within and from without, including the states of protoemotional engorgement that occur, and those that occur in the other.

The psyche is thus not something that comes from the transformation of drives, but rather from the transformation of everything that is perceived as disturbing and which therefore becomes the 'perceived evacuated'.

Once this perceived evacuated is accepted and transformed by a mind that has a functioning alpha function, a process is set in motion that leads to the alpha element and the gradual introjection of the alpha function.

So a functioning mind has the following structure:

Sensoriality ------ vs ------ $\rightarrow$ alpha function ----- vs ----- $\rightarrow$ alpha elements

The concept of sensoriality is far wider than the concept of the drive.

The concept of the beta element is far wider than the concept of the drive.

But when defining the mind there is an obligatory passage through the mind of the other and the introjection of the thinking function through the passage of the method of thinking (thinking–feeling–dreaming). It seems to me that Bion clearly indicates this path, and he points out that the great problem of the species is the 'mind' and all its dysfunctions.

The mind of each person also depends on the quality of the alpha functions it has introjected and how they have been assembled. To

40

use a different terminology, I would include Faimberg's (1988b) notion of transgenerational transmission.

What about the individuality of the analyst and patient in field theory?

Analyst and patient are two loci in the field that live in the field itself both at moments when subjectivity emerges (like the taking shape of two mountains: a kind of orogeny of subjectivity) and at moments of fluidification, when this subjectivity dissolves. This movement is perpetual and in continuous oscillation.

Is there anything outside the field?

Of course there is, but it doesn't belong to us as analysts. In my opinion we are analysts when we are in the presence of the patient and inside a setting. If something bursts into the setting, it breaks up the field.

An intense earthquake would be sufficient reason to leave the virtual consulting room and enter the reality of 'every man for himself' or 'let's get out of here'.

What changes in technique according to a field theory?

Let's take the example of a patient who denies all emotion, any emotional involvement, any emotional dependence on the other. Before the summer holidays he tells me that his girlfriend's cousin is very upset because her boyfriend has to go away for a long time to work in the United States. He does not know the girl, but his girl-friend has asked him to give her the name of an analyst. For me this 'person' (who does not belong to me if he or she exists outside the consulting room) is a place in the room which is becoming permeable to feelings and emotions.

The stories and the vicissitudes of this person, Pina, in her deal-ings with her analyst all pertain to the analytic field, as does the analyst cousin who is horrified because I have provided the 'cousin' with the name of an analyst; for me these are all presences and move-ments in the field. They are not collateral transferences but are components of our world, of our analytical ecosystem where analysts, patients, cousins, girlfriends coexist – all presences in transit and perpetual transformation.

Is there not a risk that the concept of field will become self-referential?

In my view, absolutely not.

Because the field is constantly expanding and it has any number of scenarios, scripts and personalities. Because a functioning field becomes a living field of which there is no perception. It's just like in a good movie: we forget our perception of ourselves and take our place next to *Ben Hur*, *Star Trek*, *Pretty Woman*, and so on.

This happens without any awareness that one is engaged in analysis. Except perhaps at those moments when the analyst for one reason or another steps outside the story to give interpretations of what is happening. This can sometimes be necessary. This corresponds to the moment at the cinema when the lights come on and another level of awareness comes into play – pending the resumption of the journey.

The field is the space–time of all possible virtualities, all possible worlds, and these will be different for each analytic couple at work. The field makes possible the continual activation of the dream functions of the mind that permits the continual expansion of the capacity for mentalizing.

This field makes not only for transference interpretations alongside interpretations in transference but also for interpretations of the field and those 'in' the field. These are never outside transference or extra-relational (I am thinking of the field as an expression of enlarged relationality).

Transformations during analysis

Of course, transformations need to be distinguished not only according to type (rigid motion, projective, in hallucinations, narrative) but also according to their degree of stability and reversibility/ irreversibility in time. Let us look first at short-term and reversible transformations, then medium-term, and finally those that are long-term and irreversible.

Natalie and time denied

Natalie is a girl with anorexia who has had to spend long periods in hospital with varying results.

After beginning intensive psychotherapy she quickly moves away from more clearly anorexic issues ('there is no place for me, there is no room for me') towards the solution already suggested by Grinberg (1981), namely that only by making oneself extremely small can one perhaps find a place in the mind of a very busy, and thus often emotionally unavailable, mother, towards a different scenario in which transgenerational separation anxiety stands at the forefront.

Natalie expresses an all-consuming nostalgia for when she was little and also good, really good. She was a shy and well-behaved girl. Then her family moved house. Actually they just moved a short distance along the same street and it was at that point that the 'strange fever' appeared that lasted for months. At the same time her father developed hernias.

She often talks in the session about what her room had been like before and then of the 'other anorexics' who were in hospital with her who manifested unyielding aspects of self.

But unyielding to what?

Change and grief seem to be beyond her. She lacks the apparatus to contain her grief and to metabolize it, or to metabolize all the emotions that every change implies.

She is desperate at the idea of not being able to go back to the way she was before.

They moved house to have more space, but everybody saw the new house as cursed: the father contracted several different diseases and the mother developed a tumour.

Natalie's behaviour – crying before a plate of ravioli, desperate because she cannot eat them – seems to be designed to stop the vector of time. Because the necessary equipment had never been installed in the house, she cannot bear the passage of time and the grief that constantly attends it. To her it is a hopeless struggle, but for now it seems impossible to abandon.

She is attempting to make a pact with the devil so as to stop time.

This brief reference to the case of Natalie is a way of saying that there are no unifying interpretations and that even a well-defined symptom such as anorexia can have very different facets: in Natalie's case anorexia seems to be a pseudo form – a solution to the fear of a depressive collapse in the face of an impossible change.

Other forms of anorexia, on the other hand, as we have just seen above, point to the problem of a plethora of split-off and denied protoemotions repeated continually in waking dream thought that shows them in what to all appearances is a misperception.

Marcella and the paralyzing spray

Marcella is an adolescent who is attending a school specializing in classical studies.

Since being told of the impending separation of her parents she has had pantoclastic crises alternating with periods spent in a catatonic state in bed, in the dark, during which she doesn't bother to get dressed or eat.

She comes across as superficial and vain; she wants to become a model or a showgirl, and seems to shift between silliness and depression. There are times when she shows the depths of her desperate loneliness, but then others when she covers it over with utter frivolity.

The relationship between her parents had entered a state of crisis when a blood test made necessary by surgery had shown that Marcella's blood group was incompatible with her father's. It came out that Marcella had been conceived during a relationship her mother had had – and continued to have – with an office colleague.

Marcella is terrified by immigrants and in particular she is afraid of being attacked and raped by Albanians, Moroccans and Senegalese. So she carries around with her a paralyzing spray bought on the Internet. On a couple of occasions she has used it to defend herself against threatened aggression and once to stop a violent motorist who was on the point of attacking her mother after a risky overtaking manoeuvre.

Another distinctive feature of Marcella's is her constant use of lies as a way of life. She tells lies to teachers, to her parents about her marks at school, she tells lies about her boyfriend and the things he does.

At this point it is clear that the spray she always carries with her is the lie with which she paralyzes overly powerful emotions she would otherwise not know how to handle.

The only alternative is that the 'spray can' might explode in a pantoclastic crisis.

Suffering in its turn can only be put to sleep.

This behaviour also seems to be the principal way of functioning in the family. For more than fifteen years her mother had hidden her relationship with her office colleague from her husband, hidden the true paternity of her daughter until everything exploded with the (blood) analysis.

Marcella herself is extremely afraid of the analysis because she fears that it will bring her into contact with intolerable despair. Superficiality and frivolousness are in turn the intrapsychic sprays with which she avoids contact with emotions that would be too intense to handle and by which she feels raped, just as she fears she may be raped by illegal immigrants.

Illegal immigrants seem to stand for everything that cannot be shared with others or with oneself and therefore can only be paralized, denied, split off, until the defence mechanism fails and an explosion occurs, and so on.

The therapy also takes on this characteristic oscillation between lethargy, lies and explosiveness but this (or rather the contagion of the field) is the first step towards initiating a possible change in register in Marcella's mental functioning.

This situation leads to some reflections about 'lies' – which I believe should be tolerated and 'played with' by the analyst. In many cases, the analyst cannot be a champion of truth or psychic truth: one can get progressively closer to psychic truth but one must still tolerate that certain quantity of lies necessary, in various doses, to survive: again I would refer the reader to Bion's comments about liars (1970) already mentioned above:

> The liars showed courage and resolution in their opposition to the scientists who with their pernicious doctrines bid fair to strip every shred of self-deception from their dupes leaving them without any of the natural protection necessary for the preservation of their mental health against the impact of the truth. Some, knowing full well the risks that they ran, nevertheless laid down their lives in affirmations of lies so that the weak and doubtful would be convinced by the ardour of their conviction of the truth of even the most preposterous statements. It is not too much to say that the human race owes its salvation to that small band of gifted liars who were prepared even in the face of indubitable facts to maintain the truth of their falsehood. Even death was denied and the most ingenious arguments were educed to support obviously ridiculous statements that the dead lived on in bliss. These martyrs to untruth were often of humble origin whose very names have perished. But for them and the witness borne by their obvious sincerity the sanity of the race must have perished under the load placed on it. By laying down their lives they carry the morals of

the world on their shoulders. Their lives and the lives of their followers were devoted to the elaboration of systems of great intricacy and beauty in which the logical structure was preserved by the exercise of a powerful intellect and faultless reasoning. By contrast the feeble processes by which the scientists again and again attempted to support their hypotheses made it easier for the liars to show the hollowness of the pretensions of the upstarts and thus to delay, if not prevent, the spread of doctrines whose effect could only have been to induce a sense of helplessness and unimportance in the liars and their beneficiaries.

There is otherwise no explanation for all the devices we use to absorb the shock of our finiteness and in particular the shared delusion of places and spaces for a 'life after death'.

Giulio and the guinea pigs

Giulio has been diagnosed as suffering from Asperger's syndrome.

The description that Giulio's psychotherapist gives of his mother is of a person who is 'neither tall nor short, neither fair nor dark, neither thin nor fat . . .' and so on – the portrait of a person impossible to portray, someone who seems not to exist nor to have any salient features. His father owns a well-established company in the north-eastern part of Italy and is always away on business.

Giulio is capable of complex language, but he lacks any emotional variation; he 'speaks like a book'. At long intervals he has crises in which he scratches himself to the point of ripping the skin on his body and his face, screaming that he is a failure and incompetent. Once the crisis is over he goes back to being 'a young mechanic, a robot'.

Asperger's syndrome seems to occupy a sort of no man's land, with autism at one end and hyper-obsessiveness at the other. Whilst the autistic world is two-dimensional and the obsessive world is three-dimensional, but within the walls of a rigid container (the rigidity is guaranteed by the rituals that transform the fragility of the container into the inelasticity of the *claustrum*), in Asperger's it is as if there were a halfway house, a sort of shallow cupboard where things can be put as long as they are thin: an aquarium for flat fish.

There is room for language that is not affective; however, periodically, when the aquarium contains a plethora of soles (emotions compressed to the point of two-dimensionality, as in an animated cartoon) it bursts, demonstrating all his split-off despair.

In autism we have a nearly total evacuation of the alpha function, and in obsession a functioning alpha function but a defect in the container that gathers and squeezes the alpha elements. In Asperger's, on the other hand, alpha elements are formed that are 'stretched' and thus lose all emotional characteristics; they are pure representation unrelated to an equivalent transformation of protoemotions or rather of sensoriality into an emotional pictogram.

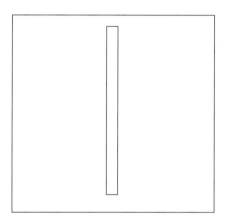

Figure 3.2 Mental space in Asperger's syndrome.

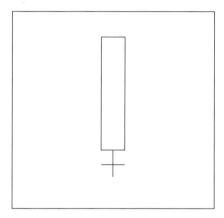

Figure 3.3 Claustrum with hypercontents that are compressed and partially split.

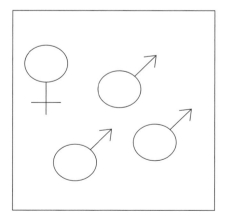

Figure 3.4 Container dealing with content that is not easy to manage.

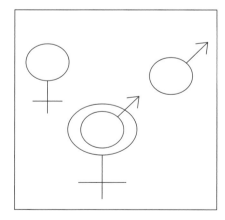

Figure 3.5 Container and content in creative oscillation.

The small number of functioning lumps of alpha function are 'persecuted' by invasions of stimuli. The result is the enormous mental pain these people are exposed to when they encounter more stimulation than they can alphabetize.

After a period of therapy Giulio begins to speak and draw his own guinea pigs. In particular, he becomes interested in their sex life, describing their couplings, which always turn into out-and-out rapes. This seems to be his simple description of what the meeting or the coupling of minds is like for him – a sensory impact similar to rape. Also the relationship with his own emotions has the same characteristics.

One day he describes the penis of one of the guinea pigs as enormous and fiery red: here what happens is that the fiery ♂ emotions rend and tear the totally inadequate ♀ container.

Gradually he goes on to draw the guinea pigs as they couple and depicts violent scenes in which they are strung up, crushed. The ever more obvious arrival of these violent operations coincides with the appearance of emotions that Giulio evacuates violently in the consulting room: increasingly the mind of his therapist becomes the space that is 'abused' by these evacuations, so not only Giulio but also his therapist plays the part of the abused guinea pig; or rather he necessarily becomes the object of Giulio's evacuations.

The therapist's generous acceptance of such evacuations seems to be the first move towards creating an additional space, the 'room' that will become the place for Giulio's emotions as they gradually become be more alphabetized in the encounter between his projective identifications and the therapist's ability to engage in reverie (see Figures 3.2 to 3.5).

4

Bion: theoretical and clinical comments

It is significant that the Bion I am most fond of is Bion during the period from the 1960s up to his later work and especially the author of *Seminars* and *Discussions* (1974, 1975a, 1978, 1980). For me the Bion Edna O'Shaughnessy (2005) describes as 'less disciplined' is the most fascinating precisely because of the unsaturated nature of the texts he wrote and the constant stream of new thoughts they stimulate. For years I have been leading a Bion reading group and I find myself coming out of each session enriched with new discoveries and new ideas. I believe that a systematic reading of Bion can only start from his many *Seminars* and once one has grasped the spirit, the way of thinking, the courage that emanates from each of the seminars, one can then go on to his more theoretical works, which I suggest should be read in groups because they are like freeze-dried food requiring continuous hydration to turn them into something unexpectedly and extraordinarily alive.

What is impressive about the last seminars is their constant striving towards what we do not know: theories just formulated (and which were all the more fertile with innovation) become limestone, lifeless, incapable of carrying us towards new horizons, hypotheses, questions. Of course this way of looking at things stands in diametrical opposition to that taken by all supporters of 'isms', whatever they may be; in opposition, that is, to all those saturated theories that already know the answer to the patient's problems. In fact, if one knows how to listen to the patient, he is the 'best collaborator'; he will open up new horizons of knowledge and dare to create 'wild' thoughts as long as the analyst, the analytic establishment, the Society do not stand in their way for the sake of maintaining the peace and quiet that every institution craves.

The purpose of analysis is to develop the poet, painter or musician who, often unbeknownst to the patient himself, lurks silently within him. Or we could say that for Bion psychoanalysis is synonymous with the development of the creative potential of the human being whose misfortune it is, however, to structure his mental functioning on the basis of the experience of acceptance or rejection he has been exposed to in his early attempts to relate to others.

On the question of the continuity/discontinuity of Bion's model, in my opinion, there can be no doubt that Bion started from a strongly Kleinian matrix, but I think that from a certain point on he gave birth to a new model that was no longer a linear expansion of what came before but that achieves a quantum leap, a break (as indeed Klein's model did vis-à-vis Freud). In my opinion between these three models there occurred what Bion would call a catastrophic change (Bion 1966) which, although it entails the persistence of certain invariants, in fact creates a new gestalt.

Although not interested in creating new conceptual apparatus – he often says that there are already too many in psychoanalysis – Bion provides us with a set of tools for thinking we previously did not possess and which enable us to think things we previously could not think. These tools are not only a formal enrichment; they allow us to perform new operations or to acquire an awareness of the operations performed in the consulting room previously we did not have.

(Personally I think this is a way of doing research in psychoanalysis – using the invaluable laboratory of the consulting room to name and give recognition and shareability to 'mental events' that have always occurred but of which we previously were not yet aware. This is, for example, what Melanie Klein (1946) did with projective identification.)

I should also like to say something about the ephemeral nature of models: it is logical that in psychoanalysis we model 'things' that have no real structure but are provisional ways of understanding certain functions; a model is something that gives us a provisional view of the phenomena we observe. For it to be fertile, each model has to be ephemeral. A model that does not imply its ultimate transience would be supremely anti-knowledge.

The most important concept in Bion's work and the one that for me has had the most significant implications is 'waking dream thought'. Our mind constantly dreams even when it is awake. The function that creates this dream thought is the alpha function and the product of this function is alpha elements.

A fundamental characteristic of alpha elements is that they are constructed in a way that is peculiar to each mind. The protoemotional sensory inputs (beta elements) are 'pictographed' (Rocha Barros 2000) by each individual mind in different ways (unlike primal phantasies, which belong to the species, and unconscious phantasies).

If the alpha element (the way in which each mind creates a pictogram of sensory inputs) is extremely subjective – it is as if the alpha function were continuously working through an untrained painter who puts into images what he perceives – what is even more subjective is the continuously produced chain or sequence of alpha elements which constitute 'waking dream thought'.

In the session we have therefore the 'waking dream thought' of the patient and the 'waking dream thought' of the analyst, both of which are in constant formation (this, according to the modalities of interaction of dream thoughts, is at the origin of the various theories of the field (Ferro 1992) which have their precursors in the Barangers (Baranger and Baranger 1961–62) and are at the root of concepts such as the analytic third (Ogden 1994b)).

What's more, the analyst's mind (Bion 1962) may be put to the test by quotas of beta elements evacuated by the patient which are transformed by the analyst's alpha function into alpha elements (Grotstein 2006). This constant play between the mind of the patient and that of the analyst leads not only to transformation into the 'basic building blocks' of thought but also to the progressive introjection of method (the alpha function) which will continue to develop where it is missing (as in serious pathologies).

When sequences of alpha elements are not directly available, they give rise to the unconscious.

Other tools intervene at this point to weave the sequences of alpha elements into fuller images and these are the PS-D oscillation (considered to be operating all the time) and the ♀ ♂ relationship, where the container made up of 'emotional threads' (also between the two minds?) allows emotional content to enter the scene – somewhat like trapeze artists who perform if they know that there is a net to catch them. I would also add the oscillation between negative capability (the compelling expression borrowed from Keats's letter to his brothers that refers to the ability to remain in doubt without a sense of persecution) and the selected fact (opting for one fact, which means ignoring all other possible facts and creating a particular gestalt).

The moments when the analyst is in deep contact with his (ever-forming) waking dream thought correspond to his reveries: preverbal stimulations are syncretized into an image with which the analyst comes into contact.

Projective identifications are also seen as a normal communicative phenomenon of the species and are not only evacuative in nature (and even the violent evacuations of the 'beta screen' are seen as designed to generate countertransference (Bion 1962) with a dramatically communicative intent). Behind this lies the original relationship between the mind (or perhaps a preconception of the mind) of the newborn child who evacuates sensoriality that he does not know how to or cannot metabolize ('nameless dread') into the mother's mind on a massive scale. If the mother is receptive and available, she not only transforms beta into alpha but progressively passes on the method for doing so. The basic model is therefore that of projective identification, also to be seen in continuous ♀ ♂ play (Gaburri and Ferro 1988).

This is enough to produce a series of cascading effects in the consulting room (and in analytic technique).

The patient is considered the 'best collaborator' (Bion 1978, 1983) because he is the only one who through what he says (or does not say, do, draw, etc.) after an interpretation gives us the chance to understand how an interpretation has been experienced and how the whole of our interpretative activity should be modulated so that it can be a factor leading to growth and not persecution. Bion says that it is not simply a question of what you understand as an analyst, but whether the patient is able to understand the interpretation you give him: 'You can't launch into a great explanation of the biology of the alimentary canal to a baby' (Bion 1987).

The mental state of the analyst and the quality of his mental functioning ('without memory and desire') become one of the key variables in the field (Bion 1970).

What matters is not only the patient's mode of functioning/ dysfunctioning for it must always be seen in relation to the functioning/dysfunctioning of the analyst's mind. The only person who can tell us about the quality of this function/dysfunction is the patient: 'we can become what the patient is saying' and the borderline patient 'always knows when the analyst has become mentally absent' (Bion 1983). This also raises the question of the quota of truth about the patient and about himself that the analyst is able to tolerate mentally.

The patient serves as a mirror reflecting the analyst's distance, making it possible for him not only to remedy the relationship but also to observe which emotions the patient has not been able to tolerate (because of his dark occluded areas or painful residual scars); in this respect what happens is not unlike a countertransference dream by the analyst. He can also be a mirror of the excessive close-ness of the analyst to the truth when the patient is not yet in a posi-tion to tolerate it (Barale and Ferro 1993).

Looked at this way, the patient becomes someone capable of telling us continually how and where we are for him from vertices unknown to us (and whilst this may not always be to our liking, it can still satisfy our need to seek the truth) as well as having continual experience of our mental functioning.

So there is always a vertex from which the story told by the patient is the story of the effective mental functioning of the couple: whether to identify and explain this through interpretation or through an interpretative mental reorganization is a technical decision to be made at that moment. This puts an end to the illusion that it is always possible to find the point where anxiety emerges, making it necessary for long periods of progressive mental movement (Bezoari and Ferro 1991a). Interpretation at this point is something that comes after the play of projective identifications and must be propor-tionate not to the analyst's truth but to the patient's ability to take it on board ('in practice we have to have a feeling about what the patient can stand': the interpretation may be given 'six sessions later, six months later, six years later', Bion 1987).

In this way the interpretation can take on a character of insaturation and polysemy which allows a dialogical construction of meaning and does not involve the holder of the truth imposing himself on the other ('Perhaps one would need to give an even more vague interpretation than the statements he is making', Bion 1987) Interpretation, with its need for 'closure', can often come up in column two of the grid (lies told to pacify the analyst and to avoid going to unknown places).

Here we have another characteristic of Bion's thought that becomes increasingly clear: being able to not know, being able to wait, and being able to wait for meaning to develop.

Analysis is a probe that expands the very field it explores (Bion 1970) – this assertion protects us from the notion that the analyst possesses some kind of assumed and preconceived knowledge; he must always 'dare' to go towards the unknown, a kind of Dersu Uzala (as in the film by Kurosawa) and not a 'geographer' in need of mapped certainties.

The unconscious itself is not given as formed once and for all, but since the alpha elements that make up the unconscious originate in the relationship with the other, the unconscious becomes something much more dynamic and open to transformation.

Bion's courage to embrace the new is also reflected in the last lines of his last work (1987) where he expresses the hope that the revolutionary method of psychoanalysis will not be used for anti-revolutionary purposes – and that what was revolutionary will become respectable.

This leaning towards the unknown, as clearly emphasized by Edna O'Shaughnessy, is also found in Bion's preface (1972) to the Italian edition of *Learning from Experience*, where he says that the greatest gift the reader could make him is to render obsolete the theories expressed in the book. Bion (1970) is never orthodox; he is much more a mystic who knows that truth is unattainable, but equally that the path towards it is essential, albeit painful and at times even impossible.

In a passage of *Clinical Seminars* (1987) Bion also says that if one day he were tired and did not know what to say, then and only then would he be able to make a Freudian or Kleinian interpretation. His point is that the interpretation should always be cooked *ad hoc* for that patient, for the first time. Sometimes, though, you realize that something has been discovered that was already known.

Inside myself I have always made a distinction between different periods in Bion's production. The first period was more frankly Kleinian (it could hardly have been otherwise). Then came the period when with (sometimes sharp) oscillations he developed his own way of thinking about psychoanalysis. I deliberately now don't use the word model because Bion said that one cannot be Bionian (Bion Talamo 1987). (In this context Bion himself (1980) says even Melanie Klein claimed not to know what it meant to be called 'Kleinian', to which Betty Joseph made the witty riposte: 'It's too late now – you are a Kleinian whether you like it or not!'). Every analyst, Bion believed, must be himself all the way without being afraid of his own originality and uniqueness. 'The analyst you become is you and you alone, you have to respect the uniqueness of your own personality – that is what you use' (Bion 1987). During this period Bion gave us the tools I mentioned earlier, that is, the conceptual instruments that enable us to think new and unknown thoughts. Then came the period of *Seminars*, during which he tested his psychoanalytic instrumentarium in increasingly original and creative ways, giving invaluable and continual technical guidance. Then came the works in which he re-narrated his theory, this time no longer in abstract mode along the highest rows of the grid but along the C row. This took the form of the wonderful, visionary narratives contained in 'Memory of the Future', where he presented his thinking in a highly figurative manner, embodied in films and tragedy – and behind which, held up as it were against the light, one can read his life-long dialogue with the mind of Freud (Baruzzi 1998).

Returning to the question of the impact that Bion's conceptualizations have had on technique in psychoanalysis, I would add, if I am allowed the metaphor, that the kitchen has grown but not the restaurant. From one point of view the customer is always right; that is to say, we should be interested primarily in seeing and sharing his point of view before working towards transforming it (Bion 1987).

Concepts such as transformation in hallucinosis, bizarre objects, inversion of the alpha function, hyperbole, reverie and beta screen open up new horizons and enable us to lend form to previously unthinkable concepts.

Basically, the analyst and patient co-generate a field which, in order to be transformed, must 'fall ill' with the patient's disease. Bion's instrumentarium also makes it possible in a linear evolution (by simple addition) to open up doors to the possibility of continuous monitoring of the field (Ferro 1992, 1996a, 1996c, 2001a, 2001b, 2002a, 2002b), to the earliest mental functions and to those mothers (and indeed fathers) incapable of reverie who, instead of opening the doors of the mind to the child's projective identifications, draw them on the surface in the form of *trompes-l'oeil*. The concept of reversing the flow of projective identifications and inverted reverie is a logical consequence and is a phenomenon that can also be seen in the session itself.

We also have the opportunity to describe pathologies according to very simple criteria: absence of alpha function; absence of the apparatus for the narrative weaving of the alpha elements ♀ ♂, PS-D, NC-FP; excess of undigested beta elements when the structures of the mind are intact.

Nevertheless, I see three risks in Bion's thinking. The first is a drift towards mysticism which has two consequences: a language is used that is designed for initiates and not to make explicit concepts which are, after all, simple and useful (speaking at a conference in France about the concept of the container and the usefulness of expanding this idea to contain more contents, I talked about the size of the 'casserole'; only later did I discover that in argot the word also refers to the female genitalia, which is all right, since the symbol is ♀); likewise the language used to speak to patients becomes a kind of jargon that communicates nothing transformative and instead simply celebrates a rite of membership (for example, 'this is not a thought').

The second is a hyper-subjective drift whereby the creativity of the analyst (the result of a genuine meeting of minds between patient and analyst during the session) is replaced by an esoterically odd state in which everything is permitted.

The third is a formalistic drift whereby the use of Bionian language and Bionian jargon takes the place of real communication.

In conclusion, I wish to emphasize once again the point that after Bion the analyst enters the scene in a totally new way, with all the density and weight of his own mental life and an awareness of how rudimentary his apparatus for thinking is (Bion 1978, 1980). The analyst knows that in the session he is dealing with 'two frightened and dangerous animals' (1980) and it is important not to tame them straight away. The analyst remains in the PS position in search of unpredictable thoughts, just as the officer stays together with his soldiers on the battlefield (Bion 1978, 1980, 1983). What matters in the analyst is not his teleological anchorage in cure as a point of arrival but his awareness that he himself is a 'bad job', because he has 'not been fully analyzed', and that when the analysis ends he will have to make 'the best of a bad job' (Bion 1980).

The alphabetization of beta elements will be the result not only of verbalized interpretations but also of sequences of emotional and relational movements between the two members of the couple, both engaged in the growth of their own minds, growth that cannot be measured in terms of the number of new ideas acquired but in an increased willingness to accept such ideas (Gaburri and Ferro 1988).

Bion (1980) also demonstrates his full and modest awareness that it is the analyst who is the highly delicate tool that makes the analysis possible when he says, 'I do the best I can with what I am'.

As I said at the beginning, considering dreams as a continuously operating level in the session enables us to work within a virtual space, a field that is created by the encounter between a patient, an analyst and a setting without having to address so-called 'external reality' – which does not belong to us as analysts in a consulting room with a patient. It speaks to us continually of other things; the other things are what concern us, notably the development of tools for managing, weaving, metabolizing, digesting, and giving both meaning and depth to these 'other things'.

Another not unimportant peculiarity of Bion's thinking is his view of man not as brimful of instincts or as a battlefield where the struggle is between the death instinct and the means for overcoming it, but exactly the opposite: the problem for 'homo sapiens' is that he has a mind, a mind which is in need of care if it is to develop harmoniously and the failures in whose development lead to various modalities of evacuating untransformed beta elements. It is only a short step in my opinion to the view that our species has an utterly archaic apparatus for thinking – a mere rough draft of what it could, hopefully, one day become. This apparatus is primitive and delicate at the same time and at all events inadequate to the overall level of the species. So what we usually think of as the death instinct or drive may in fact be merely the result of the present inability of the species to transform sensory input: what cannot be alphabetized will be evacuated in hallucinations, psychosomatic illnesses and unreflected actings-out. This is the source of the 'madness' of the species we see around us.

In the consulting room, analyst and patient are two frightened, dangerous animals; the hope is that one of the two is less so. The problem, however, is not the violence of our instincts but the inadequacy of what we call the 'mind' (Bion 1980).

The analyst's capacity to be in unison with his patient constitutes a factor of evolution and transformation. Every time the analyst mentally mates with his theory he in effect engages in a primal scene with it and thus creates the living contact between minds that is the only possible growth factor.

Personally I am amazed by the sections in Bion's *A Memory of the Future* (1975b) where he manages to enact his theories by means of a dramtized use of mental functioning. These passages combine great analytical creativity with an extreme freedom of expression; I would say that in such passages he enacts his thoughts in a way that can only leave the reader transfixed (although many were in fact shocked). Bion showed remarkable courage in deciding to leave England at an advanced age to live out the last years of his life in Los Angeles (from where he also went on trips to Brazil to hold his seminars) for fear that carrying on in an environment where he had received important institutional awards would stifle the vitality of his still evolving thought. For a long time Bion met with much incomprehension in the United States, even though today it is one of the countries where his 'truly pioneering' thinking has met with analysts who are now creatively developing many aspects of his work that had previously remained implicit; one need only think of Grotstein and Ogden.

5

Bion's thinking and its fertilization: clinical implications

It was Bion himself who said that his concept of 'waking dream thought' had hardly ever been taken into account despite its theoretical and clinical implications. To my mind, this concept revolutionizes not only theory but also technique and the theory of technique. As I have repeatedly argued, in my view it is Bion's most significant and powerful conceptualization. Our mind not only produces night dreams but constantly, via the alpha function, carries out the alphabetization of all the sensory protoemotional stimuli we receive. The culmination of this process is the formation of alpha elements which, when put in sequence, produce waking dreams:

Stimuli (beta elements) ↔ (via) alpha function ↔ alpha elements ↔ waking dream thought.

It is no accident that he introduced the use of double-headed arrows because all these operations are reversible and in various situations can also occur in the opposition direction. There are situations where we can experience visual flashes, transformations in hallucinosis, hallucinations, and the formation of bizarre objects; situations where the alpha function is reversed and works through evacuation.

Of all these phenomena, that of transformation in hallucinosis seems to be the most valuable because we constantly come across it, also in relation to our theories, every time we see with certainty what we have projected.

There are a number of important consequences that flow from waking dream thought, from its function and dysfunction:

- It allows continuous monitoring of the analytic field. In this way the analyst can be informed as to how he (and his interpretative activity) is accepted and/or rejected, making possible a continuous modulation thereof. An interpretation may be followed by a broadening of the field, its collapse, or even the emergence of phenomena evacuated by a part of the patient in the form of visual flashes often in response to visual transformations in hallucinosis carried out by the analyst. At an international meeting of colleagues interested in clarifying possible models in psychoanalysis, I suggested a start to the session that I made up on the spot:

Patient: Yesterday I didn't like what my mother made for me to eat. She always makes the same old things.

Analyst 1:   The envy you feel for what I say prevents you from enjoying and accepting my interpretations.

Patient: Yesterday I saw a tram that was about to run over a child, but fortunately the child managed to get out of the way at the very last moment.

Analyst 1:   The anger you felt about what I said was about to crush you but the memory of the work we have done together stopped you from being overwhelmed by anger.

At this point, however, I suggested a different version of the same session with a hypothetical second analyst:

Patient: Yesterday I didn't like what my mother made for me to eat. She always makes the same old things.

Analyst 2:   I understand that you were disappointed not to get what you wanted.

Patient: That's true but my mother tries to understand my tastes if I am brave enough to express them.

Analyst 2:   And that allows you to feel both the moments of harmony and the disappointments.

At this point the discussion focused on the following questions. Can each session really be co-determined by the interaction between patient and analyst? Can what the patient says after receiving the interpretation be his dream about that interpretation? Can unsaturated interpretations be considered equally of transference or at least in transference without direct explanation, as long as the explanation is clear in the mind of the analyst? Is the second analyst being kind or is his interpretation the only acceptable one for that patient at that specific point in the analysis? And what is the analyst attempting to achieve by means of his interventions? Is he trying to make conscious what is not conscious? To reveal the patient's unconscious phantasy? To enable the expansion of the container through the experience of unison?

- It cancels the problem of external reality, for what concerns us as analysts is what happens in the consulting room, in other words, how analyst and patient function or fail to function. This is because both the most abstract and the most concrete of communications can be understood as narrative 'derivatives' of waking dream thought as it is being formed at that particular moment. Other vertices for listening to the patient's communications coexist, of course, but are not specific to analysis and its method.
- In my view this reduces the problem of truth/lies in the consulting room virtually to zero. Normally a book, and the process of reading that book, sends us back to the encyclopaedia we share with the reader. There is some kind of agreement in place, and the reader has specific expectations about each particular type of book, or rather each possible literary genre. If it is a historical novel or a biography, there is no place for the supernatural (unless perhaps in a history of saints). In a work of science fiction it is generally agreed that anything can happen, although even here the genre requires there should be no surprises. Recently I found myself reading a book (*The Eyre Affair* by Jasper Fforde) which initially I found frankly irritating. All my expectations as a reader were immediately confounded. Ostensibly it is a novel with a realistic setting and realistic characters. However, even though it doesn't actually turn into science fiction, it does introduce temporal and logical breaks – alongside normal facts, events and characters – which thwart all expectations and predictions. The only way to read the novel is to play along with the author and to partake with him in the incredible/normal world he presents to the reader – a world where time has a habit of bending suddenly and the boundaries between reality and fantasy are blurred. The uncle in the story has found a way of physically entering and exiting from works of literature. But the invention falls into the hands of a diabolical criminal who steals Charlotte Brontë's

original manuscript and kidnaps Jane Eyre in order to ask for an huge ransom . . . the plot continues along this double track, with the absurd on the one hand and the perfectly realistic on the other (Woody Allen did the opposite in *The Kugelmass Episode*; he was the first to have thought of a machine capable of transporting someone into a novel, but the whole thing is written according to the conventions of the grotesque). As I see every session as a dream, the problem of lies for me ceases to exist. For there to be a truth or a lie there also has to be a holder or Holy Inquisitor of truth and for some time now this is absolutely the last way I would behave in a session. It's amazing how the number of lies diminishes when there is no one trying to discover them. I've experienced everything in sessions: dead brothers who were only in intensive care, animals like the 'dodo' of Thursday Next (the main character in *The Eyre Affair*), ghosts that wander around the house interacting with the living and with the living-dead. Analysis can be just like a fantastic video game!

- It shifts the analyst's attention from the content of the dream to what the dream generates. It is no longer a question of analysis seeking to lift the veil of repression or to repair splits. Here psychoanalysis looks to develop the tools necessary to foster the development and production of thought itself, that is, the apparatus for dreaming and thinking. Here we have an analysis that poses itself the problem of the development of the alpha function, the development of the container and consequently of the greater number of contents that can be accepted, the development of the oscillation between PS and D on the one hand and NC and FP on the other; an analysis that looks at how the mind functions/fails to function and how the analyst enters into resonance/dissonance with all this, how he makes himself permeable to it or protects himself from it.
- It allows us to look at the phenomena of the 'casting' of new characters that become indicators of the development of the ability to think. Casting is no less significant than the plots the characters create and the constant underlying factors that are necessary for everything to happen (a permanent and available theatre, sufficient funds, necessary subsidies, etc.) – these are all metaphors of the mental operations that analyst and patient must continue to perform to bring the ever-expanding analysis to an end and which are such as to make the patient want to come back the next day (as Bion pointed out).

The constant interplay (again indicated with the double-headed arrow ↔) between *projective identifications* and *reveries* becomes one of the crucial operations in an analysis. Beyond all words and beyond all interpretation, what matters is what is 'done!' in the consulting room, by which, of course, I mean the continuous coupling of the minds of analyst and patient. Projective identification is recognized as a basic activity of the human mind in communication. Most projective identifications flow from patient to analyst, but this is not always the case: sometimes the flow can be reversed and a tired, occluded, unavailable or suffering analyst evacuates anxieties into the mind of the patient, and in these cases this mind temporarily takes on the function of a receptive-dreaming hub.

This continuous interplay is what also leads to the formation and development of the container and the development of the contained, as well as the constant physiological oscillation between PS and D; or in other words, between disaggregated and brutal emotional states (the painter's palette with its full range of colours) and well-defined and completed moods (the picture the painter creates using his paints).

Another equally valuable oscillation is between 'negative capability', that is, the ability to remain in a state of mind open to doubt and uncertainty, and the 'selected fact', i.e. what the analyst identifies as the dominant emotion at that moment or in that session.

But let us not forget, as I mentioned earlier, that the phenomenon is reversible and that the patient may become a witness, a consumer, the editor of the projective identifications that come from the analyst. The essential point is the frequency and intensity with which these phenomena occur. Once again what is important is listening to the field with its cast of new and unexpected characters (the doctor with tuberculosis who infects his patients, the Ticino river polluted with illegal industrial waste, the mad cow that will make you crazy if you eat it, the classmate with a cough who passes on his fever, and so on).

The *modulation of interpretation* is one of the most significant consequences: Bion focused very sharply on how the interpretation ends up — whether it becomes a factor of growth or of persecution. His famous statement that an interpretation ought to expand the field of meaning, myth and passion (Bion 1963) is also a way of saying that whatever affects the senses of the analyst and the patient can in some way be interpreted (to pull a rabbit out of a hat you must at least be able to see its ears). He also tells us that the interpretation should not be of the decoding type but should expand to include a mythical narrative, that is, it should be put in the form of a scene, a story, a 'film' that lends depth and visibility to what is said and that ultimately expresses 'passion'. In other words, the interpretation must entail a passionate and current link between the analyst's mind and what is interpreted.

In this way, I would say that the classical concept of interpretation often gives way to activities on the part of the analyst that trigger transformations in the field, transformations that can also result from a change in the analyst's mindset, from minimal enzymatic actions. Saturated transference interpretations remain of course among the possibilities of intervention the analyst may deploy when he deems them useful.

The *mind of the analyst*, in many ways the focus of *Attention and Interpretation* (Bion 1970), becomes a key variable in the analytic field. The analyst's mind becomes an invaluable and delicate laboratory that requires ongoing maintenance.

In *Cogitations*, Bion (1992) argues that even the number of hours of sleep an analyst gets has implications for various functions of his mind at work. In particular, the analyst's mind must possess the basic skills I have already referred to as 'negative capability', namely the ability to remain in doubt in an unsaturated state without the need to find full and exhaustive answers immediately.

Mind maintenance becomes part of the analyst's work. This involves an awareness of the caseload of patients every analyst feels he can take on at a given time of life, awareness of his needs in terms of the interval between patients, taking notes after the session (an example of a constructive evacuative activity!), leaving enough time for other roles outside the consulting room, time of life and so on.

The similarity between the analysis of adults, adolescents and children

This is a further consequence which I'll only mention very briefly. If attention is shifted on to mental functioning, dream thought and what forms dream thought, every analysis has the same characteristics; languages and means of expression may change but the main features remain the same.

Let us imagine a field that is saturated with beta elements which are then expelled violently; this could then be embodied in the story of a child suffering from enuresis, encopresis or vomiting, or in the story of an adult who evacuates through violent actings-out and character disorders.

We would then have a basic identity of fabulae and a diversity of plots or narrative modules.

A game that I often play with trainees is to ask them to take a session of child analysis and then to rewrite it, pointing out that the same basic issues can be expressed be it in a session with a young adult or with an elderly woman – but in a different language. A later chapter will contain exercises of this type.

At this point we need to go on an apparent digression. My real aim, however, is to provide a map that enables the reader to orientate himself clearly vis-à-vis my reference model, which I consider as resulting from a mutual fertilization of the concept of the field, several conceptualizations of Bion's, and certain contributions coming from narratology.

Since its initial formulation by Willy and Madeleine Baranger (1961–62) the *concept of the field* has gradually become more complex (Baranger 1992; Corrao 1986; Ferro 2005d, 2006a). Initially seen as a place created by the encounter of analyst and patient in terms of cross-resistance, and then by the formation of bastions and their subsequent demolition through interpretation, the product of the analyst's ability to take a 'second look', the field has increasingly become the locus of all the various potential skills of analyst and patient and of all the possible worlds that open up as a result of their meeting. It is, in my view, not only a spatial but also a temporal locus inhabited by both present and past and continually open to the future.

Such a constantly transforming field implies the impossibility – after the big-bang of all the possible worlds generated by the encounter between patient and analyst within the setting – that something should remain outside it.

Places in the field include the current relationship between analyst and patient, their stories, transferences, defences, emotional turmoil, their alphabetization and de-alphabetization. The field has a breathing pattern of its own: the inhalation phase signals the arrival (or the un-freezing) within the field of lumps of unthinkability; the exhalation phase signals the collapse that follows any saturated inter-pretation and which reduces it to a point in preparation for future expansion. Needless to say, this is a constant movement.

Another characteristic of the field (described above) is that sooner or later it will be infected by the patient's illness and may even contract his illness, becoming a place of treatment and hence of transformation.

So the field is in continual oscillation, alternating between a constant opening up to meaning (negative capability, Bion 1970) on the one hand and an inevitable closure to meaning, on the other. This means setting aside the whole range of possible stories in favour of the one story that clamours to be told (the selected fact, Bion 1963).

Analysis finds itself oscillating between 'The garden of forking paths' by Borges (1941) with its constant unpredictable developments and the opening up of possible worlds, on the one hand, and *Jacques the Fatalist* by Diderot (1796), on the other. In this latter work the author confides in the reader that if reader and writer are to proceed together and to complete their journey, the writer must give up all the possible stories he could tell in order to focus on the supreme story, the one that must be told. Sometimes the patient's story is not repressed, split off or impossible to reconstruct, but tells of the part that is missing from his apparatus for thinking. Accordingly, analytic work consists in adjusting looms that fail to weave. In these cases, then, there is a function that must be repaired – or sometimes made from scratch. So instead of an analysis that can be compared to a driving school that provides its own well-running car we have an analysis that – long before the driving school and the instructor come into play – needs a mechanic to repair the car and sometimes a workshop to supply or make (even the most basic) missing pieces.

The path taken by analysis becomes a function of the modes of functioning of that particular analytic couple at work and the very idea of a natural process is lost. Each couple will have its own way of carrying out analytic work, and even the events of an analysis, the negative therapeutic reactions, the psychotic or negative transferences (and countertransferences) will belong to that couple.

Of course there are limits to the subjectivist drift, and these are anchored in the analyst's ethics, in his personal analysis and training as an analyst and his sense of responsibility towards the fact that the events narrated are those that urgently await alphabetization by the analytic couple – and not others (such as confirmation of the analyst's theories or the avoidance of possible mental pain). In this context concepts taken from narratology such as 'limit to interpretation', or limit to the opening of all possible worlds, can be of considerable help (Ferro 1996e; Eco 1962, 1990; Petofi 1975; van Dijk 1976; Pavell 1976; Platinga 1974; Ryan 2001).

Thus defined, the field takes on the following characteristics:

- the field becomes the space-time where the emotional turbulence activated by the analytic encounter begins;
- the field is a function with respect to the two members of the couple that possesses a high degree of unsaturation;
- the field becomes a place-time for promoting stories and narratives that are the alphabetization of protoemotions in the couple;
- the field is the matrix that generates the development of the alpha function and the container from the capacity for reverie and the capacity to be in unison present within it (Ferro 2006c).

The transformations of the field take place through a continual process of co-narration by both analyst and patient, who become 'two authors in search of characters' (Ferro 1992) who alphabetize protoemotions and allow them to evolve continuously.

In the field the semantic halo around the concept of interpretation spreads to encompass all the analyst's seemingly conversational unsaturated interventions.

Central to the field is the analyst's reverie, understood as his ability to make contact with his waking dream thought (and the sub-units that form it) and to narrate it in words that activate the transformation of the field. No less central, however, are the narrative derivatives of the patient's waking dream thought, and the alpha elements that form them.

From a certain point of view, the patient's narrative can easily be seen as a continual retelling of how he 'frames' the components, the events, the lines of force within the field. From this point of view we cannot talk about the patient as not belonging to the field.

The earlier focus on observing the patient's communication – the focus on countertransference – is shifted to the figures that come to life in the field and act as continuous indicators of the life of the field. This makes it possible to continually deconstruct in a subliminal way the tangled 'ball' of transference into narrative sub-units that, one by one, can be transformed and constantly reassembled.

It is essential to enrich the complexity of the current field – which is horizontal and exists in the here and now – with a similar complexity of the vertical field, which includes the multigenerational: time enters the consulting room.

So we enter into a geometry that not only reflects the 'inner world' and the 'relationship' but is a geometry of stories and their transmission: analyst and patient are no longer active and present with their two-dimensional 'photos' of parents, uncles and grandparents to be interpreted and revealed in the transference interpretation; they are presences, three-dimensional characters, belonging to a different time-frame that ask to enter, or need to enter, the scene on their own terms. At this point any interpretation which is 'in the field' is of transference.

In this dimension, the analyst, in my view, should let these 'freeze-dried' transgenerational elements (Faimberg 1988a) pass through him; they are just waiting for the life-blood of hospitality coming from the field to take on 'density' and history.

We thus find ourselves facing a complexity we are not always equipped to cope with.

There needs to be space along this path for many other considerations: for example, how the narrative function of the field can 'marry' the pockets of non-thinkability:

- The transgenerational component of the analyst that enters the room, as a quota regarding the person and as a quota regarding the transmission of the analytic function, including any blind spots he may have (and which fortunately the field can signal – if it is listened to).
- Going over history again, even our history as analysts, not in ritual fashion, but as a way of discovering transgenerational legacies.
- Broad reflections open up about the concept of projective identification and emotional turbulence: to use a film reference, we can think of the beginning of *Jurassic Park* with the DNA fragments still included, and how the development of the mind cannot be separated from certain re-enactments of what had been split off.

While previously the 'double multipersonality' opened up a myriad of possible universes along the spatial axis (Baranger and Baranger 1961–62) between analyst and patient, now it necessarily opens up ramifications in time, what Borges called 'This network of times which approached one another, forked, broke off, or were unaware of one another' – a world of uchronias or historical utopias. For the history of civilization such possibilities are mere exercises ('What would have happened if Custer had won at Little Big Horn?') but in personal history they can, through *après-coup*, become thoughts of new realities that can be both part of the future and even of the past; and this possibility of rewriting a story that never happened seems to me the most fascinating prospect and the richest gift analysis can offer.

Returning to Bion, I would like to develop further the dialectic between waking dream thought and narrative derivatives. Pictograms (although I continue to refer to the visual world, obviously the same applies to audiograms, olfactograms and so on) remain unknowable, it is true, but one can get closer to them by means of their narrative derivatives.

Figure 5.1 (Ferro 2005a, 2005g) summarizes what happens in an adequately functioning mind or in an analysis that works. Thus far this scheme has been implicit and obviously follows Bion's thinking on this point and my own development of his conception.

The first activity to set off the big-bang that switches on the mind – in our species – is the massive evacuation of protosensorial, protoemotional states by the child. If these evacuations (beta elements) are gathered, processed and transformed by a mind that absorbs and metabolizes them (the alpha function), they are gradually converted into meaningful pictograms (alpha elements).

The mind of the person carrying out this transformation not only transforms the protosensorial and protoemotional chaos into meaningful emotional form, but also, by continuously repeating this operation, passes on the 'method' for doing so (alpha function) (Bion 1962, 1963, 1965, 1987). The constant repetition of this cycle of transformation – a veritable Krebs cycle of the mind – produces other effects as well: the game of projection–introjection–re-projection–re-introjection makes it possible to differentiate between hollow space and convex space, between receptive space and solid space, in short to differentiate container ($♀$) from contained ($♂$). The first interrelation between 'projective identification' and 'reverie' is actually the first sexual relationship of the mind with another mind, and this is what will go on to underpin the creative abilities of each individual (Rocha Barros 2000).

By way of illustration: if a patient had a protoemotional sequence involving alarm–doubt–relief, the sequence of pictograms could be:

fire tanker – puzzled face – birth of a child

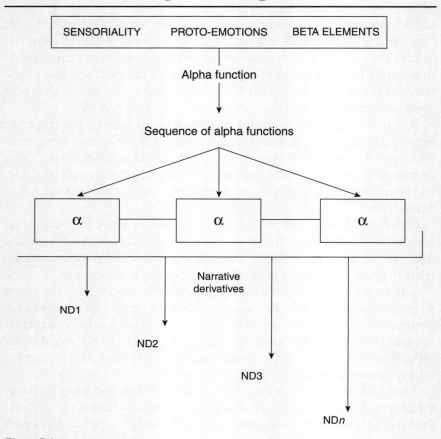

Figure 5.1

In the field this sequence (itself unknowable) could come to life in an infinite number of different narrative derivatives:

- A childhood memory: as a child I was scared the day it seemed that no one was coming to pick me up, but then I saw in the distance a man with a stick who looked like my grandfather; I was really pleased when I recognized him.
- A narrative of sexuality: it seemed to me that Licia did not want to make love to me when I finally reached her house. I thought she was perplexed by my late arrival, but the way she embraced made me realize that she was not angry with me.
- A diary entry: I saw a scene at the university that made a deep impression on me. A girl was trembling with fear before an exam,

but once she entered the exam room she seemed less frightened. She smiled at the first question because she knew the answer.

This exercise could go on for ever. One could look at ludic derivatives, graphic derivatives, motor derivatives (often found in the analysis of children) and even dream derivatives, namely, when a dream appears more significant as a dream derivative of waking dream thought active at that moment than as a night dream, but what I am anxious to show here is how – if we make the situation a bit more complex – the patient constantly becomes the place in the field that continually describes the evolutions and transformations of the field.

In these examples, we have a field where there is a movement from fear to doubt and then on to a feeling of calm. It may sometimes be useful to interpret this to the patient, and it may sometimes be useful to work on this communication only in the mind's kitchen without interpreting it, unless in a largely unsaturated way.

What I have described normally happens after an interpretation given (or withheld) by the analyst, but the example of active interpretation lends itself better to my purpose.

The analyst makes an intervention. What the patient says after that can also be understood as the description of what the interpretation has triggered in the patient. After interpretation X an infinite number of answers can come from the patient: from 'yesterday on TV I saw a bombing raid on Baghdad' to 'yesterday I saw some Santa Clauses giving gifts to children'; from 'yesterday a dog tried to bite me' to 'a kitten came up to me affectionately'.

Projective identifications (hopefully more flow from patient to analyst than in the opposite direction), activation of the alpha function(s) and swirling protosensoriality would all operate in the session. The alpha function of the field begins to generate a 'waking dream thought' in the field which remains unknown.

Narrative derivatives arise from this.

The transference of the patient who conveys beta elements (balfa elements, or only partially alphabetized beta elements) and alpha elements comes up against the analyst's mental functioning, thus immediately generating a group-of-two situation, a situation in which the field itself is always being dreamed and re-dreamed. The transference undergoes a kind of diffraction into a multitude of stories, characters who are 'chimeras' of 'then' and 'inside' but also of 'now' and 'here' and of the interaction between the two minds.

If we immediately consider the oneiric functioning of the field at work, there is no communication that cannot be seen as activating and relevant to the field itself.

Also the facts apparently closest to reality would have more value as 'narrative hooks', bringing us closer and allowing the signification of dream thought. Even more subjective elements, such as the patient's dream, are part of the field, and their job is to signify and indicate the movements of the waking dream relative to the moment in which the dream is narrated.

If a patient talks about her daughter who cannot bear being touched, or about her younger son who is fond of displays of affection, about a father who is not authentically emotionally available, and then talks about a very depressed girlfriend who has a friend who is furious because his wife has left him, and then a film seen on television in which a husband who has been cheated on tried to kill his wife, and so on, she is describing what emotions are present in the current field. They could all be brought together in a transference interpretation, but that would be like bringing all the week's shopping, including all the frozen food, to the table in a raw state.

The field allows you to describe, collect, group together these emotions, clarifying them, focusing on them, using the characters as 'oven gloves' that make it possible to touch hot contents, because the analyst is certain that the patient's communication is a diffractogram of the current situation of the field, whose ingredients (which are waiting to be focused on, processed, digested) are relevant to, say, an inability to tolerate contact (perhaps inadequacies of ♀ with respect to hypercontents), lumps of developing affectionate feelings, occluded containers, fury and anger, jealousy, murders, etc.

These emotions can be 'cooked' using narrative transformation, unsaturated interventions and by constantly 'tasting' the patient's response to determine what ingredients are needed to enrich or lighten the dish. Certainly it is a story of jealousy, abandonment, rage, anger, affection, rejection, and some of these emotional and narrative elements are already 'cooked', already narratable: 'it must be painful for Lino to be abandoned by his wife, it is no wonder he is full of anger' rather than 'Lino's anger is understandable, even Medea when . . .', i.e. one can use tangential interventions that carry on the cooking process, that put things in order, creating links between the various things the patient expresses. But sometimes there is a share that is still frozen and has yet to become thinkable; for example, the patient's action of beating rhythmically with his fist as if holding a dagger would become: 'When one is hurt, vengeance seems to be the only way to find peace. So what can one do with protoemotions that have not yet been named?'

The transformation of protoemotional states into images entails naming something that was previously nameless – 'revenge', for example, represented as a 'pirate with a sword'.

Other 'narremes', however, are already narrative derivatives introduced by the patient.

My next digression concerns the way of conceiving characters, in narratology but above all in the consulting room (Ferro 1992, 1999b; Arrigoni and Barbieri 1998). To take an example from Manzoni's novel *The Betrothed*: Renzo and Lucia want to get married while Don Rodrigo wants at all costs to stop the marriage from going ahead. If one took a realistic-psychological approach, one would investigate the psychological traits of these characters, their mental and emotional lives. From a structuralist point of view, say from Propp onwards, what is significant is the function that the characters have within the story: Don Rodrigo is the engine of the story, precisely because he is the one who delays and prevents the happy ending, namely the marriage of Renzo and Lucia.

Another model of extreme cooperation between reader and text would see each reader constructing and making sense of the different characters in different ways (Eco 1979; Marrone 1986).

In a session of analysis (Paniagua 2002), a patient who is due to finish his analysis on his return from the summer holidays is distraught because of his daughter: he explains that he is afraid she is afflicted with precocious puberty and that she will have to be operated on. It is clear that there are different ways of considering these characters ('daughter with precocious puberty' and 'operation') depending on the analyst's model:

(a) The real problem is the daughter and the set of emotions that are triggered in a patient suffering from hypochondria.
(b) The subject of 'precocious puberty' acts as a brake on the plan of finishing the analysis, and the difficulty lies in finishing the analysis.

The patient's concern about his daughter's premature puberty and whether an operation is a good idea are what the field has to give an answer to – in relation to the problem of when to terminate the analysis and the anxieties it triggers. Only the analytic couple at work will be able to give an answer, as yet unknown, and the answer will come from the script of the previous sessions.

To put it radically, this corresponds broadly to the three major models of psychoanalysis, which, however, never exist in a pure state. The first is historico–reconstructive, the second relational, and the third represents an attempt to combine the two extreme views by acknowledging the existence of a 'here and now' that oscillates in a constant transformative fashion with 'there and then' and which opens up to a 'not known' that calls above all for the development of tools of knowledge.

Let us imagine a female patient who is still in the early stages of her analysis (this brings us back to the subject of sexuality). After some interpretative interventions by the analyst, she says: 'When I was a child I once went, in a spirit of perfect trust, to visit a friend of mine, never expecting that her grandfather would touch me under my skirt in such a shocking way. I remember that I left immediately, determined never to go back.'

In the first model, the analysis would start from the given narrative by progressively dissolving the repression of real childhood experiences that actually happened; gradually they would be 'remembered' or repeated in transference, and thus processed and detoxified. What was previously unconscious because of inhibition and feelings of guilt would, by becoming conscious, melt away like snow in the sun. The analyst would be a kind of Poirot or Homer singing and exploring the patient's Odyssey until she reaches self-knowledge at Ithaca.

In the second model the same story would be understood and interpreted as an experience that has a lot to do with the current relational situation: the patient is saying that she suddenly feels touched on a deep level by the analyst's interpretations, in a way that is too intimate and shows disrespect for her emotions, and that she doesn't want to continue such a disturbing analytic experience.

In the third model (which I would call the model of the 'ever-expanding unsaturated field') the analyst listens to the patient's manifest communication about her childhood and fundamentally respects this level of the narration. However, he also listens to the second relational level, the current level, without feeling the need to interpret it, regarding it rather as a signal coming from the field of excessive closeness and depth of interpretation. Accordingly, the interpretation will be modulated and the door will also be left open to the experience, in the particular situation created by the analytic setting, of a patient who feels her emotional world invaded by her most tumultuous and passionate aspects. By keeping in mind all three of these scenarios the analyst will, with his 'unsaturated' interventions, open himself up for further narrative operations belonging to the patient's infancy, to the here and now, to her inner life, in a constant oscillation between listening vertices. A new and unpredictable 'novel' will flow from the mating in the session of the two co-narrators who will constantly have to contend with what is unthinkable, with the repressed and split-off elements that enter into the current analytic relationship, and with what has been 'transformed' in the interaction of minds that will return to inhabit the patient's inner world and history – although the last word on this narrative and transformative weaving will never be spoken. It will be more important to learn to read new languages and new alphabets rather than to become familiar with any particular story.

The 'grandfather' character referred to above could of course be seen in terms of all three modalities within one session of analysis.

In the first way of thinking (both with regard to the character and the patient's communication), the grandfather is an altogether historical figure, with his own psychology, his own incontinent impulses to satisfy, and so on.

According to the second model, the grandfather is there to promote the dialectic between desire for peace and desire for knowledge, between reliability of analysis and its disquieting aspect. He could be interpreted as the part of the analysis that disturbs and frightens and thus enables the analysis to continue.

In the third model the grandfather is all this and more: he signals the degree of tolerable tension in the field (to make sure that the book is not closed) but then also many other things depending on whether the text is *Lolita*, *Madame Bovary* or *The Betrothed*, depending on what needs to be told most urgently and how this material is collected and transformed. But above all, it will open up the pleasure of reading.

Theories about characters can also be applied to the analyst and patient in the session.

In a 'psychological' theory we have two people, analyst and patient, each with their own personal characteristics and their own subjectivity (Renik 1998).

In a structuralist theory what matters is the role played by the one in relation to the other and the complex interplay of their actions (the patient projects his projective identifications, the analyst has his reveries). These are the roles that matter and that permit the development of the analysis that has some sort of structure-process such as admirably described by Meltzer (1967).

According to the theory of total interaction, analyst and patient are loci and functions of the field: the analysing function, the receptive function, the function of meaning-giver, the function of interpretation, the function of waiting. They all belong to the field that flows from them and they occupy different locations in the field, which becomes a sort of self-interpreting, self-expanding context. The asymmetry in the field is merely a factor of the analyst's greater responsibility.

Given this, we can distinguish between three types of transference: in position one, it is a repetition transference; transference in position two belongs to the model of projective identification/reverie where the relationship has two strong poles: analyst and patient. Transference in the third position is pervasive, co-determined, indistinguishable from co-presence and co-generation.

Needless to say, no situation is entirely pure. The fact is that adopting model three gives me the impossible task of describing the more frequently projecting pole (the patient) and the receptive pole (the analyst), and this is an expedient to see the functions carried out by both. We are still in a kind of solid Euclidean geometry and we have not yet made the leap to consider patient and analyst, transference and countertransference as loci/functions of the analytic field.

The same session can be seen (at least predominantly) from each of these vertices.

Guido and immigrants

At the beginning of his analysis Guido describes the scene of a prison, where he has started to do some consulting work as a doctor. Most of the inmates are Arab immigrants and it is difficult to understand what they are saying. I decide not to interpret this communication either in terms of the difficulty of entering into contact with unknown aspects of self or in terms of the difficulty of understanding what I say. However, it helps to develop the subject of these 'Arabs', each of whom gradually becomes recognizable and takes on his own characteristics. As our work continues, the narrative becomes more complex, which helps Guido to focus on the various emotions of which each individual Arab becomes a 'carrier'.

The claustrophobic experience at the beginning of the sessions shifts to an agoraphobic register towards the end: the fear that the Arabs will carry out attacks along the stretch of the Metro he regularly has to take (the path from Thursday to Monday?) or the fear that he won't see his 'dear friends any more'. Here, too, I refrain from offering any decoding type of interpretation, seeking instead to help Guido to focus, modulate and metabolize his anxiety with regard to separation by remaining 'apparently' inside his manifest text.

At this point I would say that I see his manifest text as resembling the inside of a trolley bus (Figure 5.2), where various characters sit and interact, and I think the trolley bus draws its motive power from the thread of thoughts present in my mind (the Italian word for trolley bus – *filobus* – contains the word for thread or wire; hence, thread of transference interpretation) that allows me to introduce into the trolley bus 'characters', comments and interventions that help generate narrative dialogic transformation whilst sticking to the manifest meaning that many patients need to

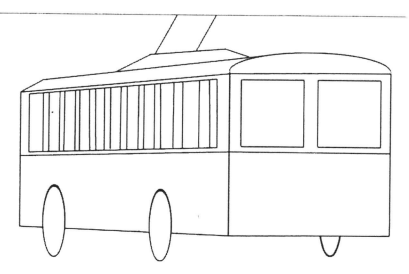

Figure 5.2

see respected as such for a long time. Besides, the narrative transformations that occur through the weaving of the analytic dialogue do not imply
a lesser degree of transformation than more decoding-type interventions
which give a more explicit meaning but often trigger off unwillingness on
the part of the patient to take on board the analyst's contribution.

6

Psychoanalytic scales and light pollution

This chapter consists simply of psychoanalytic exercises and some free-wheeling reflections.

Like a concert pianist who does finger-exercises when he is not performing, the analyst, Bion recommends, must do his exercises in the manner that suits him best. Bion, for example, suggested the use of the grid to review clinical material outside the session; I prefer to perform variations on a theme using small segments of sessions, also re-examining old material or even inventing possible clinical situations.

'My father works too much and never has any time to spend with me.'

This is a short communication given by a patient in analysis.

How should we listen to it? Where do we think this scene is played out? What characters are involved?

Of course, the scene can be placed 'outside' or 'before' the session, and clearly one possible listening vertex is the complex affair of a depressed father who fills every void with work, thus denying the patient the emotional availability she feels she needs.

But it could also be a communication within an internal scenario. The father could be an internal object that saturates everything and leaves no space for simply being together, an internal object that also becomes a mode of being of the patient herself. Then the scenario would be the 'inside', the 'inner world' of the patient and the time would be the present.

Another vertex might involve relational listening to the communication: you as the analyst are preoccupied with your own affairs, and you leave little space, you signal little willingness to 'be together', to show an interest and a closeness that the activity of interpretation alone fails to provide.

Naturally, different analysts (or the same analyst at different times) may choose to privilege one particular listening vertex. In the case of relational listening the problem would then arise whether it is more useful to the development of the analysis to 'interpret' this communication or whether it would be better to use this communication to change one's own internal structure and thus one's interpretative framework. Perhaps one can even ask oneself where and how the father came on the scene, or whether he is something that relates to one's own way of being, a blind spot (Guignard 1996) that will remain such if it is not lit up by the patient, or whether it results from the reception of projective identifications coming from the patient who thus manages to bring this problem to life in the current field.

Later the same woman patient has a dream: 'My father touched my breast.' Clearly this dream, given its unsaturated nature and the absence of associations suggested by the patient, lends itself to an almost infinite number of variations on a theme and it is a matter of some importance from which listening vertex it is received. Again we have to ask the classic questions of British journalism: when, who, where.

A wide spectrum of possible theories presents itself: a theory of repression that is made to fade away, thus bringing to the surface a traumatic childhood memory; a seductive and intrusive internal object; an analyst feared and seen as someone who triggers an erotic touch; or an analyst contact with whom the patient eroticizes defensively.

How should we deal with this? Perhaps by adopting an interpretation of the type we call in Italy unsaturated or narrative (Bezoari and Ferro 1994a; Ferro 1996a; Gaburri 1987; Corrao 1991) and which is widely used by French colleagues under the label 'interpretations in transference'. It could be worded: 'I think that the dream expresses an excessive, indiscreet and deductive closeness'. In this way we recognize the emotions conveyed by the dream and expect the patient to choose the narrative scenario in which to place it.

From this perspective, anxiety acts as the signal of the arrival of an excess of beta elements (bags of rice) while the emotions are the risottos (alpha elements) we cook with them.

Of course, what are needed are time, patience and adequate equipment.

80

Anxiety as a signal of the arrival of beta elements that we have not yet metabolized may be the prelude to metabolization, and such a transformation gradually lightens the 'burden' of anxiety. If the signals of anxiety are not immediately picked up and metabolized, this can activate the projection of the beta screen (Bion 1962), a last resort to generate countertransference and to see one's protoemotional states accepted.

It is just like a dynamite attack, which should be accepted for its value as a way of communicating despair that otherwise is not seen. It is, however, probable that excessive quotas of beta elements are in turn driven back, which generates NTR phenomena or examples of psychotic transference.

Part of the art of the psychoanalyst involves marrying – even for a moment – the point of view of the other.

One particular type of anxiety, as I have pointed out elsewhere (Ferro 2002a, 2002b), is that which results from the breaking up of the agglutinated nucleus (Bleger).

Usually this becomes stratified in the setting. We can imagine it as being made up of lots of cats (or panthers?) that, when placed side by side, form a kind of soft, furry carpet. Any violation of the setting results in a rip in the carpet and all the cats (panthers?) leap out biting and scratching, just like protoemotions that have yet to be transformed.

But let us carry on with our exercise.

At our first meeting to discuss a possible analysis a patient says: 'I am being pursued by judges, they give me no rest. They want to ruin me, particularly Dr Dentoni (in Italian, this means 'big teeth') and Dr Uccello (= bird, and penis). I am looking for any possible strategy to escape from them, whatever the cost.'

What is the problem this potential patient is referring to? Certainly, on one level he is talking about an actual legal question in the external world but this concerns us as analysts only very marginally. Another vertex is intrapsychic: the patient lives in a state of great inner persecution which, it is possible to imagine, is caused by archaic objects that generate a sadistic superego the patient is unable to elude. He cannot bow to its judgement, either because of the particularly archaic nature of the superego or because he has to deny his own misdeeds; only lies and flight can save him. Again, one need only think of Bion's defence of liars.

Sooner or later, once the analysis has begun to take shape, the analyst will very probably take on the guise of Dr Dentoni and

Dr Uccello. Then it would become clear that the patient feels 'bitten' by guilt and intruded on by Dr Uccello, perhaps because of a level of interpretative activity he cannot stand.

The important thing would then be not to provide the patient with defence lawyers, who would confuse the context even more, but lawyers who help him to face up to the verdict and to recognize his wrongdoing, both his phantasmatic misdeeds and those that have perhaps become 'real' as a way of representing the drama of being a child who never felt defended by good and welcoming objects.

The consulting room should become the kind of courtroom where a trial is held in order to stop flight from perpetuating the confusion, if only as a manic defence from profound depressive feelings to which the excitement of fight–flight had for some time been a useful antidote. Giving up on megalomania, narcissistic scaling down, mourning for time past are all painful undertakings, but at least they are not as destructive as the emotional 'cooking the books' constantly needed to make ends meet in one's inner world.

Besides, the superego should be thought of as a transgenerational precipitate of persecutory internal objects (Ferro 2002b). It's like snake venom that spreads intrapsychically. It is not enough to 'analize it'; it must also be sucked out and drained away by means of receptive reverie.

According to the patient's second communication, he 'only finds solace with whores he can pay for without any problems'. It is obvious that prostitution stands between 'stimulants' (gamblers) and 'antidepressants' (essentially, prostitutes treat the depressed and despairing aspects of themselves and their 'patients').

The fear is that one will not be able to receive the love one has never had (and whose place has been taken by persecution). All one can get is a surrogate one has to pay for: besides, it is clear that the analysis is immediately seen in this light.

An old motif, I don't know how relevant it is today: anal masturbation?

This was a subject dear to Meltzer (1996) with regard to which there were two principal modes of interpretation. One focused more on the description of the unconscious phantasy underlying its consequences, the other more on the emotions and feelings involved (fraudulence, cheating, pseudo-maturity, denial of need).

A supervisee recounts a series of patient's dreams: in the first, the patient could not find the car that gave her a sense of security; in the second, she was about to take the wrong road, one that would lead her to a rocky ledge, but then she discovered another road; and in the third, she found herself in a street full of stinking excrement. Then the patient went on to speak of a small girl who was horrified by dirty things.

I immediately rule out a possible interpretation in terms of anal masturbation (in any case, the patient had previously talked about this practice) and I suggest the following path: for the patient, being alone, the time that passes between one session and another is a source of despair. She could even end up on a ledge (suicide?). But then she takes another road, which is dirty and full of scary things; that is, she clings to the anger and hatred she feels in order to survive. To the child they are ugly and dirty, but ultimately they are the things that help save her from despair.

Even masturbation can be a life-saver, although it means descending to the level of desperate exclusion and abandonment felt by the 'Little Match Girl'.

The supervisee takes on board this point of view and communicates it creatively to the patient. Hatred and anger will begin to appear as feelings expressed in this way in the second column of the grid, where we find lies – albeit white lies – which offer protection from an encounter (which is as yet too difficult) with fear, pain, suffering, despair at finding oneself alone and feeling abandoned. She remembers that as a child every time her mother was about to go away she would sing to her a famous song entitled 'Balocchi e profumi' ('Toys and Perfume') and beg her not to go (a request that went unheard). Today she makes the same request to the analyst who likewise goes away, but with whom it is possible to make the 'non-thing' thinkable (Bion 1963).

The Oedipus complex: an example of light pollution?

I believe that today's psychoanalysis is suffering from a phenomenon similar to light pollution in cities: the excessive artificial light that prevents us from seeing the stars. I am thinking of the phenomenon of the overexposure and over-illumination of the Oedipus complex in psychoanalysis.

This is true from various points of view. There can be no doubt that the Oedipus complex is a structure and a conceptualization (but also a preconception) that is basic to the human mind; it is like the wheel in the history of civilization. Often the richness of this concept prevents us from looking elsewhere – for two additional reasons. The first is that as a species we are more tied to what we know and what gives us certainty (one need only think of religions, not to say ghosts) than to the various facets of the unknown; this point was made again and again by Bion. The second is that the success of the

Figure 6.1 The Oedipus complex. Freud's theories generally only explain the male psyche. When he later finally got round to looking at women in more depth, there were many who wished he hadn't bothered.

Oedipus complex is due especially to Sophocles, who created a masterpiece that acted as a vehicle – today we might say a winning 'logo' – for psychoanalysis.

Other psychoanalytic truths, on the other hand – comparable to the invention of the plough, the discovery of fire, metals, alloys, the steam engine, radar, space probes, and so on – have not been blessed with a 'creative writer' who has managed to come up with another equally effective 'logo'.

I am thinking of Klein's idea of the centrality of an inner world that is as real as the outside world and of the idea of the centrality – in the functioning and development of the mind – of the constant game of projective identification/reverie, and again of the alpha function. Whatever you wish to call it, this is the basic equipment that allows us to 'cook' sensory stimuli at their first appearance. It is 'basic equipment' whose preconception is a legacy of the species but which becomes operative only if it is 'activated' through the encounter with the mind of a more receptive other, a kind of trans-generational freeze-dried food requiring hydration provided by an other to become 'active'.

All dysfunctions that occur at these levels are the seeds, the loci, the cracks and the faults of most future pathologies.

It is not uncommon for such basic dysfunctions to be ignored for a long time until they are discharged in different ways into psychic life in forms that can even be very serious.

After all, the mind is the 'variable' or 'mutable' part of the brain, and the mind will forever elude any other category of knowledge that is not the mind itself (we also need the illusion that Freud entertained but belongs neither to Green nor myself, namely that one day new tools will allow us to access the biology of the mind!).

So I see two sources of crisis in psychoanalysis: the light pollution of the Oedipus complex and the loss of its special nature through blending processes that would be enriching if they came via implicit or metaphorical references but whose effect is toxic when psychoanalysis is levelled down to empirical research, to the development of infant psychology, the observation of development (including the practice of infant observation, which can be valuable if it is conducted as a metaphorical–intuitive study of mental development).

Psychoanalysis is relevant to other territories; namely, the mind, its various facets, its dysfunctions, and, today I would add, everything that itself belongs to the mind and brings the visible mind to life. This happens not only on the verbal level but also via those mental operations that have to be carried out and not simply talked about. I refer here to the analyst's capacity to take on board not only what comes from the patient in verbal terms (sensoriality, evacuations, actings–out, stagings, projective identifications, etc.) and to transform all this into lines of thinkability, into images that can then be variously re–woven into a narrative–constructive–interpretative fabric together with the patient.

In this way psychoanalysis moves from being a psychoanalysis of contents, conflicts or deficiencies to being a psychoanalysis of instruments that foster the very development of the possibility/capacity to think.

> A young man asks for a consultation because he wants to become a woman. He has had a tragic childhood: as an adolescent he beat up his parents several times and later, on two different occasions, was on the verge of raping two girls. Now married, he has two sweet girls, and just wants to be a 'good mother' to his/her children, a mother who is a source only of gentleness. The reason he has decided to work towards becoming a woman is that it is impossible for a male to be what he wants to be. He has started to shave his body hair and to grow his nails long like a woman who puts on red nail-polish in the evening.
>
> The problem at this point is not a question of interpreting the segment (----- →), the hyperbeta segment, but giving the patient that certain something that will help him to introject a digestive-metabolic-figurative-pictogramatic function of the mind that enables him to choose the unthinkable split up into possible narratives.

An analysis that focuses on content, or that activates it before having thought of developing apparatuses for thinking it, could become a psychoanalysis that sets off iatrogenic pathologies – like a particle accelerator that triggers processes it can no longer contain.

It is my view that clinical psychoanalysis is much more responsible for such situations than one might think – situations which are often called negative therapeutic reactions or psychotic transference, and which often take the form of psychosomatic illnesses during the course of analysis.

In other words, before triggering 'nuclear fission' we should have at our disposal the equipment to handle it – otherwise we run the risk of mental Chernobyls, when what is activated by the analysis sweeps away the ability to manage and/or transform it. This is particularly true for patients with a significant presence of 'aggluti-nated nuclei' (to use Bleger's term), a source of possible changes or possible and traumatic evacuations into the mind and the body.

Nevertheless, there are authors like De Simone (2004) who give what I consider a very modern reading of the Oedipus complex by seeing it as both a complex and a triangle situation. She suggests 'thinking of the two situations connected to the Oedipus complex as the transition from a situation of linearity to a situation of trian-gularity (complexity). The passage from a more biological linear drive (incest as directly derived from the sex drive and patricide as a direct deviation of aggression and rivalry) to triangularity would stand in relation to the ability to tolerate the space of deferral that leads to thinkability and symbolization.'

But this is so far removed from the original meanings that it would be more useful to make a leap of language and to focus our thinking on the definition of 'what' it enables us to think. I believe that at present this 'what' (a model of this 'what') has been given us by Bion and by those who are developing his model of the thinking apparatus.

Again, De Simone (2004) in her reading of the Oedipus complex points out that the Oedipal preconception of the mind 'is config-ured as a natural endowment of the human mind waiting to meet with the other in order to develop'. She also quotes an important passage from Bion (1963):

> I am postulating a precursor of the Oedipal situation not in the sense that such a term might have in Melanie Klein's discussion of the *Early Phases of the Oedipus Complex*, but as something that belongs to the ego, as part of its apparatus for contact with reality. In short I postulate an α-element version of a private Oedipus myth, which is the means, the preconception, by virtue of which the infant is able to establish contact with the parents as they exist in reality. The mating of this α-element Oedipal preconception with the realization of the actual parents gives rise to the concep-tion of parents.

It is difficult to disagree. However, I would postulate that behind this lies the problem of the development (formation–framework–delyophilization) of an alpha function that would permit the formation of the alpha element. In short, I believe that when the mind is able to produce alpha elements we are already in a state of 'abundance' (or *fat kine* (cows); see *Genesis* 41:20). Today's 'famine' (*lean kine*) corresponds to situations where there is a hypo-function or an alpha 'a-function' (a defective or missing alpha function).

A patient is now nearing the end of her analysis. Initially her predominant mode of functioning was autistic with protoemotions erupting in panic attacks or psychosomatic manifestations, but she has moved on to a new situation where she is able to create freely and deal with emotions. After a particularly intense session working on issues connected to the end of the analysis and the 'new' that lay ahead, she talks about her 11-year-old daughter (the daughter's age corresponds to the length of the analysis) and going out to buy new clothes with her. At each item of clothing the daughter let out squeals of joy and almost started dancing. But then she said to her mother: 'I do not feel very well, it's too bright in here, too noisy.' Her mother suggested she should stop for a bit, get her breath back and then carry on shopping.

If a previously insufficient alpha function is exposed to an excess of protoemotional sensory data, there is a return to 'pain', to fatigue, an announcement of weakness as if it were an old war wound. All one needs to do is catch one's breath and the session can continue – with the various emotional stimuli that involves.

Bollas (1999) makes the point that Sophocles' *Oedipus Rex* is not the tale of an Oedipus complex but 'the story of a family that did not happen', and that 'the Oedipal stage is, in many respects the discovery that one's fate is to be inside a complex, consisting of the family and an internal world of one's own making'.

Once again the film is at quite an advanced stage; the Lumière brothers have been and gone, we already have projection, lenses, celluloid.

It's about time we looked at the background to all this with some passion – before the Lumière brothers, before the lens, before celluloid – and considered how these things are gradually constituted (constructed).

What I am trying to say is that we need new myths, because if a myth is the precipitate of a group dream that resolves a nodal point in our emotional life, there is equally a risk that it might become a brake, a marsh that restricts access to other unforeseen paths not contained in that myth. So we must make a constant effort to

88

generate new myths inside the consulting room, private myths that belong to each pair but also new collective myths that can act as narratable precipitates of experience and can open up ever new perspectives.

Reading psychoanalysis: the pleasure and adventure of exploration

'Galeoto was the book and the one who wrote it' is one of the most memorable lines in the *Divine Comedy*. The readers of the book were – as everyone knows – Paolo and Francesca, whose overwhelming and irrepressible passion was kindled by reading the book together.

This is one of the characteristics of a real book and a real book of psychoanalysis: the power to kindle a mood of curiosity and passion that makes us say, as we lie in bed at night, 'I'll put the light out in a moment' – not once but many times.

Every true book is essentially a book of psychoanalysis, and Freud taught us how writers and poets often anticipate psychoanalysis. Writing and reading are, and were, privileged tools for investigating the depths of the human soul: Tolstoy, Dostoevsky, Proust, Mann, Flaubert (I'll stop there because otherwise I would use up all the space I have just citing names and works).

So every book can be a book of psychoanalysis.

This is my first assumption, which I shall develop only partially. Were I able to develop this idea more extensively, I would look at Joyce, especially the Joyce of *Finnegans Wake*, then Balzac, as well as various playwrights from Shakespeare to Molière, from Ibsen to Pirandello.

If I may be allowed a touch of hyperbole, I would say that three of the best books on psychoanalysis among those I have read in the last few years are: *Red Dragon, Silence of the Lambs* and *Hannibal* – all three by Thomas Harris.

Why do I say they are about psychoanalysis? Because they investigate and describe in a psychoanalytic way very deep states of mind which otherwise – outside literature – only psychoanalysis can fathom.

Red Dragon has the following story:

In psychoanalytic language: the inversion of a flow of projective identifications of a mother incapable of reverie prevents the child's proper development of the alpha function and causes the evacuation of uncontainable anxiety through acts of violence. An encounter with a person capable of receptivity momentarily arouses hope for change, but once again destructiveness prevails.

In ordinary language: a serial killer, Francis Dolarhyde (!), kills entire families every third moon in a ritual that involves the mortification of his victims, the shattering of mirrors and arranging dead bodies so that they look at him. The protagonist had a tragic childhood: he was abandoned by his mother, a beauty queen, who let out a cry when she saw him for the first time because he had a severe cleft lip and palate. He will never be able to look at himself. An attempt to return to his mother and her new family fails miserably and after the death of his grandmother, the only person who ever cared for him, he begins his killing spree. This goes on until he meets a blind girl (who is not horrified by his face), who has a relationship with him characterized by tender affection and full acceptance. This results in a sort of split between his two sides: one that will stop at nothing to get revenge (the Red Dragon) and the other that wants to save the girl and the affectionate relationship they have together. (We are in the consulting room with a borderline or psychotic patient.)

Silence of the Lambs has the following story:

In psychoanalytic language: the search for a stable container in the absence of the introjection of a psychic skin causes the protagonist – incapable of symbolization – to use fetishes that delude him into thinking that self-containment is possible.

In ordinary language: Jame Gumb, another serial killer, kills big women. He has a history of early abandonment and lack of maternal care. He kills because he wants to make a suit of human skin that will function as a new skin and a new identity. He kills young women to create a kind of sheath, as if he were a tailor. An important figure in both novels is Dr Lecter, a psychiatrist who is himself a serial killer imprisoned inside a cage in a maximum security prison. From the second novel on, Agent Starling is the heroine who is determined to find the killer and who experiences a thousand adventures on the way.

The third novel, *Hannibal*, has the following story:

In psychoanalytic language: the psychotic part of the personality is capable of seducing the healthy part and, consumed by a sense of guilt at being unable to save his tender infantile part, he has turned to cannibalism in the absence of food for the mind – the maternal reverie; his tender parts are destroyed by his violent parts which end up cannibalizing the mind itself.

In ordinary language: Hannibal escapes from prison and is again hunted by the police. Meanwhile his cannibalistic perversions come to light as does their childhood origin: he lost his beloved little sister in childhood when she was the victim of acts of cannibalism. In their desperate hunger, bandits who had invaded the farm where the children lived had eaten not only a scrawny deer Hannibal used to play with but also the little girl. Hannibal wishes for a non-linear temporality to allow him to reverse the course of time and bring his sister back to life through Agent Starling, who he manages to mesmerize . . .

What kind of reading excites passions?

'I sing of knights and ladies, of love and arms, of courtly chivalry, of courageous deeds' are the first lines with which Ariosto addresses the reader in his *Orlando Furioso*. Rivalry, love, hatred, adventure.

The recipe must be 'spicy'.

The other factor that makes the recipe appetizing is, in my view, the bringing forth of the *visual quality* of the narrative.

The reader, who as we know co-constructs the text, should be roused by action scenes, characters, a highly spiced atmosphere and a degree of unpredictability and sometimes mystery and fear; it is even better if the reader's encyclopaedia is occasionally severely tested.

These qualities are what we find in all successful novels and they are also what account for the growing popularity of 'detective stories' or 'crime stories' in recent years.

Todorov (1971), a writer I already mentioned in 1992, describes three types of 'detective story'. In the *whodunit* we have the story of a crime, which is absent but real, and the story of an investigation, which is present but insignificant. In the *thriller* the two stories merge, or rather the first story is suppressed in favour of the latter. There is a previous crime: action and narration coincide, looking forward replaces retrospection.

Intermediate between the two is the *suspense* novel, which maintains the mystery element of the whodunit and tells two stories (past and present), although it refuses to reduce the story of the present to the simple gathering of data. As in the *thriller* the latter story plays the lead role. The reader asks himself about the future as well as the past. He is curious to know what happened, suspense plays a part. I have always found it intriguing that these three descriptions correspond to three models of thinking about analytic work: one is archaeological and reconstructive, the second is centred around the 'here and now' and the third attributes value both to a past history to be revealed and to what is new, what comes to life in the present story between analyst and patient (Ferro 1999g).

I – reader and reader of psychoanalysis

The books that made me into an avid reader were, alas, the works of Emilio Salgari. I am consoled by Claudio Magris's view (1982) that 'the adventure novel is a kind of sally into the open and at the same time a homecoming . . . the Malaysian cycle is a crudely naive and childlike version of the adventure that *The Odyssey* and *The Phenomenology of Spirit* told in the more elevated and mature words of poetry and thought'. He then goes on to say that 'having loved Salgari at the age when one first encounters the book is to have oriented one's fantastic passion in one direction or another'. Adventures, struggles, injustices, travel, storms, losses, victories, passions, mysteries, Tremal-Naik, the Tigers of Malaysia, Mompracem . . . The joy of adventure, the anticipation of 'what happened next' have always been an enduring hallmark of my taste in reading.

I shall spare the reader a further excursus into my later literary tastes and turn instead to how I began to 'savour' psychoanalysis.

I started (was initiated into) reading psychoanalysis with *The Psychopathology of Everyday Life* (I was 15). I then moved on to *Some Elementary Lessons in Psychoanalysis* (in the old Italian Astrolabio edition).

What was it that captured my attention? The clarity of the text, the tangibility of the examples, a structure that somehow resembled a 'detective story' in that it constantly exercised the reader's 'little grey cells'. The years pass and I continue to read Freud, but what was it that impassioned me to the point where I even read him on the beach during the summer holidays? The answer is Freud's *Case Histories*, and in particular, the visual evocations contained in his narration, his stimulation of associations, his construction of scenes.

I even studied the more theoretical works and got the same pleasure from discovering his 'evocation' and use of images and metaphors. Ever since then I have always enjoyed the adventure of reading case histories (and the worlds created by every theorist of psychoanalysis) – this happens with Klein and the infernal circles of the most primitive phantasies and with Bion in his *Seminars* or *Memory of the Future*.

What kind of psychoanalysis should the non-specialist read?

First of all, the works have to be 'understandable'; they should 'evoke images', have a distinctive 'flavour' that carries the reader into the consulting room, they should open the way up to unexplored worlds, to underground worlds, basements, to parallel and possible worlds.

For me the definition of a good book of psychoanalysis is that it should have the same effect on the reader as chivalrous romances had on 'Don Quixote': it should transport us into another dimension. That is what happens to me and what I think happened to many with the classics of psychoanalysis, from Freud to Klein, from Winnicott to Bion.

The oft-cited food metaphor comes to my aid. According to Alberto Manguel (1986), this metaphor apparently dates back to 593 BCE, when Ezekiel had a vision in which an angel told him to eat a book. Later St John had the same vision.

Subsequently this metaphor became a common figure of speech.

Apparently Samuel Johnson was such a voracious reader that he would keep a book in his lap during dinner, ready to start reading after he had swallowed the last bite of his meal.

'The world [. . .] is a book that is devoured by a reader who is a letter in the world's text,' writes Manguel (1986).

I often talk about visual phenomena because I believe they occupy an essential place in reading. For me the perfect example of this is a book by Luigi Serafini published by Franco Maria Ricci, which created a kind of medieval encyclopaedia of an imaginary world. Every page illustrated something specific (and non-existent) and the notes and comments were written in a fantastic and likewise non-existent alphabet. A book composed entirely of invented images and words, with a preface by Italo Calvino: *Codex Seraphinianus*. Here we could also talk about children's picture books, comics, films, the need for wonder and magic reflected in the enormous success of Harry Potter.

Finally, if a book on psychoanalysis is to be read it must fire the 'imagination' and meet the 'taste' of the reader: that is, it must inspire delight and pleasure.

Writers on psychoanalysis

I have always considered the writing of psychoanalysis (and the experience of being inside an analytic session) very similar to the activity of a painter, someone intent on making verbal pictures that undergo constant change, construction and deconstruction both in colours and forms. This stimulation of the visual faculty was one of Freud's masterly characteristics as a storyteller (Petrella 1988). In my way of thinking about painting/writing I have always regarded as fundamental the 'tonight we improvise' approach and the 'taste for not knowing where you are going'.

Two frightened, dangerous animals in a room whose only hope is that one is less frightened, less dangerous than the other – this is the pictographic expression Bion (1980) used to describe the situation of analyst and patient alone in the consulting room. It was also Bion who called psychoanalysis the probe that constantly expands the field it is exploring. These are the strong flavours we should be able to pass on. The psychoanalytic method provides us with a wonderful spacecraft that hopefully is archaic compared to tomorrow's model – which will bring us towards dimensions of the mind as yet unknown.

In this context it is extraordinary that Tolstoy – in an Italian book recently edited and translated by Carla Moschio – has his hypothetical characters (a country school-master, a very parochial school-master, a pedantic school-master, a school-mistress, himself, and finally an intelligent farmer) describe how a ship is powered by steam. By using these different approaches to the same topic Tolstoy poses the problem of how to construct an effective narrative that manages to capture the reader's attention – to the point where the reader says: 'a little more, please'.

7

Thinking the unthinkable (the analytic kitchen and grandfather's recipes)

Alessia's snakes

After several years of analytic work, Alessia recounts a dream in which she is at a market lined with lots of different stalls, one is which is full of snakes. Her mother hands her a bag and says: 'I've bought a rolled up one to cook for you tonight.' In the dream the patient gets angry. Then the analyst comes along to comfort her in her dismay at what her mother was planning to do.

It is clear that the analyst in the dream is represented according to the two functions he fulfils: one is to console her and the other, disturbing but no less important, is to be the person who cooks the snakes for her.

Emotions, emotion-snakes that poison and suffocate, have always been Alessia's big problem. Early on in our analytic work she often had to contend with poisonous snakes or with boa constrictors she thought might crush her. So she had invented a strategy of both avoidance and control of the emotions she felt threatened and persecuted by because she knew that they would poison her existence or take her breath away.

Accordingly, she only had relationships with married men. Of course this meant jealousy, anger and exclusion, but somehow all this was taken into account right from the beginning. An unattached man would have meant trusting in the relationship and then maybe one day finding herself suddenly dealing with a cobra or a boa.

The same strategy was at work in the consulting room . . . she was always aware of the limit put on any possible emotional relationship in analysis: it was after all work!

In this way she had a kind of ever-ready antidote to jealousy, anger or feelings of exclusion.

I think that seeing the analyst as someone who cooks snakes is an excellent way of describing one of the functions of the analyst, namely cooking and making edible, assimilable and digestible emotions that previously could only be split off and kept at a distance.

Another defence mechanism that Alessia deployed, this time against a tyrannical and intransigent superego, was her continual use of lying to save herself from presumed accusations or disapproval. In her analysis the cooking of emotions went hand in hand with the 'cooking' of the superego that gradually became softer and more malleable, thus making emotions, even the rawest emotions, more approachable.

Leoluca's polyps

Leoluca is a young engineer who is unable to have stable relationships. If a relationship becomes more intimate, he immediately feels suffocated, he runs away and changes partners – and this goes on in an ever-repeating cycle.

One day, however, a dream opens up a new perspective: a gastroscopy and colonoscopy show that he is full of polyps. He talks about the film version of the book *The Secret Garden*, where the main character, a young boy, is kept alone in a room for fear that might be allergic to everything. It seems clear that what Leoluca fears is the attachment of the polyps, their hunger, their need to establish tentacular ties. He is terrified that if these links are established, he will be exposed to emotions such as jealousy and terror of abandonment, as well as his fear of being allergic and not able to withstand such toxic emotions.

Over the course of a few weeks he continues the story of the film and the book (in the meantime he has bought himself a copy) and eventually he has a dream in which he finds himself outside a door, terrified that it may be Bluebeard's door, whereas in fact it is the gate that gives access to the 'secret garden' of the film/book.

He realizes that what scares him is the intensity of his need for a tie that exposes him to possible powerful emotions which he exorcises by breaking off any significant relationship.

Marzia's Arabs

For a long time Marzia was unable to tolerate frustration. Every time someone went away or separated from her she had panic attacks. This continued until she experienced a situation in analysis of lack of response that provoked two reactions in her, one which she calls 'Catholic', in which she is well aware of the reasons for the rejection, and the other, which we will call 'Arab fundamentalist', which appears in a dream featuring rejected Arabs who, condemned to poverty, prepare terrorist attacks (panic attacks). The arrival of the Arabs who do not listen to reason is, however, already an initial representation of what comes to life in Marzia when she is faced with the frustration of having her duality with the other confirmed.

★　★　★

Some of the functions of the analyst seem to me to be clear:

- cooking snakes,
- cooking polyps (the Italian word refers both to polyps and to octopuses),
- depicting Arabs and finding ways of 'cooking' them.

In the presence of lumps of emotions (or protoemotions) that are difficult to manage, the human mind activates a series of defences.

Sometimes the problem is further upstream, because there is not even the possibility of depicting the element that burns, that scorches; that is to say, there are situations where there is as yet no figuration for the snakes, polyps or Arabs.

These are the *most 'mute' situations*, those in which suffering is expressed through evacuation or expulsion, which can occur in different ways, from psychosomatic illnesses to hallucinations, from character disorders to delinquency. In these situations it is more difficult to activate a more effective and functioning metabolic function such as might lead, by reversing the evacuative flow, to thinkability – or at least early forms of thinkability – through figuration, pictographs of what had previously been totally silent. This can happen at any place in the field. This place can also be the analyst's mind – with his reveries, figurations and countertransferences. Once the 'evacuated unthinkable' finds a place somewhere in the field, we are already at a turning-point with regard to the seriousness of the problem. Now it will 'only' be a matter of finding more economic and gradual ways of managing it in the field and getting closer to a possible digestive-metabolic solution. Once the unthinkable enters any place in the field as 'the depressed friend on the point of suicide', previously unspoken despair finds a leading man who can voice it on stage.

It is at this moment that the various defence mechanisms come into play. They are less archaic than evacuation, and serve to make tolerable in the field – at any place in the field – the protoemotional lava that as yet cannot be 'held' directly.

There is also the possibility of splitting (again inside the field). Here this primitive function, this part, this aggregate of beta elements or this 'betaloma' (as I have termed it elsewhere) is labelled 'a friend', 'an acquaintance', 'a colleague', or in various other possible ways, from a terrifying pit–bull to a dinosaur. Another possibility is the recourse to disavowal, repression, phobic avoidance, obsessive control, hypochondria, and so on.

Each of these different mechanisms also implies a different narrative strategy: the undigested element is concealed or revealed in the narrated text in different ways.

A patient who had extreme difficulty in keeping under control the violent emotions triggered by the summer break in the analysis starts off the first session after the holidays by talking about how wonderful her holidays had been and how good she had felt during the summer, adding at the end of the session that she had read a book that had made her cry a lot. The book, *History: A Novel* by Elsa Morante, is about a woman who is widowed, raped and then forced to deal with the child who is born from this rape.

So in a small corner of the narrative fabric of the session appears the feeling of abandonment over the summer, the holidays experienced as violence, and an awareness that emotions and feelings arise that one has to deal with.

After all, denial (or perhaps negation) all of a sudden leaves open a sort of crack in which emotional history takes form and comes to life. Of course, a defence mechanism against violence or anger could take the form of a phobia of knives, the obsessive ritual of making sure the gas is off, or hypochondria: all of these can become places to accommodate and monitor a frightening danger. It matters little, of course, which defensive strategy is chosen; the important thing is to find narrative/interpretative strategies which remain close to the problem that triggers the fear.

It's not a question of reinforcing or criminalizing the defence mechanism, but making it gradually less and less necessary by progressively negotiating the 'lava lump'.

Of course, this can take quite a long time; the defensive constellations of the analyst are also called into play, and the work of emotional re-weaving can be carried out either in a grey, technical way or with dynamism and creativity. This reflects the qualities of the analytic couple; but equally I would say (to some extent at least) it reflects the qualities of the analytical group one belongs to.

The narrative text of the session continuously indicates the changes that occur in the patient's inner world and in the field. If a patient who has a fear of his own emotions, which he copes with by keeping them under strict control and maintaining a computerized distance from them, should talk about having been to a concert of 'live music' and explains that he now adores Brazilian music or that he has given his son 'carioca' pastels, this would signal an ability to get closer to his emotional world in a different way.

So if a patient says he enjoyed going dancing with his girlfriend, that would indicate that that day the session had followed the right emotional rhythm, and had done so in an atmosphere of warmth and closeness.

The field is therefore the keeper of the truth about the functioning of the field itself, no matter which place in the field becomes the expression of that functioning.

Possible places in the field include: the dramatic component of the field (the continual formation and transformation of characters), the mind of the analyst, countertransference, the place where images are formed (waking dream thought), derivatives thereof, the counter-transference dreams of the analyst, his reveries, the inner worlds of analyst and patient, their histories, their relationship, enactments, projective identifications and all their vicissitudes, and the transgenerational places of both.

Narrative balls of wool and the fabula

A 'character' that becomes the bearer of the patient's 'lava lump' is a kind of narrative 'ball' (as in a ball of yarn) that is waiting to be woven by analyst and patient. If that ball were called 'Mario' and referred to violence or uncontainability, this would have to be deconstructed and narrated in a way that can be 'worn' by the patient.

Inappropriate interventions (usually rejected by the patient) include: 'Mario is the part of you that . . .' or 'Mario enters the scene when . . .' and even 'I think that Mario is the function that . . .'.

99

Then there are intermediate forms such as 'Mario has perhaps similar features to you when . . .' or 'Mario reminds you of something about yourself'. And finally there are the more telling narrative formulations in which Mario the ball of yarn is deconstructed into the threads that compose him and are then re-woven.

'It would seem that Mario is jealous of Caterina when . . .' thus introduces the yellow thread of jealousy or 'what angers Mario . . .' introduces the red thread of anger, and so on. There is no need to go as far as an exhaustive interpretation; it is enough to disentangle the 'Mario ball of yarn' and to re-weave it with a pattern and a design that the patient can understand and take on board. Nothing stands in the way of the occasional exhaustive interpretation – and indeed at some point there must be one.

What applies to Mario also applies to any 'ball of yarn' narrative which takes its place in the field in any way or any form. Often, more tangled balls may enter through projective identification.

The incompetent head physician

Luca is at the early stage of his analysis. He tells me about a patient of his who is considered to be very bad, who is very angry, and who some people find frightening.

It is true that he has started working but at his workplace he is afraid of his employer. He perceives him as someone breathing down his neck, someone who might even bite him on the neck.

Without thinking, I say: 'I would bark first'.

There is a brief silence. Then Luca carries on talking about his patient, about the fury he sometimes feels and the terror that accompanies this fury.

Then in a deep voice he says that he wonders whether he might ever have points of contact with this person; he would be terrified by any possible similarities.

Feeling that the atmosphere is too saturated with anxiety and that my approach is excessive, I say: 'Who said you had points of contact?'

Shortly afterwards Luca says (or I could also say he responds by saying) that his head physician doesn't know how to use a computer: once he had a file containing an article, and another containing a bibliography, and he was amazed that it was possible to put them together. Luca adds: 'He's really a troglodyte as far as computers are concerned. I have to teach him how to operate them' (said with a relieved tone of voice).

The next day he dreams of a dinosaur, a *Tyrannosaurus rex*, but he was Spiderman and was able to save himself.

I say that to me it at least looked like an even combat, because Spiderman had his strategies for saving himself. He carries out a further transformation by talking of gladiators fighting with nets against lions.

★　★　★

The following drawing:

may be interpreted as the raw material of a story that can be told in a thousand different ways, that is to say, there are relatively few *fabulae* and an infinite number of *sujets* (to use the terminology of narratology).

This is what in effect Sandra does when at our first session she reports that she has been 'suffering from ulcerative colitis'. This follows the first reverie that comes to her analyst on seeing her: he finds himself, despite Sandra's extreme beauty, in the presence of a transsexual, as if he had recognized her surplus of protoemotions.

Sandra then describes a number of love affairs, involving being left, fights, scenes – which apparently evacuate all tension. It had been a turbulent period, albeit without disease.

She then tells the story of her childhood, in particular the onset of asthma at the age of two and half.

She goes on to tell how she was upset when her grandmother, who had not seen her for some time, said: 'Who is this boy?'

There follows a story of sexual abuse suffered at the hands of the 'grandfather' at the age of seven, 'shingles' at the age of ten, and finally an uncle whom she had to masturbate to placate his terrifying fits of rage. It is clear that through these multiple scenarios Sandra narrates over and again the same story of a superabundance of protoemotions she is unable to cope with by means of transformation but which she evacuates or blandishes with various strategies.

Psychoanalysis used to have a horror of the analyst infecting the patient, the pollution that would ensue if the threshold of analytic neutrality were lowered; the analyst was not allowed to introduce any phantasies or use metaphors or reverie. This principle was applied without considering that 'neutrality' belonged to the fabric of the field just like any other emotional colouring.

I think reparative activity is essential also when it involves the grafting on of extra pieces, provided they come into being in the field and in the dream thought of the analyst.

A patient dreams of running free and naked, feeling a renewed contact with nature, but then dogs come on the scene, he gets frightened, covers himself up and leaves. The analyst participates in the construction and transformation of the dream by saying: 'I think that there is a character missing, an Eve or a Jane who emerges from somewhere and who is forced to cover herself up by the arrival of the dogs.'

A woman patient recounts a recurrent masturbatory phantasy which is always accompanied another phantasy of being slapped by her governess. The analyst leaves a theoretical hypothesis unexpressed but adds the missing piece, 'who knows what she had done before, in the missing scene'. The patient is amazed and describes how once her mum had caught her letting her cousin touch her.

Different symptoms point to different ways of coping with the same problems. For example, there is at root a very close kinship between narcissism, autistic aspects and psychosomatic manifestations.

Here we are in the presence of protoemotions (or often protosensoriality) which cannot be transformed and thus made capable of being thought and experienced emotionally, and from which one defends and distances oneself by taking up position some distance away (in narcissism), by insulating oneself (*isolazione*) from them (like the plastic encasing around electric wire) in autistic defences that involve 'isolation' (*isolamento*) or by evacuating them more or less 'silently' into the body.

I say 'more or less silently' because there are some bodily symptoms that reveal something of their origin and yet others that are now totally disconnected.

Lisa and the pilot

When Lisa began her analysis she was suffering from Crohn's disease, which frequently caused her to evacuate blood. After years of analytic work had given her a greater ability to dream (I refer to alpha dreams) and to experience emotions (I refer to the development of ♀ ♂), Lisa began to experience more and more intense emotions.

The way a bond is structured (which is the basis of emotional vicissitudes) is narrated by means of an 'ultrasound scan' that reveals the presence of some polyps. It is logical that the analytic status of the communication should reflect the presence of a drive towards a very strong bond and that jealousy, disappointment and anger are tentacles that are in turn activated by the polyp(ous)-bond.

The scenario proposed by Lisa involves an airline pilot who regularly comes close to her and then withdraws (the analyst leaving, the analyst arriving) and who still has a relationship with a hostess he is jealous of. So jealousy also appears in the field. The pilot involves her emotionally but that also upsets her. Referring to the analysis, she says that she had self-harmed in order 'to avoid coming' (she skips a session); likewise she does not abandon herself to the pleasure of the (mental and sexual) relationship with the pilot. The pilot (this time part of her) wanted to tail the hostess to see if she were having relationships with other men. Lisa meanwhile spent an afternoon staking out the analyst's house to see how many other patients he had.

Lisa then goes to the cinema to see a movie about tigers while a friend moves to a house in Viale Eritrea, Africa, and the hottest emotional areas come to life and tell a story.

Other, truly African emotions gradually come to life: her rivalry with a colleague at work, anger at the pilot, disappointment over a friend who leaves her . . . This continuous alphabetization of emotions in fact coincides with fewer bloody evacuations, as if now the protoemotions could become pictographs and be woven into an ever livelier scene.

Alessio

This is also what happens with Alessio. At the beginning of the analysis he would always bring a computer with him (Alessio deploys obsessive-autistic defences). His computer breaks down completely after the first interpretation: when he speaks of wanting to repair his Eaglet (referring to an old scooter), I make the remark: 'God knows how the eaglet got into the scene.'

Subsequent sessions are all about imagination: dreams of barbarians, Huns, Visigoths, tornadoes. Again, in Alessio's case it is the existence of an immediately strong bond with the analysis (and with the 'girlfriend') that causes him depressive anxieties at the end of the session, exposing him to typhoons of jealousy whenever he imagines his girlfriend with someone else.

Cristina

At the root of emotions there is always the coming to life of the bond and its vicissitudes (and we're not actually that far from naive Propp-like formulations): Cristina tells me in the session about feeling spied on. As we are

103

close to the end of the analysis, on the one hand this alarms me, while on the other I think it is a reawakening of 'spy-like' aspects of Cristina that were present at the beginning of the analysis when she watched my every gesture, posture, tone of voice in order to find in them motives for anxiety and anguish. Then I think that 'being watched' is what has happened to her in the consulting room and further that this is an analgesic way of not feeling loneliness.

Cristina reverses the vertex: being watched is being alone, one is not part of the group, one is excluded.

I mention *The Truman Show*. In the film, whilst it is true that the protagonist is 'spied on' and seen by everybody on television, it is also true that he is the loneliest person of all because he does not belong to the 'group'; he is excluded. At this point I think of the reality of the end of the analysis as a prototype of exclusion, of the last session of the week (which is where we are), of the revival of the historical roots of the problem of 'exclusion', namely that Cristina had always suffered from parents who were strongly attached to each other; but I also see how in the last session I was 'paired off' with my own troubling thoughts, and that made Cristina feel the bitter taste of the exclusion one experiences when one is with someone else but the other person is absent mentally and is tied up instead with other thoughts.

The bond, as I mentioned before, can be a source of storms, pain, disappointment, and even joy, a way of finding things. But some patients often take time to give up these narcissistic–autistic defences that protect them from engaging in an emotional tie. Naturally, it does not matter in what area of the field this happens: it can be an explicit link with the analyst, but it can also be narrated and enter the field as a link with a girlfriend, or with a pet cat or dog.

When the bond is structured, then its trials and adversities become easier to narrate. A case in point is Eva, who avoids getting too close to intense emotions, but who tells me that her little daughter affectionately exclaims to her, 'Mummy, what would I do without you.'

And when I suggest to her (after several years of analysis) that perhaps she also experiences this feeling of fond need towards me, even though she is afraid of it, she again makes the point she has often made before, namely that I say the usual stupid, obvious things that analysts say, adding immediately that she has met an acupuncturist who unexpectedly had given her some figures for a nativity scene. Something – trust – is coming into being and her inner world is enriched with a presence where previously there had been an apparent emotional desert of narcissism and self-sufficiency.

Berto's poodle

A child starts the session in a manic way, saying that he had been to the theatre with his mother and had felt really good. Then he speaks of his desire to follow in Berlusconi's footsteps in the future and strings together a series of perverted plays on words that refer to anal masturbation (as described by Meltzer).

There is a moment of happy exchange with the analyst that allows access to some lively and strong emotions: 'the illegal immigrant who burned down the house', 'tortured and abandoned animals', the 'puppy saved' by animal rights activists. Towards the end of the session, Berto talks about a 'poodle' and asks whether it is true that snakes can eat small animals.

The structuring of a bond in the session allows this little Berlusconi to feel like a 'little tramp' (literal meaning of the Italian word for poodle) at the moment of parting and to be afraid of being devoured by separation anxiety. We are in effect in the paradoxical situation whereby a bond must be formed and gradually recognized but at the same time that same bond exposes us to a series of extremely intense emotional vicissitudes.

The bond exposes us to suffering but it is also the matrix of our ability to feel and experience emotions and their possible expressiveness to the hilt. There is nothing to stop defences against links from delivering us at particular moments from emotions we fear are too intense to manage.

Until a patient acquires the ability to manage emotions and the distress that a bond implies, this choice must be respected. When the bond begins to grow shoots, I think one has to avoid rushing in to clarify them and bring them into the transference. One needs rather to be a prudent and trusting gardener who tends their development. When the links become obvious and evident, this means not only that they can be explained but also that the patient has all the necessary tools to cope with the hardships that the vicissitudes of each bond imply. The purpose of the analysis is to progressively add to the patient's set of tools that enable him to recognize, name, manage and metabolize emotions. This is a psychoanalysis that is more concerned with tools for thinking and feeling than their content. Not that the content does not matter but if the piano is in good working order, it can produce all kinds of music depending on the individuality of the pianist.

It is also true that initially analysis exposes patient and analyst to a traumatic situation that arises out of the disorder created by the mind in its continuous, albeit discreet, coupling. This implies a total change of policy in dealing with Pandora's jars (boxes, by the way, are a mistranslation) when these exist. Often we find ourselves having to make the jars themselves, or indeed even needing to manufacture, together with the patient, the necessary potter's tools.

On transference

Transference also comes into play in the choice of the object: in the case of still encysted, unworked-through mental situations, transformation is only possible by bringing them to life again in a situation where the chances of a positive outcome are greater than in the original trauma. The transformation that is 'naturally' triggered in fortunate cases allows the selection of ever new objects to replace the original traumatogenic ones.

In analysis, the re-proposal of forgotten, split-off, repressed history is one of its driving forces.

The positive thing is that this allows for transformation and change; the risk is that the analyst may fall into the trap of taking on a specific role and that the field will contract the patient's disease (as normally happens) but then not heal.

Continually falling ill (in the Barangers' terminology, the formation of 'bastions') and continually getting better (the dissolution of the bastions) correspond to the breathing pattern of the field as it expands and collapses all the time.

If a patient has had an emotionally unavailable mother, this will sooner or later be experienced in the consulting room and in the field, and this can happen in the form of any character. It can be digested and metabolized through the peristaltic movements of the field or through interpretation, provided one remembers that for the interpretation to be effective it can only be the final act of a previous digestive process.

But the question of transference does not end here; it is beyond dispute that there is also a transference from the analyst on to the patient that requires continuous (often silent and automatic) processing.

However, what needs to be emphasized even more (because they have received less investigation) are the continuous 'transfers' (just like airport shuttle buses) that not only go back into the past of the field, and into the inner world in the field (of which the analyst is one of the loci) but also pass continuously from the field to the patient's inner world and from the field into his story. This constant coming and going of tangled fragments of sensoriality and protoemotions makes possible their transformative weaving and the neoformation of inhabitants of the inner world and the story. The patient's inner world and story constantly enter (and feed) the field by means of repetition and projective identification, and they are constantly transformed through mini and macro *après-coups* that guarantee the multi-directionality of the movement.

Emily Brontë's *Wuthering Heights* is very useful in helping us to see transference at work on the object. Heathcliff is an abandoned orphan who is in effect adopted by old Mr Earnshaw. The bond that ties him to Catherine, Earnshaw's daughter, is symbiotic and full of passion. This causes nothing but pain, jealousy, despair and hatred. All this is enacted, however, with Catherine, who is herself an orphan. What was unthinkable and unspeakable in the primary relationships is now made thinkable and bearable: otherwise atrophic parts of the mind are infused with life. Only long and hard transformative toil will allow the children of Catherine and Hindley (new aspects of the self), born from transformative digestion, the chance to have a relationship that brings with it joy and not only tragedy.

In psychosomatic situations the outstanding achievement of analysis consists in turning back into tragedy what was evacuated in a symptom that is nevertheless a memento towards future hope for thinkability.

Even everyday micro-tragedies continually enact what demands to be improvised. Sometimes the scene freezes and the repertoire remains unchanged; in these cases the analyst is called upon to act as an entrepreneur/theatre manager who knows when to introduce variations into the programme for that season.

Tonight we improvise Pirandello

In the theatre of analysis the silence of the analyst is often feared because the impression is that he has failed to make the constant adjustment to the pH of the session that should be reflected in his words. The analyst's silence is like darkness in the room for small children: a darkness peopled by ghosts and scenes of fear. Certainly, in order to hear the noises and see the film one needs to lower both sounds and lights, but the little lights that ALWAYS remind you that you are at the cinema or at the conservatory – they have to be left on. The exception is when you have patients who are sufficiently well-structured from the very beginning to know how to throw themselves into darkness and silence with curiosity and passion. Such patients are, however, not very frequent. More common are those patients who need the little lights, the intermission, the soft lighting, the presence of the usher; maybe one day they will relish the great leap into the darkness of silence.

The analyst who 'speaks' softens the harshness of certain scenarios; he becomes a Virgil able to guide Dante through the circles of the inferno. When the time is right, Beatrice will come on the scene and the patient will be able to enjoy an analysis of which he is no longer afraid.

The silent analyst lends himself to any number of faces. The analyst who intervenes illuminates with the reality of his non-phantasmatic presence and with the tenor of his emotional life the real soundtrack of the film/analysis. It might be argued that the silent analyst pollutes the field less. This is true with patients who are not afraid of the emergence of the 'Nessies' (in all senses) that live inside them, but it is also true that the colour of silence sometimes becomes something that cannot be received or digested by the patient.

On defences

There are various defences against agglutinated modes of relating. One possible defence is to insulate and waterproof oneself against the link, another is claustrophobic avoidance.

For patients who have found a defensive solution against an agglu-tinated/agglutinating core (which tends to form differentiated and symbiotic links) analysis poses a big problem. From one point of view it is the only way of metabolizing these areas without their becoming such heavy baggage as to make life difficult or even give rise to a range of symptoms. From another point of view, however, 'giving way' to the analytic bond means plunging back into a somewhat agglutinated situation, the sole hope being that the analyst (along with the setting and the patient's contribution) knows how to guide the patient out of the symbiotic bond; but this will only happen through the re-proposal and the alphabetization of anger, jealousy, pain, and more.

> Luisa begins to speak of 'polyps'; her way of treating them is to miss a long string of sessions. She is reproached by her partner, who says 'at home you don't make the bed', 'you don't work', 'why don't you bring your stuff here to wash?' – all ways that in the field express her distance from the analysis. Louise is afraid that the polyps will return her to the undifferenti-ated link she had escaped from by deploying autistic-counterphobic modal-ities. She says she 'thinks about him (her partner but also the analyst) all the time'. She then speaks about her mother who talks about a child who has to separate and who is bound to suffer. For many patients, re-proposing a link they are afraid will swallow them up is a kind of Tarantalus-like torment that forces them once again to endure suffering for which they had found a pseudo-solution.

Going back and starting again implies a certain degree of courage and recklessness. The criteria of analizability have long protected analysts from the risk of daring.

It is not easy for a patient to go back into an agglutinated nebula of undifferentiated protoemotions, nor is it easy simply to alpha-betize this nebula into emotions that can be named and transformed. It means venturing back into the protoemotional jungle from which one has managed to escape, while keeping in one's luggage a gorilla that will be the cause of a symptomatic crisis.

Going back means being faced once again with undifferentiated protoemotions to which one ought to begin to give a name (anger, jealousy, exclusion) and then metabolize these protoemotions so that they become permanent inhabitants of one's inner world.

The Count of Monte Cristo

An unexpected separation caused by my absence prompts Giulio, now at an advanced stage of analysis, to say that he feels 'offended, offended, offended'. He adds that he feels that when he loosens up and comes closer, I 'drop' him, and when he gives himself up in a spirit of trust, I abandon him. The casual sequence of events – he approaches and I withdraw – is experienced by Giulio as a 'forced contingency' and the mere realization of this shows him how he in turn, each time a link was formed, moved away both to pre-empt the pain he was sure he would feel (being dropped/abandoned) and as a kind of revenge, similar to that of the Count of Monte Cristo who, abandoned and betrayed, can only heal an otherwise irremediable pain by resorting to revenge. It is also true that in the end the Count of Monte Cristo is able to forgive the woman who had betrayed and abandoned him. He also manages to discover the profound love he had never stopped feeling for her, even though he had long been unaware of it.

Silvia and the southerners
Every time she experiences the separation caused by my going away, Silvia wonders whether the price of the 'new home' she is about to move to is not perhaps too high; she is especially afraid of the southerners and illegal immigrants who live in that neighbourhood. Separation breaks off a tie, which causes suffering, a high price to pay especially because it triggers frightening emotions akin to her fears of southerners and illegal immigrants. One of her children has told her about a woman who put her trust in an Arab but was then stabbed by him.

Rino and Frankenstein
Early on in the analysis, Rino – again a patient who finds himself facing a break in the analysis caused by my absence – describes an incident that happened to a friend of his. This friend had driven up into the mountains at night because he wanted to stay in a mountain inn. When he found it closed, however, he was so disappointed that he didn't even think of going to another hotel (Rino had not wanted to make up for the missed session) and drove back to town despite the fog. On the way back he had run into a lorry and broken several bones. If you saw him without any clothes on – Rino added – this friend looked like a scourged Christ or a Frankenstein. I point out that the drama of Frankenstein's monster was that he felt unwanted by the person who had given him life. It was only this feeling of hurt at having his love rejected that had driven the creature to its terrible acts of revenge.

A different order of magnitude

What is seen in the consulting room with the aid of an electron microscope can be seen using an optical microscope in a place like a child psychiatry clinic.

Renato and the little black man

Twelve-year-old Renato arrives accompanied by his parents; his problem is that he is haunted by a 'little black man' that follows him around and terrifies him. The little black man first appeared when his parents forced him to go to school against his will.

The 'little black man' becomes the evacuation of a terror that cannot be described or transformed and is therefore evacuated. This is not a 'true hallucination' but what is called a 'dream flash', something that has been alphabetized, transformed into an image and then evacuated, but which at the same time still has some relationship with a possible sense and meaning. The 'little black man' is a kind of cluster of psychotic lumps to be got rid of by means of evacuation: this makes it possible to keep relative order 'in town' (in his mind).

After several sessions with a neuro-psychiatrist who has taken on his case, Renato begins to collect figurines. This takes up a lot of his time and energy, and he spends most of the day putting them in order.

An obsessive defence mechanism thus starts to take the place of persecutory anxieties that have been evacuated.

Under the guidance of a psychomotrist Renato then starts going to a painting and sculpture studio, where he makes monsters out of paper, which he then uses to invent and co-construct stories. This activity not only involves containing (as did the obsessive mechanism), but also transforming and processing the 'monsters' through narration. Meanwhile, the 'seen' little black man progressively leaves the scene and is only present in situations of high emotional pressure (when Renato attempts to go back to his school class). Later Renato reaches a kind of compromise. He won't go into the classroom but he will spend time in the school library with a support teacher and a reduced timetable which will then be gradually increased.

At this point the 'little black man' leaves the scene for good and is replaced by some 'panic crises' Renato suffers during the time he spends in the library, especially when unfamiliar people come in.

Gradually in the (twice a week) therapy that he has begun with me, the 'little black man' fades away somewhat and is narrated in emotions of extreme anger and depressive pain. At this point the 'little black man' reappears but this time as the protagonist of nocturnal dreams. The evacuative fissure is closed and the black man finds a kind of habitat where he can live (the representable world of dreams) without causing any more panic crises.

Gradually Renato's mood improves and he starts meeting his classmates outside school. Behind this brief story was a family history in which the symbiotic bond was a kind of shared code.

111

His mother had also suffered from school phobia and his father had been unable to cope with being away on military service. The panic attacks this caused had exempted him from continuing his military service.

The idea of the bond was 'if you go away, you die', 'if you go away, I die', 'if I leave, I die', 'if I leave, you die'.

Renato's symptomatic explosion came after the death of his grandfather with whom he had a very strong bond. His grandfather's death coincided with the need to change school when the family moved to a new house and a new neighbourhood.

This breaking of bonds had triggered emotions in a situation where he had no apparatus to manage them (alpha function and ♀ ♂), or rather it had produced over-intense protoemotional states which were only partially digested and could only be evacuated.

Somehow the 'little black man' was also a kind of transgenerational legacy that found expression in Renato's story.

In the history of the family there had been an excess of 'projective identifications' which had not been accepted and cooked (transformed into images, into alpha elements) and these had accumulated. The result was not only a superabundance of 'protoemotions' (hyperbeta) but also a lack of tools to deal with them (hypo-function of alpha and hypo-development of ♀).

The 'outpatient services' that I offered in this segment worked like a mind, a mind capable of providing laundry facilities (for cleaning anxieties) and at the same time buckets and soap.

To use Bion's terminology, one might say that the 'little black man' was an aggregate of partially digested beta elements (balfa elements) that had found a sort of alpha group function capable of generating alpha elements and thus thoughts and emotions instead of sensoriality and protoemotions that had not been fully imagined.

Rosina's 'guinea fowl'

The story of Rosina has some points in common with the story of the 'little black man'. Rosina is a Ukrainian girl adopted at a young age by a very emotionally available couple. She says that since the beginning of therapy she has had a friend who she can see and who she talks to – a 'guinea fowl'. She has begun therapy because her parents are concerned about Rosina's risky behaviour now that she is an adolescent: she has started to hang out with gothic rock bands and satanic sects.

From the beginning dreams are a space for processing very primitive ghosts. At the last session of the week she dreams of a vampire that flies up into the air but lacks the strength to keep flying. She then dreams of a woman with long red hair, then a woman with blood-red nails. . . .

Rosina calls the therapist the 'lamp-maker' because he provides a soft light as he accompanies her through a world populated by blood, witches and monsters, a world that seems to be like the previously inaccessible other side of the world of the 'guinea fowl'.

Gradually 'sharks', 'snakes', 'tigers' and 'tiger sharks' take the place of vampires and witches and bring her closer to harrowing emotions, emotions that bite and choke . . . gradually the visual flash of the 'guinea fowl' disappears . . . and a prosaic duck being cooked for poor children on Christmas Eve appears in a dream.

Back to the consulting room

Luigi and reading

Luigi is a child who has been diagnosed as having 'severe dyslexia'; he is restless and often uncontrollable at school, hyperactive.

The interview with his parents takes an unexpected turn at the very beginning: the mother talks about having been dyslexic herself as a child. She immediately goes on to describe with great emotion 'the terrible experience she had with the deputy head' of a school where she taught. He had persecuted her, targeted her, made her life impossible, showing not even the slightest understanding for her situation, and in the end she had taken early retirement from school. The father minimizes everything, saying that he is only worried by things that justify concern, such as the mortgage they have taken on and which he is afraid they won't be able to pay.

It is clear to me that the minds of both parents were and are barely available for Luigi and his anxieties. They seem to be like rooms where there is no sense of calm, no space or silence. They are two rooms in which a continuous swirl of tornadoes wreaks havoc all over the place.

It is as if sheets of paper had been put on the table and now lie scattered about the room and hence are impossible to read. The only emotions that are read and approved are the mother's feelings of persecution and the father's catastrophic anxiety. Theirs is a kind of two-letter alphabet that prevents them from engaging in any emotional reading of their reality.

It is merely a natural consequence that Luigi can only evacuate his mental states through hyperactivity, restlessness and mental states he is unable to read. If you can't read your own mental states there is a sort of fog that makes every signal, every letter, every alphabet a blur. The alphabet to be learned is first and foremost emotional and only later cognitive, at least in the sense that the latter is based on the former.

The sessions with Luigi follow their own distinctive course. Luigi arrives in a state of great confusion and hyperactivity, he calms down and 'organizes' himself in the middle part of the session (when the analyst begins to read to him the emotional states of characters in his game and constructs a sort of emotional syntax by progressively tackling the more complex links between emotions) and finally he becomes disorganized again towards the end of the session.

If we take a typical session, at the beginning Luigi smears an incredible number of sheets of paper and mixes up all the colours.

Then gradually figures begin to appear as the analyst intervenes to contain Luigi's anxiety. A 'face' takes shape, to which the analyst says, 'he looks angry, but also frightened and desperate'. Luigi goes on to draw a boat, a small man, the sea. The analyst offers a reading of the drawings as a sequence of events: 'This face is perhaps that of a man at sea, perhaps the man has fallen into the sea, and is scared because he is afraid of drowning.'

The analyst is apparently sticking to the manifest text while all the time setting up links, connections, interpretations. He decides not to offer a premature reading of the transference aspect (which would amount to doing logarithms in first form): 'When we're not together I feel you sinking into a sea of anguish and I see that you're desperate.'

Luigi continues to draw. He describes a boat trip with his parents. He talks of the danger posed by large waves, and thinks that if the boat were to capsize, they would need floats and life rafts. Luigi's response is coherent, logical and emotionally coherent.

The session proceeds with a narrative co-construction, again using a text that takes in boats, ferries, dangerous crossings, waves, the risk of shipwreck – all of which amount to an accurate description of the emotions that come alive in the therapy room.

Towards the end of the session, Luigi draws some waterspouts, the game speeds up, he talks about pirates 'who are outside the law . . .', and from that moment on it becomes impossible to read the emotions present in his narratives and the game becomes mere evacuated turbulence.

There are repeated sessions like this where these features gradually make more and more evident the bond of survival that has developed between Luigi and his analyst, until it seems that the time has come to up the number of 'lifeboats' to at least three a week.

Luca and the primer

Dyslexia is very often an inability to read profound basic emotional states. It is hard to recognize or discern anger, jealousy, disappointment; it is as if a person were missing a sort of elementary emotional primer that would help him to advance to more complex reading and writing.

At one point in the therapy, Luca, a dyslexic child, says that he would like to do away with Monday because it's the day he has to go back to school. He fills the therapy room with hard rubber balls that he starts to throw violently, making them bounce around the room. This is the way he begins to depict uncontrollable emotions that are bouncing around the room and inside him after the weekend separation.

This is a kind of dream-acting-out in the session where he appears to be showing that he is having to cope with swarms of bees he feels are persecuting him. Later he introduces some cardboard rackets to hit the balls with, as if a beekeeper came along who was able to handle swarms of beta elements waiting to be transformed into alpha elements.

An adult and healthier patient could recount essentially the same experience as Luca's by, say, describing after the weekend a dream in which he was aboard a boat that was tossed violently by huge waves (emotional waves created by the separation) and adding that he was not able to read or write on board because of the severe rocking of the boat. For Luca it is the intense violence of the balls that prevents him from reading or writing because he is being struck by unmanageable emotions that constantly confuse him.

When (how much) is enough?

A crucial problem is the decision about the end of analytic work when analyst and patient are not in 'unison' on this point.

Termination may be anticipated by one of the two members of the couple, especially if the subsequent communications from one or the other are not read as signals coming from the field.

An analyst believes that the analysis of his patient has reached its end, confirmed in this belief by some of the patient's dreams, in one of which he sees very clearly the bottom of the sea, a translucent blue sea where all the fish can be easily made out. The analyst suggests finishing the analysis in a reasonable space of time, and the patient, who is about to begin training, agrees to this plan with satisfaction.

He then recounts a story in the session: in the shop below the analyst's studio he has bought 'four delightful golden knobs, genuine art nouveau, for a considerable sum of money. I want to use them to make a coat rack for my hall. The knobs are beautiful, robust and capable of holding up the weight of any object one might want to hang there.'

He seems to be saying that he is about to come into possession of a solid analytic function, the result also of the introjection of our four sessions and the work done together.

A few days later, however, he says that he has received a call from the shop assistant, who had managed to trace him through the bank (he had written a cheque to pay for the knobs), enquiring whether he might be willing to return them. As they were designed by a famous art nouveau artist they were really worth a figure ten times what he had paid for them. Of course, he was free to say no, but if he did she would lose a lot of money. The patient is disappointed, but understanding the shop assistant's position and not wanting to cause her any financial damage, he gives them back. In return, the assistant gave him a bottle of whisky.

The analyst does not interpret all this, perhaps blinded by his own need to finish the analysis, perhaps because of other commitments he has taken on (his waiting list?). The knobs are given back before the coat rack is made and before the analytic function has been permanently introjected.

The patient accommodates the needs of the analyst, gives back the knobs, and in return experiences the intoxication of access to training.

Needless to say, later the patient had to return to his ex-analyst in order to work through the end of their analysis in an authentic and non-manic way.

Bianca and her monkey cousin

The opposite can happen, too: the patient is ready but not the analyst (all in all, a preferable situation). Bianca began her analysis on account of a serious depression that was 'kept at bay' through continuously acted-out eroticization, namely by cheating on her husband, which left her always on the (exciting) cutting edge of being discovered.

There had also been a wide range of possibly psychosomatic manifestations: atopic dermatitis, various allergies, asthma attacks. Very soon 'the schizophrenic cousin who looks like a monkey' becomes a central figure in our therapeutic work. The husband is called Furio and is described as a control freak. During the course of analysis she begins to understand the excitatory and antidepressant nature of her infidelity and progressively the bond with her husband becomes more stable.

Gradually various emotions are experienced, named and at least partially processed: jealousy, rivalry with her sister, her frequent experiences of abandonment. Later she starts doing voluntary work and in particular she looks after 'Mimmo, a boy with cognitive deficits' partly caused by 'traumas' at birth. 'Since someone has been looking after him', however, he has progressively regained his sense of smell, has become interested in rhythm and music, and has also begun to paint.

She then talks about a friend who is depressed and who sits around at home 'in her slippers and dressing gown'. She goes on to describe how she has started taking care of herself, and the gratitude she feels towards her 'hairdresser' who has really given her a new head (of hair).

At this point, while the analyst still feels they are a long way from finishing the analysis, Bianca begins to speak about wanting to end it. The fact is she no longer receives the rental income that had hitherto made it possible for her to afford the analysis because her Chinese tenants have now opened a restaurant and are planning to buy their own house.

The analyst does not pick up on all the signs of the transformation that has occurred, until work with a supervision group allows him in turn to 'waive the rent' and settle for the 'change of head' he has helped the patient to achieve. Now he also notes the transformations in the patient, which are reflected, for example, in the transition from her ape-cousin to the boy who is acquiring new skills.

About narcissism

Marina goes to a restaurant where she expects the waiter to bring her what she wants: marinated salmon, fettuccine with mushrooms and sea bass in salt. She is well known at the restaurant and reasonably enough expects to be waited on with the same enthusiasm that led her to the tiny street where the restaurant is located in the first place.

Once there, the waiter, full of courtesy, brings the menu.

Marina is stunned. Don't you know what I like? Don't you know what I need? Don't you know how much I looked forward to coming here? Annoyed, she doesn't eat and, pleading an emergency, she leaves. The scene is repeated for several days in a row. Then one day Marina sits down silently at her place. Without even greeting the waiter.

Marina is offended, offended, offended, offended that the waiter doesn't know her desires, doesn't know her needs, doesn't remember what she likes. She withdraws into herself, keeps silent. She is full of anger, rage and sorrow.

Luigi says that the photographs he has been waiting for so anxiously have arrived, but he is disappointed because they had not been developed and printed by hand, as he had expected, but had been done on a computer. They did not resemble what he expected. He felt disappointed and offended.

Nando has a dream in which he goes to a big four-star hotel. They tell him they are fully booked, the only room available is in the annexe. He is offended, hurt.

These are examples of narcissistic wounds where the object is felt to be not in unison, not on top form, not fully available.

The *infans* – as Florence Guignard would say – needs to be understood, to inspire passion, to be received with a sense of expectation and dedication.

When this doesn't happen, and doesn't happen for a long time, what sufferings are activated? What name can we give to such sufferings?

What are the characteristics of the analyst?

A young colleague in training amazed me one day by asking what basic skills an analyst should have. I did not give a theoretical answer (I could have referred to reams of literature on the subject) but said without reflecting: benevolence, trust in one's method, the ability to blind oneself to any reality other than that of the consulting room.

Benevolence means getting in touch with the feeling that even the most 'horrible' of patients corresponds to an analogous lump of our own that has often not been integrated. There is no patient who does not speak to us of our own out-of-the-way and often silent wildernesses. Benevolence means the capacity to 'wish well' and, above all, the ability to have a Fra Christoforo outlook *omnia munda mundis* – or better yet, an outlook like the bishop in *Les Miserables*, who defends Jean Valjean, guilty of stealing his silverware after being welcomed and given hospitality; the bishop who tells the

118

gendarmes who arrested Jean Valjean to let him go because he had given him the silverware himself.

Trust means confidence that the method works; it may take months or years, but in the end we will be able to do something useful with even the most terrible of patients as long as we cling to our knowledge 'that analysis works'.

And third, *blindness* to all external reality: the ability to see scenes in the consulting room and not to be dazzled by external reality.

In one session we are 'the Russian hostesses' who save the patient from depression, in another 'my husband the monster who offends me deeply by asking me to make love when I am exhausted' (this after a transference interpretation), but we are also 'the bowl of scalding hot water', 'the cousin who continues to reject me even though I cannot stop thinking about her day and night', 'the dog that bit me', and so on. There are no external scenes; if we make everything dark all around, the drama of the analytic scene takes on depth, life, body, and in it we can really perform a transformative function. We can tune in to the 'jealous wife', the 'pain of being rejected'; in short the consulting room becomes a stage where the whole of Shakespeare, Pirandello, Molière, Ibsen, etc., is performed in an endless sequence of emotional plots that would lose depth and vitality if we let light in from outside. As I said, at the cinema the little lights are kept on, but we must make darkness. In the consulting room we admit life and light if we create total darkness on the outside.

This does not, of course, mean attaching no importance to historical or existential reality, but we should allow it to be embodied in the consulting room, the only place where it can be transformed; and if the boyfriend does not answer the mobile phone, we must live through the pain of this failure to respond together with the patient, knowing that we are the ones who did not pick up the phone, and that it would be too simple to interpret this event; first we must answer the phone.

Thinking of the internal object that does not respond, the mother who did not respond in the past, prevents the drama from coming fully alive in the consulting room; we are aware, but the patient who continues to call us 'her boyfriend' remains unaware.

And if a patient asks us what we think of homosexual relations and tells us of her ongoing argument with her husband, this is an enactment of our homosexual relationship with the patient: neither

119

of the two hears the point of view of the other and, wanting to be heard, we impose our will on the other. Only what we think lives there can be seen and transformed by us.

Emotionless metaphor: Gino and underwear

There are some patients, especially highly narcissistic, obsessive patients or those with autistic characteristics, who drain away all emotional value from the communication; thus the communication is (apparently) meaningless.

A good child psychotherapist once told me about treating a boy with Asperger's syndrome. What he was trying to do, he said, was 'to invent anything as long as he could maintain some kind of communication'. He also told me that he had the sensation in the session of listening to a record that has got stuck.

In one session Gino pulls out a Barbie doll and asks 'how's the ballerina?'. The therapist understands that the question is addressed to him and answers 'fine and how are you?'. 'I went to the cemetery' (apparently a real event, something that actually happened: it is the only way Gino can handle the despair he has experienced between sessions). He adds that his favourite class mate had not been at school that day and that the school mistress wasn't listening. Gino immediately perceives that the therapist has not picked up on his depressed state and adds that he likes to touch his class mate's thick long hair.

The bemused therapist (whose hair is very short, almost a crew-cut) has not understood the boy's desire, expressed in a concrete communication, for a soft feel and touch, and asks: 'is that an erotic sensation?' Gino is now disorientated and responds by talking about a girl he knows who pushed away his hand as he tried to touch her hair. He goes on to describe a boy he saw blowing the hair of a girl. Feeling alienated makes Gino snort, but the passionate emotional component of snorting is lost in the blowing.

Then he says, 'the school mistress came to school in a vest, can kids put on a t-shirt over a sweater?' 'They speak double Dutch,' he adds. There is a coded message, which gives back the freeze-dried emotion that has been sucked away. The communication becomes: you told me something about yourself (eroticization), can I in my turn reveal intimate things rather than cover them up?

It's as if Gino were constantly extracting the emotional life-blood from the metaphor and what the therapist has to do is to give emotional and affective vitality and depth to what must be (apparently) completely neutral if it is to circulate.

In another session Gino starts off by saying 'are you wearing a short-sleeved shirt? Take off your pullover.' So what he seems to be saying is: reveal yourself, show your hidden emotions. Then he adds: 'Is my hair clean?' He is afraid the therapist might think there is something dirty about his communication (the therapist's eroticization), whereas Gino's communication is in fact perfectly innocent. He then adds, 'I want to have a pony-tail, I also like people who have Mohawk haircuts.'

This could also be thought of as the analyst interpreting Gino's communication in a sensual or erotic register. I do not think so. Until shortly before this moment in the session Gino had been leaning across the desk, coming right up to the therapist's face. It was like a plant's tropism towards the light source, it was vegetal behaviour. (This after years of petrification, of being locked up inside a gestureless mutism.)

He cannot say 'I feel attracted to you', but he moves in that direction, like a climbing plant. Now he feels that his next evolutionary step is to make the leap from the plant world of physical metaphor to the animal world of protoemotions, a world of pony-tails and crests as representatives of a realm that is no longer vegetal.

There is nothing stopping us from also thinking on a sexual level, seeing a shift from pollination to a more sexual functioning of minds: an emotional thread now comes into being that binds two minds even though it is still wrapped up in thick layers of sweaters, insulating tape and double Dutch.

Reverie/projective identification

In my view there is a constant basic activity of reverie which is the way the analyst's mind continually receives, metabolizes and transforms 'what' comes from the patient in the form of verbal, para-verbal and non-verbal stimulation. The same activity of reverie is at work in the patient in response to interpretative stimulation as it comes (or doesn't come) from the analyst. The purpose of analysis is first and foremost to develop this ability to weave images (which are not directly knowable). Access to these images may be indirect – through the 'narrative derivatives' of waking dream thought (Bion 1962; Ferro 2002a, 2002d, 2004g).

This basic reverie activity is the fulcrum of our mental life and health; illness and mental suffering depend on its function/dysfunction.

The same goes for the existence of *basic projective identification* activity, which is the essential trigger of all reverie activity.

There are situations where there is an explicit and significant manifestation of reverie – generally in the visual register, of course, but not exclusively.

Reverie and *après-coup*

The way I listen to the presentation of a case history is to treat the story of the case as if it were preceded by the expression, 'I had a dream about this patient.' This mode of listening is not very different from the one that I adopt in analysis sessions with patients: the beginning of the session always contains the implicit expression uttered by the patient, 'I had a dream', whatever the actual content of the narrative may be. This, of course, concerns my work in my 'analytic kitchen', in the 'analytic restaurant', i.e. in the part that is in contact with the patient. The 'dish' of interpretation can be presented in a variety of ways, and can – if necessary – be accompanied by the sauce of sharing manifest content.

The operation I find myself carrying out is a deconstruction of the patient's narration and a reconstruction of a scene through the transformations I carry out. The deconstruction also occurs through the increasingly 'de-realistic' process of listening and 're-dreaming' what is said, organizing its meaning according to 'dream organizers' which are spontaneous and to some extent arbitrary and which generate a scene that continually needs to find its subsequent validation.

Sergio and the feather duster

Sergio first comes for treatment after a suicide attempt, and he appears rigid and emotionally frozen. He says he 'feel hatred for the people who love him, and he wants to escape from them', even if that means moving to another city or country.

For years he has been on the run from one continent to another. After his first attempt at sexual intercourse, during which he was 'scratched bloody by a girl', he has never had sex.

He often vomits and has sudden attacks of diarrhoea. Sometimes he feels like he is suffocating and he runs away.

Sergio describes his childhood as one of abuse which was both physical – he was beaten by his father who also beat his wife – and emotional (his mother often ran away from home, disappearing for several days at a time).

Despite this tragic history he also has, despite his imposing size, a gentle and affectionate air about him. He's a renowned and much-admired glass artist who makes precious glassware using long-standing craft techniques.

He's afraid of women who make advances, those he is afraid might want a sexual relationship. He is always afraid of 'suffering and causing pain'.

The fantasy that comes to me even this early in his story is to imagine the experience of a delicate crystal object when the cleaning lady comes along with a delicate feather duster.

What would I do if I were the glass object?

I would run away, I would move to a different bookcase if I were in a library, to a different shelf if I were in a cabinet. I would be afraid of being smashed to pieces; I would feel hatred for that soft duster, however soft it may be.

Here, in my view, is the key to Sergio's communication: fragility, afraid of being smashed to pieces if he has a relationship, a relationship with anyone.

Sergio is swamped with emotions that choke him, so he has to vomit or have diarrhoea. He must necessarily hate whoever loves him, who is the same person that might shatter him while 'dusting'.

The shards of broken glass can of course hurt the other. If the core of extreme fragility shatters, then it will be violently evacuated into the other.

All he can do with a woman is have a coffee, nothing more; everything serves his avoidance of the violence of disappointment and abandonment. A child abused, choked with feelings, who has to avoid any relationship because they cause unmanageable emotions and hurt. Sergio's 'narcissistic vulnerability' leads him to hate those who come close to him because they might smash him to pieces.

Another of Sergio's characteristics is his tendency to adapt totally to what women want from him; this would seem to be the result of projecting onto women the 'crystal child', the dream that was cherished in the womb of a young woman.

This crystal child cannot be exposed to any trauma, otherwise it will be smashed to smithereens. Many of Sergio's paranoid aspects appear to be attributable to narcissistic fragility, as if a thousand eyes were on the lookout for the arrival of a thousand possible threats, as if a thousand radars were always on the alert to avoid and prevent any trauma.

123

With analysis already well under way, for a long time Sergio begins sessions with communications such as 'time is running out already', 'I'm going to be seconded to another workplace', which indicate how the theme of the trauma of separation needs to be headed off at the very beginning of the session.

Referring to a foreign friend who is about to get his 'residence permit' is a way of narrating the early formation of a bond.

The theme of the tyranny exercised by the glass child (tyranny when viewed from the point of view of the other; necessity if viewed from the perspective of the fragility of this infantile aspect) is expressed in 'I have to satisfy women as if they were giving me orders to carry out immediately'. It is as if there were no chance of deferral in the face of the imperious shrieks of the crying baby who might disintegrate if frustrated. One day, however, Sergio is able to say 'I need sex' – an event that coincides with the appearance on the horizon of a possible girlfriend.

Dino and fear

The first thing I am told is that the patient's real name is Bernar-dino, but the Bernar remains unsaid. Immediately I think that the second part is also missing: Saurus. I am then told that he has hypochondriac symptoms, that he is phobic-obsessive and homosexual. This drawing renders my mental picture of him:

```
[♀          ♂          ]------    Dino    --------
[Bernar     ]-----      -----     Dino    Saurus
```

The association that comes to me is that in a situation where the container is insufficiently stable the 'saurus (or lizard)' contents can be managed by relegating them to a part of the body (hypochondria), through avoidance/ hypercontrol (phobias-obsessions) or by giving in to them (homosexuality understood as a kind of Stockholm syndrome with regard to his primitive parts).

I am also told that every time he feels the slightest pain (in Italian *dolorino* – which I deconstruct and reassemble as dolo-Rino-ceronte, i.e. pain- rhinoceros) he consults a doctor. Recently an x-ray showed up 'a dark spot' . . . he is also 'afraid of thunderstorms' . . . even though he had served in the heavy artillery (*artigli* = claws) in the army.

There is a dark, black spot that cannot be thought and that perhaps begins to be alphabetized through my reverie: the rhinoceros, the stormy emotions, the claws.

I am told that he is often prey to apparently unmotivated fits of anger and jealousy. So in the story of the supervision an emotional jungle begins to take shape which was previously the 'dark spot'. At bottom 'these black spots' are like lumps of beta elements waiting for the narrating-dream function of the analyst to turn them into stories that can be shared.

Short vignettes

Mathematics and the *tragadà*

Twelve-year-old Anna is no longer able to go to school. Within the space of a few months she has stopped attending her second-year classes completely. At our first consultation session she says that she is not good at maths, not even able to do basic calculations. Then unexpectedly she also describes the fear she felt when she went on the *tragadà* ride at the funfair, a sort of swinging platform on which she could not keep her balance.

Already this brief narrative suggests the association between not knowing how to do (mental) operations (calculations) and being shaken by emotions she is unable to cope with and which constantly catch her off guard and put her off her (emotional) balance.

This first hypothesis is confirmed when Anna said that she does not like boys (O). She likes small children and small animals, adding that she stops liking them when they grow older. Immediately afterwards she talks about the two kittens she loves, Margherita and . . . Tiger!

The sad sadomasochist

Nicola is twenty years old and asks for a consultation because he is disorientated by his sexual conduct. He likes his partner to 'dress up in black leather' and to 'engage in anal penetration wearing high-heeled shoes'.

He also takes drugs, in particular ecstasy and cocaine.

The excitatory value of these practices seems clear from the start: it is like having to turn on a turbo-charged propeller so as not to sink. The rest of his story adds further factors: he lost his mother at the age of 12 and from then on his father was emotionally distant and increasingly taken up with his many adventures with various women.

The polysemy of the practices he engages in seems clear: not only is there the excitatory factor, there is also the idea of letting himself be sodomized (at the same time placated) by the 'black' depressed part that he does not know how to accept and transform. What is striking about Nicola is also the slumped way he walks: his gait accurately suggests a child suffering from terrible loneliness and grief. He is unable to work through his grief and instead offers himself to it in sacrifice at the same time as continually seeking to distance himself from it.

Evacuations and containability

(a) Giuliana

Giuliana is actively trying to get pregnant, but then is forced to have an abortion.

Since the beginning of the analysis it has been clear that the origin of Giuliana's problem lies far back: contact with others immediately triggers in her emotions and tensions she is unable to cope with and so she immediately has to evacuate the product of conception – of any relational conception. It is like a form of enuresis or encopresis.

After three abortions and after two years of analytic work the world around Giuliana begins to change, and this is reflected in her dreams.

In one of them her mother is pregnant – as is her brother's girlfriend. Then in another dream there appears a big flat, a loft, and the husband of a cousin who is in a mental hospital, lots of rooms, and next to the loft there is a dilapidated old house.

The third dream is a comedy in which a couple invent a child and play with this idea.

The mummy-analyst is really pregnant, s/he keeps the emotions inside which the patient cannot tolerate. New spaces are created. The most suffering aspects are contained, an idea can start to find room 'jokingly': the strong emotions no longer need to be expelled immediately.

When the patient becomes pregnant again and is still undecided whether to have another abortion, the analyst feels invaded by a terrible rage. But it is precisely the act of offering a mental uterus to anger that may enable the authentic development of a container in the patient and thus give her a place for the gestation of emotions – and possibly children.

(b) Lucio

The situation of 12-year-old Lucio is not dissimilar; he has been diagnosed as having Asperger's syndrome.

All Lucio's emotions are miniaturized to the utmost; obsessive mechanisms protect him from anything new that might involve excessive stimulation.

One day Lucio's mother is puzzled: she describes how a girl gave him a micro-machine, at which he exclaimed 'how nice' and then immediately proceeded to throw it away.

An excess of emotions, even positive emotions, has to be wiped out.

This episode accurately reflects Lucio's mental functioning: in the event of excitation, the agent causing the stimulation has to be eliminated.

As it turned out the girl then put the micro-machine in his backpack without his knowing and when he got home he was happy to find it.

The same applies to the analyst's interpretative activity: it can be immediately evacuated if it causes an excess of stimuli and must be deposited 'cold' in small doses to be preserved.

(c) Manuel

Manuel is 5 years old. He suffers from primary encopresis and all he does is play motion games in a totally incontinent way. Even from the very first sessions with his analyst he feels welcome; he speaks of a fish that is at home in an aquarium and then adds, 'at home I thought of doing a drawing, but now I can't remember what'.

He then builds a pen for pigs, goes on to speak of nice things to eat and immediately tells a story about a 'treasure'.

If Manuel finds an area of containment, this immediately triggers emotional bonds inside him that stabilize him.

(d) Rosanna and stuttering

Similarly, the way Rosanna is introduced by her analyst already casts light on the key aspects of her suffering: hypercontinence and incontinence alternate – as in the stuttering she suffered from as a child.

Rosanna suffers from uncontrollable anxiety and a number of phobias. She has depressive issues and as an adolescent she was also anorexic. Her phobias are impassable places, perhaps the same places where in adolescence she deposited the most primal aspects of her mind that were split off and 'starved' in the hope that they would be easier to manage if they were weak.

I am also told that she has a father who is an 'angry man' and an elder sister who is very rebellious. These are clearly her 'uncontainable' aspects. Naturally, I carry out a narrative deconstruction whereby I consider all the people and events I speak of as 'protagonists' and interpreters of the current emotional-affective scene.

To me the narremes, the narrative sub-units are all 'vans' that transport ways of being from one place in the field to another. The examples of incontinence also include the story of nightmares that wake Rosanna up at night and leave her terrified (when the dream was insufficient to contain primitive aspects of her mind), the enuresis that had afflicted her as a child, and lastly the seizures whereby she evacuates whatever has eluded hyper-continence or splitting.

From a field perspective it is not necessary and often not useful to relate what the patient says to the here and now of the session. What from a relational perspective would be 'collateral transference' that should be related to an interpretation inside the relationship itself, according to a field conception can be 'played out' here in the field without necessarily being related to the present situation of the relationship. The field has so many pathways open to it. One is 'the pathway of relationship', but there are many more. Moreover, the field covers both space (including all split-off elements) and time (including all periods and ages of life) – and it is also in constant temporal and spatial expansion.

If, let us say, from a relational perspective a negative transference must be interpreted immediately – to nip any revolt in the bud, as it were – in the field, it is useful to understand how, where and when negative transference comes into being and to understand which mental operations the analyst can undertake to transform it. After a content-based interpretation, which the patient is not ready to hear because he wants first to be accepted and listened to (both *accolto* and *ascoltato*) by an analyst who at that moment is not receptive, the patient speaks of attempted homosexual seduction and of a gay acquaintance who wanted him to give him a taste of this form of sexual encounter. From a field perspective it would not be difficult to see how the homosexual couple of patient and analyst (♂ ♂) was generated in the session as a pictogram of two non-receptive mental states, including possible abuse or submission. Other models would have suggested other things. In the field model we are aware of the constant capacity of the field to generate characters in a time-delayed (almost live) account of the functioning of the minds of patient and analyst in the consulting room. Of course, the option of seeing the field as continually replenished by the patient's story and by the inhabitants of the inner world that constantly enriches the field itself is both compelling and necessary. The field becomes the great receptacle of what cannot be remembered and what is projected from the inner world, which is also able to continuously monitor the transformations that occur in the field. This monitoring allows the analyst in his asymmetric position of 'chef' to keep on tasting the food and to continuously make adjustments while cooking, adding either salt or sugar as well as introducing new ingredients.

Let us look now at two brief extracts from sessions (without any context) that demonstrate this ability of the patient to tell us where we are.

Patient: [*arriving 10 minutes late*] Yesterday I went to my yoga class and I didn't like it.

Analyst: [*thinks that the patient is making reference to the previous session and makes an unsaturated intervention*] You were disappointed because you didn't get what you expected.

Patient: Yes, I expected a more fruitful session with my yoga instructor, and I felt bad.

Analyst: [*thinks it is appropriate to use transference, but then thinks that he should cushion the effect by using the word 'we' in the second part of the interpretation*] Maybe you were disappointed here as well because we didn't manage to work profitably.

Patient: I look at a man and I like him, I look at a woman and I like her, and I also like feeling bad.

Analyst: [*thinks that the patient has not heard that the first part of the interpretation was more invasive and the second part more comfortable, and tries to hold back his own bad feelings*] There is then a part of you which is evil and sadistic towards yourself.

Patient: I dread the holidays. I'm afraid of my sister leaving me behind. I've decided to go on an intensive summer riding course with some friends.

Analyst: [*realizes that his intervention was inadequate and that the patient feels left alone even though he tries to equip himself to 'override his emotions' in the holidays (whether they be real holidays, or holidays understood as moments when the mental presence of the analyst is diminished). He now feels he can intervene in containing mode and by using a reverie he has had*] I think it was a good decision. I understand that you are alarmed at being left alone, abandoned. I am reminded of ET when he is alone and disorientated.

At the next session the patient begins as follows:

Patient: I feel bad. I need help.

Analyst: [*feels anxiety and shifts the request for help on to others*] Maybe you could contact the psychiatrist for medication.

Patient: I feel terrible, I don't think I'll ever be able to leave the house, I feel like I don't exist. One of my mother's friends turned the other way when she saw me on the street recently.

Analyst: [*having understood how his failure to respond to the patient's SOS and his mentioning of the psychiatrist have knocked the patient off balance*] It must have been a terrible experience to be ignored by someone who was almost a member of your family.

Patient: [*after a silence*] I then went back to my yoga class and there the teacher helped me regain a sense of tranquillity.

I believe this sequence involving a young analyst engaging with a difficult patient clearly shows how continuous monitoring of the field makes for continuous adjustments of the interpretative response and a set of micro-transformations.

Giovanni and Helen (of troy)

Giovanni is a brilliant engineer who is doing a master's in business management. For years he has been engaged to Licia, but so far they haven't managed to take the big step of living together or getting married. Although very fond of Licia, he periodically goes on erotic excursions involving casual sex which sometimes get him into risky situations.

At the first session he tells the story of being abandoned by his mother when he was six months old. She went to live with a very rich man in a beautiful villa in Greece. He was brought up by his father and his paternal grandmother who had never spoken ill of Giovanni's mother and in fact had always praised her for the qualities she possessed. The father then remarried and had other children that Giovanni saw as his brothers in every respect, a feeling they reciprocated. My feeling is that Giovanni's wound is something that is not seen but produces effects: the impossibility of a bond he can rely on. Then I think that the mother was quite simply a 'troia' (translator's note: whore, but in Italian also Troy). I must add that this word is not part of my normal vocabulary; however, it continues to suggest

130

itself to me when Giovanni tells his story without a trace of the anger, hostility or pain caused by the abandonment he experienced.

Only at the moment of parting does he tell me, à propos of nothing in particular, that he has bought a dachshund, although he says he also has plans, as the house where he lives has a large garden, to buy some bigger dogs, perhaps some Dobermans or Rottweilers. For some reason he has called the dachshund – *incredible dictu* – Menelaus!

The Iliad, I think to myself, is about to begin and I can only hope the Trojan war will last slightly less than the scheduled ten years.

You do it but you don't always say it

When I was at school I had a very good teacher of Italian literature. One day she pointed out to one of my classmates, who was a good pupil but rather conceited, that he had used a form that amounted to poetic licence. He retorted that Montale used that construction, to which the teacher replied, 'But you're not Montale!' As a matter of fact, as the teacher habitually spoke in Sicilian, the actual words she used were: 'Ma tu un si poeta!' (literally: 'But you such a poet!').

The point I am trying to make is that there is a lot one has to learn about grammar, syntax and rhetoric before one can use a creative and personal approach to analytic work.

Time-limited analysis

Margot's wounds

The first dream Margot recounts after starting analysis is of a vampire (given the unfavourable exchange rate, the fee is a little on the high side), but this vampire listens and carries a lantern.

The second is of a robber, but she offers no resistance to the robbery. She does not express and perhaps does not even feel any emotions, does not ask for help. Here the idea is of 'the petrified forest'; she is always 'taken up with understanding others'. She dreams of being given a 'small coat stand' as a present.

The coat stand in the hall thus becomes a character in the analytic scene – someone to hang one's burdens on. And indeed I often wonder if my poor coat stand will survive because it is put to use every day, laden with

131

big bags full of stuff that get heavier and heavier. However, the two of us manage to hold up.

In a dream Margot is alive on the outside and dead on the inside. Unexpectedly I fall ill for a week in mid-October and on my return she says she wants to pay for the analysis right up to the following June.

But something begins to loosen. At the end of the session it often 'rains' in the sense that she gets up from the couch in tears. She dreams of 'doing ballet' as she had as a child, emotions progressively come back to live in her, performing a dance between the relationship with me (and the fear of premature loss) and her story (the loss of her mother and the impossibility of working through her grief).

In a dream a girl is afraid of a dog and a bear, a woman masturbates a bear and a dog: the emotions that frighten her, that can tear her apart, are tamed.

Stories that relate to sessions with other patients trigger jealousy, anger and frustration.

I introduce the theme of bleeding and the alternative theme of 'petrifying' or freezing the inner world.

Any proposed interpretation is taken up, developed, elaborated and becomes a source of unforeseen new openings.

At the last session of each week there is always a reference to her childhood home, which after years of silence comes back to inhabit her dreams. She lives and feels the pain of the past and the separation pain of now. In November, she begins to talk about the 'end' of the analysis 'because if we do not think about it right now, it would be an abortion and not a birth'.

Obviously I cannot recount the whole of Margot's analysis. I just want to follow the thread that concerns the different way of experiencing emotions as they develop through our work. She remembers that there are no photos of her first year of life.

In a dream she sees many corpses to bury (the mourning to be carried out) and many living people to care for.

In a dream she says to a friend that 'if she speaks and expresses what she feels, that means giving up the idea that the mother should intervene without there being a need to express herself'.

Later she goes to visit the Aquarium in Genoa (where you 'see' the fishemotions but are protected from them), then in a dream, together with Edison (yes, the very same, the inventor of the electric light bulb), she makes animal noises – dogs, cats, horses. She then lets herself go at an aquatic theme park.

She then dreams that she is at a barber's to have a painful operation, and says 'I do not want a general anaesthetic, I want to feel'.

For Margot feeling pain was the same as feeling joy; at the hairdresser's she asks for 'highlights' that lighten and give vitality to her hair.

In recent sessions she has been telling me that analysis for her was like filling an album with photographs of the first year of her life (the year in which Margot comes back to life). She has to use the traffic light of a dream and the police officer responsible for someone else to stop herself from falling in love with a photographer who has shown her many new landscapes. She must go back to her story, where there is also a husband in Montevideo who is waiting for her.

She goes to Sicily for the weekend, where it rains and the sun shines, like Margot who moves away full of nostalgia, but happy.

Swimming up to the couch

Various swimming strokes

The idea of criteria of analizability was a powerful concept in psychoanalysis for a long time. It was a way of measuring the availability of the analyst, his willingness to put himself to the test in difficult and complex situations rather than on predictable package tours designed solely for relaxation. One should also say that every patient, even the most suffering or ailing patient (according to how we approach him or defend ourselves from him), certainly embodies an aspect of our own suffering. We are sufficiently well equipped to deal with our neurotic parts but increasingly less so vis-à-vis the parts that are borderline, psychotic or autistic. None of this relates to the mind (and its functioning does not belong to us!). Even the healthiest person is a compilation of successful and harmonized defences against alien and split-off parts involving psychotic and especially symbiotic aspects (in Bleger's sense of the term) and autism. What is alien to us belongs to us, and of course all of us are tempted to visit all the possible worlds that rotate around us at varying distances from the possible world of our primary identity. I mean that there is no human being who is not the centre of rotating unexplored worlds of his own where he can become a serial killer, a catatonic schizophrenic, a pyromaniac paedophile or a Nazi, and so on. But what do we want to know about the other potentialities of our mind? Should we take refuge out of fear or should we have sufficient curiosity to go rummaging beyond the confines of the cellar, as in the book by Carla Muschio I mentioned earlier (*La cantina di Isabella*). In the book Isabella finds a hidden door in the cellar that gives access to an infinity of ever-expanding possible worlds. But let us come back to the main theme, otherwise we will be distracted and that would amount to a discursive drift that brings us off course – precisely what Diderot's Jacques warned us against.

Today many people think that it is often a question of being able to swim up to analysis (I am referring to an excellent book on dysgraphic children that came out a few years ago entitled *Ho nuotato sino alla riga – I swam up to the line*). Obviously, the prerequisite is that patient and analyst are sufficiently motivated to go on this journey. In this way it's possible progressively to reach a more consensual analytic setting. Often the difficulties give rise to new openings. The method of pointing the patient progressively towards analysis – beginning first with one session, then moving on to two, then perhaps moving on to the couch and later to three or four regular sessions – often has its origin in the difficulties candidates in many countries had in finding patients willing to have three or four sessions and to go on to the couch from the very beginning. Later the praxis was to start according to what was possible and to guide the patient towards the possibility of structuring a setting which from the emotional point of view was more 'compromising' than the classical psychoanalytic setting. It's amazing to note how many times you can guide the patient with patience and openness towards something that previously he would have found too demanding and too persecutory. Another reason was the exact opposite, namely the situation when a patient was in urgent need and at that moment the analyst had no 'room'. Beginning with what was possible and then stepping things up proved to be a humane and constructive choice. Needless to say, much of this flexibility comes from our experience with children and adolescents where we are often forced to make a virtue out of necessity.

The moment of moving on to the couch is very touching. Despite countless anxieties, it is experienced by the patient as 'promotion' in the field, which can be a source of both fear and pride: from the face-to-face experience of West Point one moves on to the Indian-infested prairies or the swamps of Vietnam. I use these war metaphors because we often pass from herbivorous emotions to carnivorous emotions that involve pain and suffering. Even so I think that in most cases the analyst is able to modulate the arrival on stage of split-off or never thought-of aspects which reflect the development of the patient's capacity for containment. I believe that everything that happens during these transition phases should be considered not as preparatory to the analysis, but as the analysis that can be done at that moment, pending the transition to the classical setting. Fra Cristoforo's saying in *The Betrothed* – *Omnia munda mundis* – is I think the best recipe with regard to the superego rigidity – whether it be personal or institutional – that some analysts may find themselves suffering from.

The progressive nature of the approach, the respect for distance, the transmission of method – these are all tools that foster the development of ♀ and of the alpha function itself. Tolerance, patience, trust in one's method are the negative capabilities that help alleviate persecution and even promote the acceleration that comes with the increase in the number of sessions or moving on to the couch, which from another point of view are the plane's engines needed to take off to worlds unknown and which will thaw out experiences pending thinkability.

Intensive courses of analysis

'It's OK to do it but keep it under your hat.' Generally little is said about this question in Italy because it does not affect us directly as we do not have the geographical problem of large distances between a patient's place of abode and the nearest available analyst. In some countries, however, the two can be separated by thousands of miles. There are various ways for people in this situation to have intensive sessions: two plus two over two days and then a week free; a period of a fortnight or a month in which a large number of sessions are concentrated so that the patient only spends brief periods in the city where the analyst lives. I have found myself doing this type of analysis, although not too intensively, with two separate sessions on the Monday and two together on the Tuesday morning so that the patient could catch a plane and be back in his normal place of residence from Tuesday to Sunday. There were no particular difficulties apart from the initial problem of finding a rhythm that would make us feel 'at home'.

Shuttle analysis

Things are more complex in the case of so-called shuttle analyses. I have had direct experience of this practice: here it is the analysts who travel to places that are not easily accessible or to particularly remote regions where there is no chance of finding trained analysts on the spot (this is a problem that arises with each new frontier that opens up for psychoanalysis on to what is usually a 'Far West' where there is a demand for training and where a concentrated series of highly intensive sessions is held several times a year). The modalities are approved and regulated by the IPA.

This shows that in certain situations it is possible to do things that are otherwise not normally advisable.

Telephone analysis

This type of analysis is much more frequent than one might think. Naturally, it is used with patients who cannot physically reach, or be reached by, the analyst.

There are patients whose hours of analysis are done by radio link – this happens in central Africa, the forests of Canada and the Amazon, the Australian bush. We can be scandalized if we want, but it works. What I'm trying to say is that conception is not dependent on adopting the 'missionary position'. I'm not recommending these practices as normal; equally, it is not normal to operate on a patient who has a perforated appendicitis using as a scalpel the lid of a can of tuna, but people's lives have been saved this way. That is to say, let's do it when it cannot be done otherwise. And I repeat and emphasize once again that a fully-equipped operating theatre is what normally should be used.

These real-life situations also tell us (and analysts of children and severe patients are well aware of this) that all's fair not only in love and war but also in analysis when there is no alternative; and that the real setting is the mental and moral setting of the analyst. One can break virtually all the rules (remember, however, that gratuitous and pathological violations of the setting are an expression of the pathology of the analyst, as Gabbard has well described). It is clear that I'm talking about something else: how to make possible an analysis that appears impossible. I also want to reflect on the number of defences the analyst erects so as not to be contaminated by the risk that always comes with anything that goes beyond the known. I think that Freudians must necessarily venture into uncharted territory.

Restitching an analysis once it is finished

As the analyst grows older, he increasingly finds himself receiving requests for second analyses, often coming from colleagues and frequently from other countries. It is not always possible, however, for reasons of time, distance and space to carry out a four-session-a-week analysis. I agree fully with what Di Chiara (2003), among others, has said, namely that often in these cases if the first analysis was good, then it is sufficient, as with vaccines, to give a 'booster shot', as it were. Or rather, it is sufficient for a variable period of time to do one session a week – even on the couch – that makes it possible to pick up the threads of the preceding analysis and restitch what has become newly frayed. Often these demands coincide with those periods of greater fragility I have elsewhere called 'crises of the hinge ages' (40, 50, 60), with a range of different types of grief that have to be worked through and with the setting off of sometimes dangerous manias. In other words, in these cases the primary issues are often related to grief and depression.

Inhibition

I would now like to look at an example of an expression of pain or pathology that is particularly difficult to treat: inhibition as it presents itself in multiple scenarios and at different ages. The inhibited patient inhibits something that terrifies him. His psychic 'tsunami' has found a way of being halted. What can we do? Basically inhibition is a possible world the patient has slipped into and which offers a solution. However, we need to ask ourselves what other possible worlds are there spinning around in search of a geographer, astronomer, astrophysicist, painter, poet or storyteller who can map them, track them, identify them, make them possible to imagine, to pass through, to fantasize about so that the patient can enter these worlds and free himself from the 'low energy' world he has fallen into. A seminarian prays and masturbates compulsively, atoning for it by going on energy-sapping fasts. He could have many doubles: a serial killer who slits women's throats on a train; in a different historical period, a Dominican friar who tortures and burns witches at the stake; a possessive boyfriend who kills and freezes his girlfriend then cooks and eats her in delicate little portions; a cloistered self-flagellating nun; a sex maniac who engages in extreme and sado-masochistic sex; a teenager who kills both his parents in bed with a knife for cutting roast meat; an obsessive archivist who blushes in the presence of the female clerks in his office and who reads the Psalms every night. In a parallel world he is a pyromaniac who slits the throats of children as they flee the school he has set on fire.

The incredible thing is that writers move through all these possible worlds without feeling any discomposure; in fact, they may even be the reason they gain well-being and fame. But what are we if not the ferrymen taking people from asphyxiated possible worlds to other possible worlds where there is a greater degree of containable energy. Daydreaming is not action, but how can we be convinced of this, how can we gain access to the terrible movies that a seriously obsessive patient told me to buy without ever seeing them. He spent the day washing himself, constantly checking his personal hygiene after he had 'trodden on a turd' soon after he found out about his girlfriend's infidelity. In another world a man crushes his shit of a girlfriend without too many problems and he then feels guilty. But the worlds are not always so close that we can hear the noise they make, other worlds are far away, in other galaxies, which is why I believe an analyst should enjoy detective stories, thrillers and science fiction – as well as the great storytellers, of course. The analyst must perforce be a Shakespeare of the uninhibited mind who can encourage the patient to enjoy the beauty of his tsunamis.

After seven years of analysis which she had begun because of severely inhibitory behavioural symptoms, a patient dreams of entering a room where there is an aquarium full of water without a glass front. The aquarium occupies the entire wall right up to the top and the water comes towards her, making her wet but not drenching her completely. A tsunami that gushes into the room but stays there, I say. We have spent years building the room for the tsunami. After a few days she experiences her first sexual intercourse with orgasm, something she had always been afraid would sweep her away. We started from a situation similar to Asperger's syndrome; only minimal voltages were tolerable. What was decisive was my containing capacity, which began when after working well at receiving her gentle and unsaturated communications she told me that she and her sister used to come up with words that had no obvious association with each together, and their aunt had to construct stories using all the words – words like ice-cream, bear, wolf, button, pea, needle. It was wonderful.

I was very tempted to say that this was the game of analysis and the temptation was enormous to collect the material into a coherent story of that day's session which included pigeons, head physicians, terrorists, electric chairs and cappuccinos. On that occasion I kept things at bay, I harnessed the interpretative tsunamis that were pushing from within, commenting only along the lines of: I felt that day that I had heard her stories with the pleasure you experience when you watch films ranging from Pieraccioni to Dario Argento (director of horror movies) and Coppola (also the name of a typical Sicilian cap).

The opposite of inhibition is of course incontinence, which in children frequently takes the form of enuresis, encopresis, nightmares, hyperactive behaviour, stuttering and so on. The problem is how to escape from the worlds of both hypercontrol and no control to reach a world where the walls of a sufficiently broad and flexible container are modulated, a world which has a kind of rumen-bag in which to stow what needs to be regurgitated for a long time and then chewed again. Needless to say, this has little to do with classical interpretations but takes place through mental operations and activities of modulation and reorganization of the field – as Claudio Neri excellently describes with the example of the game of 'cat's cradle'.

8

Variations on transference and countertransference

General reflections

In my view transference is activated at the very moment analysis (or perhaps I should say, the phantasy of the analysis) commences; this is a widely shared idea.

From the very beginning there is nothing the patient brings to the session that does not belong completely to the analytic situation (this is true from a certain perspective, but this is precisely what I mean by the use of the psychoanalytic vertex in the session). If both patient and analyst are alive, if the setting works and nothing dramatic stands in its way, the only space-time of knowledge and transformation available to the analyst is the fictional reality of the analytic scene.

Transference enters the session in various ways: through repetition, through the outward projection of phantasmatizations, through projective identifications (it is no accident that a significant number of psychoanalysts are increasingly less concerned with content than with the repair or making of tools for the development of content), and then also through all kinds of stories and a wide range of modes of expression that convey sensoriality, distress, absence of function or presence of dysfunction.

Transference acquires visibility in the session by being diffracted into countless stories and countless possible characters, involving the most diverse expressions, which we can see as either positive or negative (Green 1993).

Absurdly enough – and this is the challenge the analysis must take up – all these characters, stories and procedures relate to the present analytic situation, or rather to the present analytic field regarded as a multidimensional dream space – both spatially and temporally.

If we take this viewpoint, we need never ask ourselves the question how real the patient's story is; it is real because it is there.

A story or a silence. A story or an acting-out. A story or a series of projective identifications. A story or a dysfunction. Even possible lies are true/real for the same reason (Ferro 2002a, 2005a, 2005c, 2005g). Corrao (1991) speaks of the nature of truth as intrinsic to the narrated construction rather than something to be attributed to the events. If analysis is at all possible there is, by definition, nothing that can be outside the analytic relationship – or to put it another way, off-field. Otherwise there is the risk of creating a non-transformable blind spot or blind area that could become the site of any number of impasses (Ferro 1993c).

This should by no means imply that the patient's narratives are to be interpreted or, worse, decoded as if one were carrying out a kind of simultaneous translation: it's up to us (we are one of the two authors in search of characters) to see how the story and the stories can gradually be transformed, how they can be made more expressive and turned into an instrument for the development of the ability to think (the development of a place to keep emotions; the development of the function that makes it possible to imagine the transformation of what is not thought or not thinkable; the development of the emotional mill called the alpha function, namely the ability to dream while awake, which involves the transformation of protosensoriality and protoemotions into emotional pictograms and thus into dream thought) (Bion 1962, 1963, 1965, 1992; Rocha Barros 2000; Ferro 2001b, 2001e, 2005c).

The source of dream thought, apart from the often silent story (which is sometimes only the story of the patient's mental functioning) that insists in various ways of being narrated, and apart from the inner world which insists on being accepted, also lies in the quality of our listening, our way of functioning and being in the session that is continuously picked up, reported and witnessed by the patient (Bion 1983; Ferro 1991a, 1996e, 2003a, 2003b, 2005b).

By way of simplification, then, we can say that we, our countertransference, are the other pole of the discourse.

In a radical view of the field, what matters is the degree of permeability of our consulting room and of our mind to the urgent needs of the patient (or rather the degree of permeability we jointly generate with the patient with respect to that which demands to be transformed into narration, whereby the main source is the patient).[1]

Our degree of permeability, receptivity, penetration and implicability forms the other half of the field: the field is born from the interrelationship of these two operations (which in some ways resembles Ogden's analytic third (1994a), although it is more complex and radical). We are not only present as a response or a more or less porous filter; we clutter and co-generate the field with our real presence, our real mind, our real functions and dysfunctions (Ferro and Basile 2004).

Often in a session we defensively make breaks or shifts in the patient's story, and we acknowledge manifest meaning: these are the oven gloves we need to be able to handle scorching emotional lava. It would be completely arbitrary to say, 'that belongs to me', 'that concerns the archaic mother', 'that is a collateral transference reaction'. Everything happens in a place in the current multi-dimensional field, everything happens in that potential, transitional oneiric space which is the tragicomic scene of the game of analysis.

The field is co-determined by the patient's projections, his urgent needs, his defences, by our projections and defences, and by his and our need for lies. On average I would say that the analyst tends to be more of a liar than the patient (because he is under more pressure) and often tries to lock up what he cannot bear not to know inside schemata, whereas the patient is often a witness for the prosecution in the event of such transactions (Ferro 2001a, 2001b). This implies a continuous oscillation of transference even within a single session; in other words, segments of transference also depend on the mental attitude of the analyst or rather on the oscillation of his mental attitudes.

I have often found myself thinking, 'ultimately this story does not belong to me', 'I have nothing to do with this story (or this behaviour), neither I nor the analysis'. This is certainly true on a common sense level. Analytic sense, however, is always different, and so far I have never found anything which didn't at some point fit into in the jigsaw puzzle of the field somewhere or other; but this is not to deny the reality of other vertices (Ferro 2003b).

Nipples and salami

Laura started out as a patient suffering from severe panic attacks, agoraphobia and hallucinatory phenomena.

142

Long years of analysis have allowed Laura to make great strides emotionally and professionally. One day, a little embarrassed, she speaks to me about a certain dissatisfaction she feels in her sex life with her husband. He likes Laura to suck his nipples for a long time, which she is also willing to do to give him pleasure. But Laura would love to be touched deeply, the way doctors do when they examine their female patients, and then be penetrated. At first I am slightly bewildered and find myself thinking about what I am being told as an external scenario, something that ultimately has nothing to do with me. I also think all kinds of bad thoughts about this 'husband'!

Then, despite myself, I have a flash of insight. Laura is indicating the need for a change of interpretative register: she is no longer the little girl who needs to suck nipples, to be contained; she is now a young woman who wants to feel my presence as more active and more penetrating on an interpretative level. I realize this, however, only after the end of the session and I have no way of communicating it to her. Laura arrives at the next session carrying a gift – a large long salami.

This communication struck me straightaway as extraordinarily polysemic. She gives me a salami because I have not understood the request for a change in interpretative register; at the same time she emphasizes her desire for greater interpretative virility on my part and then finally she gives up the phallic convexity that had long characterized her by now accepting, even wishing for, a position of full female receptivity – receptive even of emotions that previously had been evacuated under excessive pressure.

Of course there are always at least three possible scenarios in each narrative (or attempted narrative): the real external scenario (which it is sometimes difficult not to be attracted by!), the phantasmatic scenario of the inner world and the scenario of the current field – which is, in my opinion, the only place where real change is possible. (We should bear in mind that what concerns us is the transformation of content but increasingly often also the transformation of the tools that generate or manage contents without giving in to defensive or evacuative needs.)

What is 'worked through' in the current field goes on to continuously re-inhabit the inner world after being transformed, and then to live inside a story that is in a constant state of transformation (Figure 8.1).

Central, then, to my thinking is the concept of *après-coup* (Birksted-Breen 2003): understood both as a focus during the session on micro

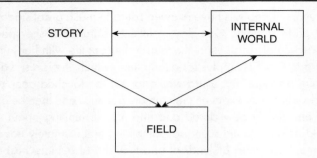

Figure 8.1 Relations between the external world (story), internal world and field.

après-coups (Guignard 2004) resulting from constant attention (Nissim 1984; Faimberg 1996; Ferro 1996b) to the patient's response to each of our interventions (responses that become the starting point for changes we make in our mental attitude, in timing, and in the quality and quantity of our subsequent interpretations) and as a constant movement towards re-inhabiting the inner world and the continual rewriting of the patient's story.

I also consider relevant to the analysis all communications made by a would-be patient at the first meeting. It is in fact a broadly shared assumption that these communications contain all the 'cooking cubes', or concentrate, of the analysis to come.

Countertransference and transference

At this point an unavoidable question comes up. What place does the concept of countertransference occupy in this model? The concept is highly changeable and is deconstructed in a number of possible lines of countertransference that can be described in a growing progression as follows:

Level 0 countertransference: when the field itself becomes narrator and metabolizer of what happens within it. The field digests, trans-forms, alphabetizes raw emotions that come to life, and by picking up the signals of its functioning the analyst makes possible its continuous modulation. This is a purely notional idea because there are always going to be various types of caesura that trigger events in the field. The characters of the session (which are not necessarily anthropomorphic) themselves take on the description of what happens by allowing interpretative modulations to shape movements in the field. The analyst presides over a process of co-generation.

Level 1 countertransference: the field can no longer absorb and shape the tensions of the field itself, but these affect a locus in the field, the analyst's mind, thus triggering an active and conscious reverie that it is perceived and utilized by the analyst.

Level 2 countertransference: when the tensions of the field are so intense that they overflow into the central part of the field, overwhelming any capacity for reverie and activating specific experiences of the analyst which he must work through in himself in order to digest and metabolize them as part of an understanding of the patient and in relation to possible interpretations.

Level 3 countertransference: the overflow is such that the analyst takes his homework home with him, so to speak. Something remains encysted and needs to be elaborated – for example using the valuable tool of countertransference dreams.

Level 4 countertransference: the overflow is such that the analyst is swamped in his analytic function, and this leads to ruptures in the setting ranging from physical illness in the analyst to unrecognized enactments, as well as breakdowns that are so dramatic as to make it impossible to continue the analysis. Here we are in the sphere of the violations of setting so excellently described by Gabbard and Lester (1995), where the countertransference has not been dissolved or thought and has become a 'thing', a 'fact'. At this point one of the constituents of analysis, i.e. the setting, is missing, which means that analysis is simply no longer in progress.

It follows that one could set up a sort of Mercalli scale of transference (the scale that calibrates the effects produced by earthquakes); then we would have an:

O *level of transference*: (not an absence of transference, which to my way of thinking about analysis is impossible) on solid ground, where transference occurs quite naturally, accompanied at most by some flaring up but certainly no telluric movements: the field *works* the transference.

Transference activates lines of force, movements of the field like watercourses or comparable to what the wind does with windmills.

145

The first session of analysis with Valentina, a seven-year-old girl seems to me a good example.

Valentina's oasis

There is little verbalization in this session; all it consists of are six drawings that filled the entire hour. I contributed to them by writing the things that Valentina asked me to write.

The first drawing (Figure 8.2) shows the 'blue river' which starts from the 'forest of the storms' to flow into the 'south sea' which at the other end touches Africa, where there is a blue oasis. You see a kind of raft in the river which is called 'hope'. The title of this drawing is 'journey of hope'. I think there is little need for comment on this beginning, no need to ask questions about Valentina's expectations or about the path the analysis will take. The second drawing (Figure 8.3) is entitled 'a camel at the blue oasis' (needless to say, there is a blue carpet in my studio). The blue drawing of the oasis could also represent a kind of pod or cover, at least that is the fantasy that comes to me spontaneously.

The third drawing (Figure 8.4) is called 'the camel drinks and two camel owners rest at the blue oasis'. Human figures appear, the customary camel

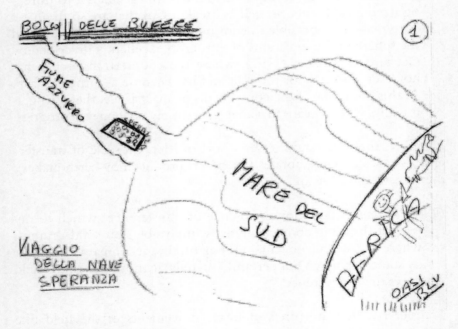

Figure 8.2 Valentina's first drawing.

Figure 8.3 Valentina's second drawing.

Figure 8.4 Valentina's third drawing.

147

that makes me think of emotional deserts to cross. The human figures are drawn with a certain skill; the camel is a kind of 'daub' – just a colourless outline. The figures have blue eyes. The drawing of the camel also refers to something more primitive.

Drawing four (Figure 8.5) shows 'the arrival of the Tartars at the blue oasis'. I remember thinking of the Tartars! And I imagined the well as similar to the pod in the film *Invasion of the Body Snatchers* – a film about the development of persecutory doppelgängers which put terror into my childhood.

In drawing five (Figure 8.6) 'The Tartars approach the camel owners at the blue oasis'. Other people arrive, there seems to be a gift, a family arrives, the camel (sense of loneliness?) shrinks, affective presences circulate.

The caption for the sixth drawing (Figure 8.7) is more complex:

'The Prampatis (primates?) meet the Tartars and the Africans at the blue oasis. . . . In the next episodes:

Will they perhaps build a village?
Will there perhaps be a surprise for people with leg problems?

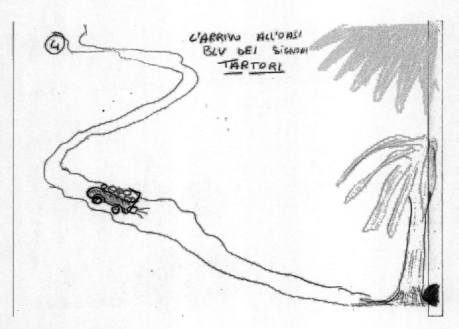

Figure 8.5 Valentina's fourth drawing.

Figure 8.6 Valentina's fifth drawing.

Figure 8.7 Valentina's sixth drawing.

149

Will they manage to build the village?
There will be new developments for the leg problems. You will find out in the next episode. Don't miss it!'

The drawing also shows a number of sketched figures, as well as a 'mysterious box' that had already appeared in previous drawings. Then there is the pod that has become ovoid in shape.

I remember thinking that this was a good start, because it showed both expectations and the shaping of narrative potential in a kind of crescendo of presences that took the place of the camel. Aridity was replaced by a large number of proto-characters – interpreters of future stories, in the customary style of old-fashioned thrillers. What also seemed positive was the fact that I was able to give life to the scenario of a dual reality full of persecutory experiences in the form of Tartars and pods from the Body Snatchers.

Valentina came to analysis because she was suffering from a school phobia or rather anxiety at having to separate from the mother (the leg problem?). The 'blue' problem was still mysterious to me, and only much later would it be configured as the blue of the bruises she received when her father, drunk with rage, used to beat her up. This kind of split-off family secret first took the form of an unusual interpretative violence on my part that disturbed me for a long time but was the field falling ill in the face of what was not sayable and barely known.

This beginning reminded me of another start, this time with an adult, which also involved the problem of a 'box', or more precisely a mysterious box. I mention this because it represents a special situation and one which was somehow not (or barely) contaminated because of the almost complete lack of preliminary contacts.

My involvement was different: in the first case I was in O transference (subliminal activity on my part); in the case of Margot we were already at a hypothetical *level 1 transference* (which is of course symmetrical with countertransference 1): this activates a significant reverie in the mind of the analyst.

Margot's wounds

I receive an e-mail from someone in Canada who tells me that she is planning to move to Pavia for a year, providing I agree to give her a year of analysis. She adds that she is a doctor and has already undergone one analysis.

My curiosity is aroused and my vanity tickled, but I am puzzled: I wonder what the point is of having a patient in analysis 'temporarily' and 'sight unseen'. Nonetheless, despite some doubts I agree to take her on.

September comes round and, as agreed, Margot presents herself: she is a young woman, newly arrived from French Canada with three children who have been attending an Italian school in Quebec and will be going to school in Italy for a year. Margot gives me little other information about the way she plans to organize her life and we confirm that the analysis will begin – as arranged by e-mail – the following Monday at the agreed time, on the basis of three sessions a week. As she is leaving, Margot hands me a large box she had left in the entrance hall, saying: 'I brought this for you from Canada.'

Again I find myself confused (I may, I think to myself, have completely forgotten to think about the problem of the criteria for analizability, but a present before we start is something else!).

However, the look on Margot's face is enough to make me accept this big box, standing as we now are at the door to my study. It also occurs to me that I took Margot on 'sight unseen' (the Italian expression *a scatola chiusa* translates as 'in a closed box').

Once alone, I open the box, and inside there is a small desk clock and a fossil, a 'slice' of a tree trunk from a petrified forest. I am impressed by the object because it seems to portray a face turned to stone with a frozen smile – like a 'laughing clown' or maybe a clown with a pained and desperate look.

I head home thinking that the clock seems to me a 'memento' as to the length of the analysis: it is temporary, a year of work.

The face immediately suggests petrified emotions, perhaps the reason for the analysis, something fossilized that hopes to come back to life.

But as I walk home the question comes to me naturally: 'why such a big box for two rather small objects?'

Now I have a kind of flash of illumination: with the apparent purpose of protecting the clock and the fossil, the whole box was crammed full of gauze, the type that is used to treat wounds. Now a third and fundamental theme lights up in my mind: the theme of bleeding and the need to staunch blood (and possibly heal wounds).

Inside myself I am aware of the importance of the reveries or phantasies or 'dreams' that I have in relation to these objects. I am also clear that I can use them as hypotheses inside myself and that it would be pointless to use them immediately as subjects for interpretation; I feel that I still need to metabolize and digest them.

What emerges in the early sessions is a tragic story: Margot's mother committed suicide by throwing himself out of a window when Margot was 16 years old. Her father was a prominent surgeon, who decided to close up the house where they had been living and to move away, together with the four children, without letting any of them take anything from the house, not even underwear or toys. A barrier of denial had petrified all emotion.

All this was to become a collection of stories in our field before being returned to a previously unknown story. Above all she was able to acquire new tools (the coat stand on which to 'hang' the increasingly heavy weights she brings to the session) and even made the 'discovery' of being entitled to an Italian passport, having discovered (?) during the analysis that she had a Sicilian great-grandfather who had left no trace.

I could provide a crescendo of examples of level 2 and level 3 transference in which what is significant is also the implication of the analyst's way of being and functioning, or rather what pertains to that particular analyst with that particular patient on that particular day of his life (always bearing in mind that they are specular and symmetrical to the descriptions of the *levels of countertransference*).

I would now like to examine two literary examples of these more intense situations, one involving a strong negative transference and the other an erotic transference.

In both cases one can see the desperate need for something to communicate and the unwillingness of the analyst to become permeable, so that basically these extreme transferences are also beta screens that serve to activate a unreceptive analyst (needless to say, I am personifying the forces present together in the field arbitrarily). The first example is taken from the novel *The Analyst* by John Katzenbach.

This is a book that can be read as a thriller, as a scathing criticism of the world of psychoanalysis – or in a thousand other ways. My first impression was that it gave an idea of the laborious process an analyst has to go through within himself to get to a 'cure' by working on the negative transference of a seriously ill patient and the forces in the field that impede any receptive availability.

To put it briefly, the story is about Dr Ricky Starks, a middle-aged analyst, tired, bored with his life and his profession. One day in the middle of the last session of the day, he hears a knock at the door and the sound of someone coming into the waiting room. (Who is it, he wonders: a patient's relative? A patient in crisis? Or someone else?) Once the session is finished, he goes into the waiting room and, not seeing anyone, is about to give up searching for an answer when he sees an anonymous note on a chair. The note contains the instruction that he should kill himself within a month unless he can work out 'who' wrote it. If he doesn't commit suicide, all his relatives (whose addresses are in the note) will be killed.

The story unfolds with growing pathos in the midst of disbelief and persecution as gradually all the analyst's certainties are undermined and ultimately destroyed (his credit card is blocked, his bank accounts emptied, his houses ruined, he is driven out of the Society of Psychoanalysis . . . and so it goes on, getting worse and worse). Finally the analyst comes to his senses and starts to take action. He changes his mental attitude and begins to 'search for' the persecutor, getting closer and closer to him, and almost reaches him. But in the end Dr Starks, now changed dramatically, stops doing what 'the analyst routinely does' and decides to be himself first and foremost, to treat people in a real way, after discovering that the person behind it all, the cause of his persecution, was the patient who was in the middle of a session when there was a knock at the door in the waiting room. These are the parts that have not had an encounter with a mind capable of dreaming. If they find this authentic availability in the analyst, they may be truly transformed, and find a receptiveness and transformative ability on the part of Dr Starks, who has now become genuinely able to take on madness and suffering.

The whole book could be seen as the 'working through' of a night full of restless dreams by an analyst who must find who his patient is and who to do so must truly find a place within himself.

The second example is even more arbitrary (of course, I am not using a psychoanalytic approach to give meaning to the text, rather the opposite; I am using the text as an effective narrative form, to make it express a psychoanalytic concept). The book in question is *Professor Unrat* (English title: *A Small Town Tyrant*) by Heinrich Mann (the novel on which the film *The Blue Angel* is based). Professor Raat takes the place of a supposed analyst and Rosa Fröhlich the place of a hypothetical patient.

The story is well known but I think it is still worth giving a brief outline of the plot.

At the beginning of the story, Professor Raat (called mockingly Unrat, or garbage, by his students) is 57 years old. He has been teaching the fifth form the same syllabus for many years – without any enthusiasm, always in the same repetitive and tired way. The set book is Schiller's *The Maid of Orleans*. 'However exquisite the lyre, the strings that are strummed daily lose their music. No one now responded to that pure Maid's voice, or thrilled when she raised her sacred sword; that armour had ceased to cover a human heart, and angel's wings spread in vain around her head. . . . the naïve spirit that, deserted from on High, became once more a helpless, bewildered girl . . .' Reading the text was only a way of catching out the students whom he hated and 'who hated him'.

The analyst is probably in a mid-life crisis; he has lost all connection with the emotional roots of his work, with the poetry of the encounter with the other and with the caring aspects of himself. His work has become mere interpretative routine, and, what's more, narcissistically orientated.

Professor Unrat wants to take revenge on some of his students and so he follows them into the sphere of attraction of an actress called Rosa (in von Sternberg's film version *The Blue Angel* she becomes the unforgettable Lola Lola). He is led towards to her by the voice of two sailors: ' "How are things, Klaus?" "Putrid," growled the other. . . . And he picked his way after them through various byways until they halted in front of a rambling old house with a huge porch, over which hung a lantern lighting up the sign – that of the Blue Angel. Once inside, . . . the woman herself seemed to Old Garbage a personified shriek.'

The analyst is not able to tolerate his own pain, his own depression. He is looking for someone who will bear for him the suffering he does not realize has invaded him. Then immediately he recognizes in the patient an aspect that is symmetrical to his own – the shriek of despair.

'Old Garbage . . . found himself able to understand what was being sung; a few words, as a cue to lift her frock and with a sly pretence of bashfulness cover her face with it. He grew angry again, feeling himself imprisoned in this world which seemed the negation of himself. Then he hears: "I'm such an innocent little thing!" '

In this way Unrat seems to have rediscovered the lost affectionate part of himself, the Maid of Orleans in Rosa (pink). Rosa herself has lost all contact with her affective side and has transformed it into a parody.

Welcomed into Rosa's dressing room, Unrat is quick not only to drink the wine, but also to drink in Rosa's youth with his eyes; he is troubled by her seductive wiles: 'He then noticed that her long black stockings had blue embroidery on them . . . he made the agitating discovery that her black-net-over-blue-silk frock did not come up to her armpit . . . Rosa is brightly coloured all over, . . . her hair was somewhat untidy, the blue bow at her neck was limp, the flowers in her frock nodded limp heads . . .'

Our analyst is drawn into a web of invisible mourning. He takes into analysis a young female patient and finds in her some of the needier and more childish, albeit mortified, aspects of himself. But the patient is plainly depressed; she eroticizes the pain, the shriek and turns them into something manic.

This is where Rosa's seduction begins: 'She bent forward, tapped Old Garbage under the chin, scratching the bare skin between his beard, and drew in her lips with a sucking sound . . . "I'd give the whole boiling of those youngsters for one sensible older man." '

Rosa traps our professor in her web of eroticized depression by touching his defenceless parts.

From this moment on Unrat/the analyst is caught in a vortex of intoxication, excitement and anaesthesia: pain and suffering are now replaced by overwhelming excitement that nonetheless seems to bring with it a taste of life.

' "Take that," she said. He took it without knowing what it was. It was black, it went into a mere nothing, and it felt warm, with a soft, animal-like warmth. Suddenly he let it slip through his fingers, for he realized why the garment was warm. It was the black cami-knickers.'

At some point there is an attempt to establish contact with pain.

' "So sails my boat, love, to my heart's repining. My heart is woe – and all the stars are shining." This is what Rosa tries to sing but it is not the song the public wants to hear. . . . Uproar . . . "Get off! Shut up!" they bawled.' Rosa has no choice but to sing a different song. 'Then she turned quickly round to them again, the old bright smile on her lips, smoothed her green silk frock, switched up the orange petticoat and broke into that quavering ditty: "I'm such an innocent little thing!" '

The attempt at analysis fails because it is not tolerated by the forces in the field. The only path open is denial of pain. Professor Unrat promises Rosa: 'I'll see you through'.

Our analyst has ended up in the quicksands. He wants to save the patient ('see her through') and himself but only succeeds in sinking ever deeper together with her.

Everything seems headed for tragedy. The various stages on the way will include Unrat's marriage to Rosa followed by the gradual transformation of their house into a gambling-den where orgiastic pleasures exorcise an unspeakable pain that asks in vain to be lived out.

Of course, at the upper end of our hypothetical scale we could put tsunami or Katrina transferences (transference number 5), in which case the configuration of the coastline or of New Orleans would only be relative (although, on the one hand, a coral reef not worn down by excessive work, or more solid defences, or, on the other hand, a deficiency of the analyst's personal analysis or a lack of maintenance – what Freud invited us to do every five years – might still have written different destinies).

In actual fact it is clear that we have good reason for saying that it makes no sense to distinguish between two different scales: one for CT and another for T. It would of course be more useful to have a scale that relates to the field, to its turbulence and storms. In other words, we should hypothesize a kind of scale going from field force 0 to field force 1, 2, 3 – by analogy with the scales used to measure wave motion.

This deliberately radical perspective could be toned down by conceptualizations that make reference to the concept of analytic space (Viderman 1979; Winnicott 1971) and which make more room for the difference between subject and object (Ferro 2006a). I find it useful to adopt a radical register so as to make things absolutely clear, although for ease of exposition later I will use concepts closer to those of analytic space to better describe the theme of connection/disconnection in the virtual channel between projective identification and reverie.

There are situations I have described elsewhere in which the field is not just flooded but overflows in many different ways (Ferro 1991b). Sometimes this is picked up by countertransference dreams or acting out, and sometimes it takes various evacuative forms that can go as far as psychosomatic illnesses in the body of the analyst, in the body of the setting (delays, skipping sessions, interruptions) and also in the body of society (violent acting out).[2]

I would like now to focus attention on the middle section of our hypothetical Mercalli scale or wave motion scale, which essentially is the point of mean oscillation in our daily work.

The purpose of these clinical examples is to further clarify what I mean by the reality of the session and the dream of the session, and to show once again that there is a daydream level that remains implicit, a night dream level and transformative work which often involves 'transformative narratives' that operate at an (apparently) manifest level. I think that for a patient it is crucial that we share in what he tells us in his dialect, whatever it is.

For me the use of clinical material is a way of embodying theory in images, of laying the groundwork for a debate that can be shared immediately; it is never meant to be a way of demonstrating a theoretical premise.

Giacomo and his animals

In the early sessions of analysis Giacomo always comes with a computer. Then at some point he starts bringing along stories about the various animals on his farm.

A day after I had raised the interpretative register, a neighbour appears who goes around with a machine gun and threatens to become a disturbing presence. I decide not to give a saturated interpretation and work with him on the emotions and fears this neighbour arouses in him; things proceed with a dialogical circularity, but then suddenly Giacomo says: 'I think that the machine gun has a red cap on the top, so it must be a toy gun he uses to play with children. It's strange I didn't notice that before.' All it needed was my playful interpretation to restructure the field. During that same period another transformation occurs that starts from a sound I apparently make unconsciously during the session more often than I thought. Giacomo tells me that his father 'moos' and he has always been scared by these bellowing noises because he didn't know how to interpret their meaning, but was afraid they meant disapproval and criticism. I try to bellow ('uuuhhm') less in the session, but meanwhile Giacomo's persecutory anxieties have been modulated by my becoming more absorbent and discursive; then one day to my surprise Giacomo tells me that as a child he was very fond of sweets called 'muh!', which his mother made sure were always available at home.

One day we end up, I do not remember how, talking about the Starship Enterprise. Giacomo tells me that in the most recent series the old protagonist

Dr Spock, the pointy-eared Vulcan, who used to frighten him as a child, had been replaced by a beautiful female Vulcan, who also had the trademark pointed ears, and that he found her very attractive. 'How strange,' he then said, 'a name like that, "Vulcan" which refers to fire and lava, as an attribute of a perfectly rational person. Perhaps behind this apparent rationality there's a fire! I remember there was a sort of rite whereby the Vulcans broke off any contact with their emotions. As a child I too had a ritual for becoming an emotionless Vulcan, but it never worked. Perhaps today my wife is a Vulcan; behind her rational appearance there must be something seething.'

A scenario like that of the Starship Enterprise, so different from the initial scenario of the prison, makes it possible to engage in further dialogic narrative transformation.

All these characters speak to a newly acquired ability to put previously inaccessible emotional states into images, to represent (Botella and Botella 2002) and contain them. Playing in the session can be understood as a kind of process of joint weaving that expands the containing capacity, involving the appearance of new objects in oscillation with the old and a movement of transformation which also works on apparently manifest meanings.

The content is purely occasional and transient; it could have entered the scene in another literary genre.

Vignettes clearly show that the process of joint narration with patients often working on their manifest texts (always seen as connected to the analytic field and not related to an 'outside' that is inconceivable to me from inside) is not important in itself but that it does imply significant changes in modes of managing emotions and thoughts through reversible and unstable micro-transformations of the here-and-now. If repeated, these micro-transformations lead to stable and irreversible macro-transformations that restructure the inner world and make for a more stable acquisition of identity which in *après-coup* will find stabilizing hooks in memories either of occluded events (Barale 1999) or possibly events that never happened (Ferro 1996a).

The plethora of clinical material also spares me writing a chapter on interpretations, however useful that might have been. I think it becomes implicitly clear that essentially I distinguish between, on the one hand, interpretations of transference and interpretations in transference (Gibeault 1991) and, on the other, interpretations of the field and interpretations in the field. To my way of thinking as a functioning analyst, 'off-field' interpretations have no citizens' rights. Of course, one could imagine a scale that takes into account the different degrees of saturation/insaturation in each interpretative intervention.

Transference and transfer from one mind to another

In analysis the re-proposal of the forgotten, repressed and split-off story (Freud 1914) is a driving force, in much the same way as are Klein's (1948, 1952) phantasmatizations of the inner world. On the positive side it enables transformation and change; the risk, however, is that the analyst falls into the trap of actually taking on a role (Sandler 1976) and that the field contracts the patient's illness (as is normal) but then does not heal.

If a patient had an emotionally unavailable mother, this will sooner or later be lived out in the consulting room and in the field, and this can be rendered through any character. It can be digested and metabolized through peristaltic movements in the field or also via interpretation. It must be borne in mind, however, that the interpretation can only be effective if it is the final act of an earlier digestive process.

If a patient had a cold mother, she must find a cold boyfriend in order to repeat and narrate the trauma. In the field she will have to experience this 'cold boyfriend', who will have to be transformed and at that point either the boyfriend will acquire new features or become irrelevant to the story that insists on being told or he will bow out of the scene to make room for other tangles of events awaiting a 'storyteller'. And somehow the analyst will also have to contract (or let the field contract) this coldness. To do this he will also have to be sufficiently nasty as an analyst (Gabbard 2004), although often it is enough to respect the setting rigorously.

The paradox of the human species is that tragedy is better for our mind than silent unrepresentability.

It is no accident that theatre, cinema and literature, but also sport, narrate and re-narrate encysted narremes of our species that still belong to the non-experienced mind and not to structural biology. The achievement of analysis in psychosomatic situations lies in turning back into tragedy what was evacuated in the symptom – itself nevertheless a memento of a hope for thinkability.

159

Even everyday micro-tragedies continuously stage what clamours to be acted out. Sometimes the scene freezes and the same play is kept on the playbill. In these cases the analyst is called upon to change the programme – both as entrepreneur and theatre director.

To come back to our main theme: I should emphasize that I consider essential the deep functioning that is established between two minds, a functioning that is also retold continually. The analyst must be a virtuoso of reversals of point of view. What the field signals belongs to what is going on at the moment but at the same time the field is at work and proceeds in its activity of receiving, digesting and transforming.

It's like a driver or pilot paying attention to all the various instruments on board a very complex means of transport, say a plane, but in fact doing so merely to make the trip sufficiently safe. The risk is that otherwise we veer off course (or cause serious incidents) by conducting an analysis that is so wrapped up in itself that it fails to continue the journey that is our goal.

What is constant is the basic activity of reverie, which is how the analyst's mind continually receives, digests and transforms 'what' comes from the patient in the form of verbal, para-verbal and non-verbal stimuli. The same activity of reverie is at work in the patient in response to each act of interpretative (or other) stimulation coming from the analyst. This basic activity of reverie is at the fulcrum of our mental life, and our health, illness and mental suffering depend on its function/dysfunction.

The same goes for basic projective identifications, which are the essential activators of all reverie. As a rule the explicit and significant manifestations of reverie tend to be visual – but of course this is not exclusively the case.

In its meaning for us today, transference – as Jim Grotstein wrote to me in 2005 in reference to my book, *Seeds of Illness, Seeds of Recovery* – can be seen as the transfer (as Meltzer would put it) of mental pain from one mind to another.

Let me clarify this point. This does not mean that we only deal with pain; in fact, what we deal with are all the skeins that cause pain for as long as they remain tangled, all the poorly functioning looms that weave tangled and occlusive skeins of protoemotions, and that absence of looms that produces mental chaos.

So these continual transfers (just like the shuttle buses at major airports) that not only move from the past to the field, from the

160

inner world to the field (within which the analyst is one of the places) but also constantly move from the field to the patient's inner world and from the field to his story. This constant coming and going of tangled fragments of sensoriality and protoemotions makes possible their transformative weaving and the neo-formation of inhabitants of the patient's inner world and story.

A possible image to express this: a cellar full of matted, musty balls (of yarn) which give off nasty smells and which, after the arrival of the parasites (symptoms), need to be taken to a laundry-dyeworks-mill where they can be cleaned, dyed and woven. From here they can return to live in the drawers of the house where they were or should have been. The metaphor (Semi 2003) is incomplete because there is something beyond and outside the cellar that presses to be admitted to the cellar itself: debris, fumes, inorganic material that requires more complex treatment if it is to become something belonging to the mind.

An analysis makes sense when it not only carries out these operations but in the long run also provides the patient with the tools to carry them out for himself.

What is needed for this transfer to take place?

First, a patient who is capable of projecting, evacuating, using the basic communication channel for this operation. This is the starting point for many patients, the point of arrival for many others, or for parts or other functions of the mind; one need only think of the two-dimensional lumps of mind for which the adjustment to three dimensions and the transition from modes of adhesive identification to modes of projective identification represents a massive change (Meltzer 1974).

Disconnections and reconnections

I am now going to describe some clinical situations that seem to me to show all the possible gradations between occlusion and receptivity, as well as the full range of possible disconnections and reconnections. To clarify this concept I shall momentarily set aside a radical theory of the field in favour of a conceptualization according to which analyst and patient are 'strong' places in the field (in actual fact there is a natural fluctuation in the field between the two positions described at different times even within the same session).

Cesare and the clogged drain

Cesare is a patient whose narcissistic fragility emerges at moments when there is least 'connection' between his mind and mine. After a session in which I interpreted, directly and unambiguously, 'the fierce anger of the patient towards a mother who neglected him', referring it back to the current relationship with me, Cesare says in the next session that he has adjusted the washing machine plug so as to stop his mother-in-law from flooding the house (as she is in the habit of doing). He also explains how he then went on to remove the waste pipe under the sink to get rid of accumulated debris and to get things back to normal.

He then announces that he will have to miss the next day's session because he has to go to a 'wedding'.

If the connection fails completely, if there is an excess of interpretation, if he fears that this might yet happen or if he suspects a traffic jam in the analyst's mind, then Cesare takes action: skipping a session is his way of protecting himself from being swamped by interpretation and also a way of unblocking the analyst's mind by giving it a rest.

This is something that actually happens in the current situation between patient and analyst, but it is also something that can illuminate the infantile emotional story Cesare reconstructs in the light of what he has seen come to life in the consulting room.

Then the current situation becomes something that activates silent fragments in search of narration, which once they come to life may be acknowledged, transformed and relocated in one of several possible stories.

Paradoxically, if monitored by the analyst with the help of pointers from the patient (→ Bion 1983), the micro-dysfunctions (and sometimes even macro-dysfunctions?) of the analyst's mind become loci and opportunities for the admission of never thought-of emotions that return to their original connections in *après-coup*.

But now we see a disconnect at even more archaic levels and with even more devastating effects.

Daniele and the analyst's 'images'

Daniele is an autistic child who, after years of therapy, had got significantly better. It is not my aim here to talk about Daniele's treatment as a whole; I want rather to focus on the moment in his therapy when there was a quantum leap, namely the moment when he abandoned the board between patient and therapist which was a kind of screen for displaying climatic and geological events (storms, hurricanes, earthquakes, typhoons, volcanic eruptions, and so on), all of them always related to moments of great turbulence associated with meeting or separation. So there comes a moment when Daniele stops these repetitive games and wraps himself up in a blanket during the hour of analysis. It seems like a moment of closure, of taking refuge inside an autistic shell. But the analyst feels he can be something other than an 'acoustic mirror'; he feels he can for the first time think in Daniele's presence.

He is pervaded by images of tsunamis, cemeteries, children's graves, murders, horror films – but also fond, sweet, nostalgic songs come alive in his mind: 'Love's Labour's Lost', 'Girls in Love'. Sometimes the therapist perceives a handicapped, tired look on Daniele's face, followed immediately by the look of a mad murderer.

One session begins with some 'puff tests', the kind you do with a pressure cooker. Then it seems that Daniele is making an effort to render his nasal cavity 'accessible'. Meanwhile all possible variations of the blanket move through the therapist's mind: metamorphosis, cocoons, but also disturbing manifestations – Kafka and the cockroach, the Elephant Man. Daniele then kicks the wall, for which he apologizes, but in the meantime other reveries flower in the analyst's mind: the living dead, gravestones with dead bodies sticking out. He experiences terror and fear, more images of horror films and then heartbreaking music and the sad tolling of bells.

At this point the channel once again becomes accessible, projective identifications are accepted and transformed . . . there is still a long way to go.

Secondly (regarding the question on p. 161), we have the pole represented by the analyst's mind, namely (what is taken to be) the receptive pole (again this is an arbitrary division, because while this is in operation in the field it is not always easy to make out what belongs to one and what belongs to the other).

The analyst's mental functioning during the session becomes – as described above – a central part of the analytic work. This takes us a long way from the idea of the neutrality of the analyst as an objective value.

If, paradoxically, such a person as an analyst capable of pH 7 existed, his presence would prevent the instances of alkalosis and acidosis affecting the breath of the field which permit the development of bacteria that could otherwise not develop in the field itself.

Given the centrality of the passage through the analyst's mind (or regarding the analyst's mind as one of the constituents of the field), the mental attitude of the analyst allows transference to develop and be transformed, even though as a variable it may contaminate transference.

But how can we tell the difference between transference, on the one hand, and what is a product of the analytic situation and the analyst's mental failure, on the other? This is the wrong question to ask, because from a field perspective what belongs to one is not easy to separate from what belongs to the other. But I must once again use the stratagem of distinguishing between and 'personifying' the operations of the field. The decision to introduce concepts such as enactment seems to me in this regard descriptively not particularly useful. However, there are some signals that need to be considered. Remember it was Bion (1987) who said that the number of hours of sleep an analyst gets determines his mode of functioning on that particular day.

When a patient talks to me I find myself simultaneously carrying out a number of alternating actions:

I listen to what the patient is saying and I participate fully in the manifest content of what he is saying. I let myself be permeated, I yield to the fascination of his story, often making minimal, enzymatic interventions which, apart from letting him know 'I get what you say' or 'I'm in synch', contribute to the development of the story itself. I participate with restraint but without being over-fearful of 'polluting', since I know that, whatever happens, the grey threads of my possible neutrality would enter the field in the very same way as the red threads of my emotional involvement.

Periodically I take on the *role of the geographer*, someone who takes bearings, as it were: now what do you want to communicate through what you are saying (it does not matter about whom, it doesn't matter where, it doesn't matter when)? The two levels of listening create interconnections. Generally, I resist the temptation to be a map-maker.

Above all I try to grasp the emotions present in what the patient says, the emotional colouring of what he says, which often I tend to emphasize. I also give great importance to the patient's response to what I say and this helps me modulate my subsequent comments.

But I also know that while this constantly changing analytic dialogue is going on, changing all the time, opening and closing worlds, what is at stake is also another deeper dialogue between the patient's continuous projective identifications and my ability/inability to engage in reverie. I absorb sensoriality, musicality, tone, protoemotional states: this often turns into images, consistent or seemingly inconsistent with other listening vertices.

There is yet another type of listening that shifts the focus from receiving content to the quality of the patient's mental functioning. I know that what he tells me on the manifest level is a way of bodying forth his dream thought; this is actually what interests me – as is the manifestation of what this produces.

For me manifest content has at most the same value as any other content: a childhood memory, an episode from everyday life, a sex scene, a film seen on television – for me as an analyst at work they all have exactly the same communicative value.

Progressively the session becomes a dream, or perhaps it would be better to say a film, which I observe and in which I participate. However, I always (or almost always) know that I am interested in improving the quality of the patient's apparatus for dreaming and hence for thinking.

I share in the contents, I use them, I transform them, I interpret them, but always with the aim of considerably expanding the set of tools the patient has available for thinking. Or to put it in my jargon: my aim is to develop his alpha function, his ♀ and then his ♂, his PS-D and CN-FP bandwidth.[3] I look closely at what we 'produce' together and what we 'cook together'. At some point I have the feeling that the session lives its own life and that the field performs on its own.

I am interested in content, but I am even more concerned about the patient's set of kitchen utensils (pots, pans, casseroles, mortars) and his cooker, his burners (alpha function). What I say in the singular with respect to the individual patient is also an exemplificatory abstraction because I too am immersed in the field. What exists outside the session is a significant moment of re-elaboration that often occurs automatically. Sometimes in situations of congestion it becomes a precious time-space for 'the analyst's homework'; sometimes it is laborious digestion that can even take up the night like countertransference dreams.

The focal problem is: what does the patient do with what he tries to 'transfer to us' if the process is inhibited? I said that the signals are there, the patient continues to talk to us in real time: there are closed doors, phones that do not work, clogged toilets, depressed mothers, uteruses with tumours, girlfriends with vaginismus, absent consultants, people who are blind or deaf, and so on.

When these indications are not sufficient, in the sense that they are not picked up and not used to reactivate the potential of the field, then the violence of the evacuation increases as a last and desperate attempt to communicate when the analyst is totally occluded (Bion's beta screen, 1962). If even this signal is not picked up, then the patient must necessarily evacuate into the body of the analysis (the setting), into his own body, by acting out or by dismantling the body of the analysis himself. Often what takes shape here are what we call impasses, psychotic transferences or negative therapeutic reactions (Ferro 1993c; Barale and Ferro 1992).

In my view it is worth investigating some of the causes of the 'dysfunction' of the receiver:

- Vertices of presentation from which we do not recognize ourselves (the example of the husband who wanted to have his nipples sucked until I recognized the message).
- Failure to receive the verbal message.
- Failure to receive 'pain' in its most primitive form (examples of disconnection). We receive tangled and snipped pieces of thread that we must weave into skeins and then into a story. This latter, more serious reason may have different roots which combine to create at one end an analyst with mental vaginismus, because he is engorged with themes of his own that are being developed (bereavement, illness, love), and at the other, the *trompe l'oeil* analyst who is drawn into the frame of the setting but who is mentally two-dimensional. (This can also be rooted in the analyst or else be the result of role-playing or enactment.)
- The analyst's mind is encumbered with theories or preconceived interpretations that essentially impede the 'marriage' between projective identifications and reveries, the marriage between the mind of the analyst and the patient's mind independently of any preconceived interpretation.

In these cases the temptation is to apply a code to another 'text' without any contagion. Essentially, Bion's abused notion of 'without memory and desire' is the only possible antidote to this defence against the new, the unknown and the authentic encounter.

Gioacchino's unavailable wife

Gioacchino dedicated the Wednesday session before a session I cancelled to the lack of availability he senses in his wife, who is affectionate but avoids sexual involvement in numerous different ways. They very rarely make love, and even then always with a certain rigidity.

There is a self-evident reference to the level of missing the session, having fewer sessions, the ensuing experience of distance and lack of interest on the part of 'the other'. Equally obvious is the transference as a reproduction of a childhood situation in which, in Gioacchino's description, the mother was not as concerned and passionate as he would have wanted her to be.

Both these levels could be interpreted in different ways and with varying degrees of usefulness. What is not so easy to detect is the affective truth about the mental functioning of the analyst that the patient is expressing.

If the analyst has the courage to look inside himself, he will recognize Gioacchino's words as an echography of their current functioning: this would reveal the analyst to be attentive and interested but with his passions elsewhere, saturated by other situations. Only this kind of listening is in my opinion able to give the analyst's receptivity a greater degree of passion in the consulting room (even when part of his occlusion is the result of having internalized the mother who occludes passionate valences or the cold side of Gioacchino himself). Working on these issues by offering premature clarification would be like decorating a Sicilian *cassata* with candied fruit and sponge cake before preparing the mixture of ricotta, sugar and chopped chocolate. Only once the mixture is ready does the decoration, however essential, make and acquire sense. Mixing is the operation that takes place in the consulting room, in the mind of the analyst in contact with the mind of the patient with the transformations that are made.

Sometimes patients come to us who only need work on the decoration or the cover, but I think that it is up to the wisdom (and perhaps unconsciousness) of the pastry chef to open his heart to the *cassata* and at least to work on the basic mixture.

I have never had a purely neurotic patient, in other words a patient in whom no psychotic nuclei emerged or, now that I have learned to recognize them, with no autistic lumps.

What ridiculous, pathetic monsters we appear if we are courageous enough to look at ourselves through the eyes of the patient and through what the patient tells us from his perspective. This is why we put up defences against sharing in his point of view (even as an absurd hypothesis). This could be a defence from seeing ourselves for what we are at that moment and from seeing what is, unbeknownst to us, our deep mental functioning.

If we dare to consider the patient, as Bion (1983) suggests in some of the unforgettable passages in *Italian Seminars*, as a kind of naive 'mouth of truth' about ourselves and the analysis, many of our mind-sets and convictions will be shattered. If we regard the patient not as someone who repeats in transference or who causes enactment but who in a naive way describes my way of being with him at a profound emotional level, this changes the whole game, often reversing it, or at the very least introducing another often disruptive dimension which brings us inexorably towards our own 'O'.

This does not mean that we should engage in self-disclosure with the patient or be treated by patients, but it does mean accepting that the other knows more about us (unconsciously) than we do; equally, the ingenuousness of this knowledge (as Bion would put it, 'the patient as best colleague') constantly helps us to carry out micro-transformations of our own mental functioning which produce macro-transformations in the field (which in turn, as I mentioned earlier, will re-signify the patient's inner world and story in *après-coup*).

After all, in the session the analyst often ends up being more alert; he uses his reveries, and the patient, in a perfectly unconscious way, dreams and re-dreams for us (when he knows how to) throughout the session.

Stefano Bolognini (2002) tells us that re-establishing contact with one's state of mind, also with the help of signals from the patient, is in itself already a *therapeutic* activity. I would add that the mind in that condition also allows the arrival of examples of phantasmatization that still await to be narrated.

Thirdly (returning to the question posed on p. 161), in these situations the concept of field allows us to carry out subtler and also safer actions in the sense that the field acts as an equalizing basin, a kind of space that can soak up much of the overflow caused by both patient and analyst, in allowing unsaturated absorption through the use of characters and narratives.

Luigi's cube

After a session in which I had put pressure on Luigi through my interpretative activity (which took place before a missed session that made the weekend longer), on the following Monday Luigi began with a dream: he was looking after a friend of his called Miriam who had recently become pregnant, and he was acting as a kind of minder to her. At one point he had to get into his father's car, a large, solid car which, however, shrank to the size of a Fiat 500, becoming a kind of small cube, or rather a cubic-shaped room which he had to leave in order to escape from danger; he would then move on into another cubic-shaped room and so on. All the rooms reminded him both of Rubik's cube and the film *The Cube*, where the characters had to get out of all the difficult situations that arose in each section of the cube. Finally, the mother, another character in the dream, asked him if he wasn't jealous of his girlfriend because she often went off with a friend.

Initially I try to grasp together with Luigi the emotions present in the dream: the idea of looking after Miriam, his disorientation at the change in the car, the feeling of uncertainty (game or threat?), and finally jealousy. Luigi in his turn adds emotional details to the various stages of the dream until I feel able to suggest that from a certain point of view the dream seems to me also to summarize his emotions about the analysis at that moment: the feeling that he is having to look after what is in gestation in the analysis, even when we are not together; his feeling of disorientation at the shorter week of analysis (missing a session); moving from one session to another without knowing what had the upper hand (the game or the sense of threat); and finally the arrival of Othello who asks questions about my infidelity–absence.

Luigi takes up these viewpoints with interest; he adjusts and corrects them and then goes on to talk about his head physician who pressurizes him a lot and prevents him from working at what he thinks of as his own speed. At this point I say something like, 'Of course, it doesn't help having a head physician like that', and on hearing this unsaturated intervention that recognizes his point of view, Luigi promptly answers by saying that 'fortunately next to "The Cube" (in-cube – incubus – nightmare?) of the head physician there is that other place where I can find relief'. Both scenes are current and reflect two places in the field.

There is no doubt that the transformations brought about by our work will precipitate a different internal organization which in turn will lead to a reworking of his story seen again through gradually transformed lenses: the different gaze that is formed in the present makes it possible to have continuous and different interpretations of 'the past', or to put it a better way, creations and recreations of the past.

Transference can be seen as a wave that becomes stratified inside the person and inside the mind of the analyst. I am referring here to a highly simplified model that leaves aside the more complex situations of the field and its developments.

The mountainous configuration that makes up the analyst's system of defences and resistances is like a kind of photographic negative, a mould within which the transference will become stratified in a continuous wave motion. One component of the transference will thus be determined by the ability of the analyst's mind to accommodate (or not) stratifications and conformations.

To sum up: the analyst's mind reacts and is modified by a series of events that have to do with:

• the patient,
• other patients,
• the group of patients,
• the oscillations of his psychic life,
• his principal theoretical framework,
• the joyful and painful moments of his life.

All these possible situations are particular orographic configurations of the analyst's mind.

If the analyst keeps his focus on his own mental state, he will not only be aware of what he contributes to a kind of transference but may also utilize and take full advantage of a situation that is in itself not desirable, understanding how the patient 'presents' the piece of transference that corresponds to the problem of his mind at the moment; when the patient's mind comes up against one of these particular configurations it will bring on stage precisely the 'piece' that fits here, as well as giving off signals that indicate how he perceives the analyst's mind.

This is of course true if the mind of the analyst is sufficiently mobile and capable of self-repair; otherwise one is likely to be heading for an impasse.

There is an interesting device they have on Finnair planes (I do not know if other airlines have something similar). While the passenger is being 'brought' to land (or during takeoff) a camera under the aircraft shows the approaching runway, its characteristics, its irregularity All this happens in real time up to the moment when the passenger 'sees' the plane's 'impact' with the ground (or the moment it leaves the ground).

In sum, what is relevant to our discussion is that we have at the same time something that belongs to the analyst, something that belongs to the patient and the patient's constant re-dreaming of the mental functioning of the analyst (or more accurately, of the field).

Luigi's farm

Luigi's analysis gets off to a good start and immediately sheds light on the coexistence of agoraphobic and claustrophobic aspects, lethargic aspects as well as other wild aspects.

The 'farm' of which he is the proud owner keeps on acquiring ever wilder new animal species.

At some point on our journey I have to inform Luigi of the cancellation of a series of Friday sessions for a few weeks, which shifts our work immediately onto a series of 'memories' (re-dreaming!) of when he was a child and was taken away to a luxury *Kinderheim* in Switzerland, his mother's home country.

He had always thought of this as a very enjoyable period of his life, but now he begins to see it as exile, being taken away, a source of anger and pain.

In the meantime his dreams are full of foxes that steal and kill geese, tearing their flesh.

My interpretation of the dream as being about the analyst who eats sessions allows him to 'digest' the anguish of separation and abandonment (however harrowing) that led Luigi to become very submissive towards his family once he came back home. Likewise he is genuinely available and appealing during the session. We are progressing along this new line of work (which started after I had informed him about having to miss some sessions) when a disturbing event breaks into my life and for a few days alters my normal state of mind. Later on, things settle down but, as happens after every decent earthquake, there are a number of aftershocks.

Luigi immediately changes the narrative scenario. He speaks about wanting to have another child in January and about his wife going to see her gynaecologist. The gynaecologist asked for some 'analyses' (Italian uses this word – *analisi* – to refer to medical tests) to make sure there is no risk of cancer and orders a scan to clear up the nature of a suspicious mass.

Luigi is enormously anxious. He is afraid not only that he will not be able to have any more children (that is, that the analysis may not produce any further results) but also that he will lose his wife (if the analyst should be irremediably invaded by his 'tumour'). What is necessary is both an analysis (the analyst's self-analysis) and an echographic scan (sounding out the responses of the analyst with a sort of scan of the analyst's availability, permeability and capacity to absorb).

Of course, if the analyst's mental situation should stay as it is, this would lead to an impasse. However, fortunately for all concerned it was transient, but it shows up the generative anxiety of the patient – which is of course part of the backlog of work still to do.

The evolution of transference is not therefore linear (unless the analyst is a robot, capable of maintaining a constant pH 7 level – the famous neutrality of the analyst) but proceeds in segments.

Of course, at some point the tasks performed may not be those planned for the day, but they will be made necessary by the particular mental functioning of the analyst or the field. This applies until the next resumption of a more linear transference.

To make things more complex, the analyst's pH 7 is constantly put to the test by the patient's projective identifications, although usually it is metabolized by buffer solutions the analyst has at his disposal.

I have always said that the field must, as it were, catch the patient's disease in order to recover from it. If an analyst does not let himself be involved in any way, for example, by the patient's symbionts, these will remain known but untransformed.

Going back to Luigi: the analyst's situation returned to 'normal', he resumed the thread of ease/difficulty in managing intense and wild emotions, but with the double risk of lethargy or evacuative acting out.

Taking stock

Only now can I say that I at least partially understand it because it has been so hard for me to unravel the concept of transference. Because I use it – even though I implicitly use concepts common to its various formulations – in a different way, exactly as it appears in the title: as the engine driving a kind of psychoanalysis that is interested in the development of functions.

Generally I do not start with the aim of seeking confirmation for theories – perhaps because I want to avoid being shipwrecked on the reefs of saying 'that's what Freud said'. I try instead to use clinical narratives to open up the path to provisional ongoing hypotheses, and so once again this time I have tried to offer ample margins for discussion and possible dissent.

I think we work continuously in the presence of a continuous dream and a discontinuous second-level dream. The constant dream is supplied by the alpha functions of both patient and analyst as they constantly seek to convert the quanta of unthinkability that transference continually feeds into the field. The discontinuous night dream constantly reorganizes the plethora of alpha elements (as well as giving a second chance of transforming quanta of sensoriality that remain undigested during the day) stored during the waking hours.

It seems to me that transference in the traditional sense is not enough. The analyst must allow the field to contract the patient's illness. A shielded analyst leaves many aspects of the patient's mind unnarrated. The patient arrives with the need to find a narrative that will give him peace, even though he does not know with regard to what or why. There is something in the classical concept of transference that leaves me with a stale taste, that reeks of the cellar. Even in the reconstructive anxieties of various types of memory what seems to prevail is an orientation towards the past rather than the future.

I see the current relationship (Schachter 2002) as a tool of transformation of transference and the precipitate of the transformations that the transference has undergone (the important thing as far as I am concerned is not reconstructing 'the trauma' but alphabetizing it by first breaking it up into its narrative units, transforming the inexpressible protosensoriality connected to it and sometimes developing apparatus to do this as a preliminary action). I agree with Fonagy (2003) (albeit with a very different angle of vision) when he says that the reconstruction process/narrative is more important than its content. I would even go so far as to talk about the creation of memories of events that never actually happened (Ferro 2006a) – or, to use the more elegant words of Bion, the Memory of the Future.

I think it is crucial to see transference (even the transference of the analyst on to the patient, when this happens) as the raw fuel of analysis. However, there is nothing linear about this, it doesn't involve repetition or projective identifications (although both are possible). It is made up of transformative and unpredictable chains which the minds of both analyst and patient will generate and jointly co-think (Widlocher 1996) through the motions of the field.

Ultimately, transference is everything the patient contributes; it is pervasive, it gets everywhere, it comes to occupy every space, every crevice. Transference is also the strength that each brings to enact the drama that will come to life and then fade away in unpredictable ways.

I regret that for reasons of privacy I cannot describe longitudinal clinical case studies, but the various vignettes I have drawn can be seen as indicative of different moments of analysis.

The analyst's mind lends itself to the complete staging of the transference. The drama needs to develop as a story in instalments (Luzes 2001); it must live, pulsate, become flesh, find an outlet.

For some analysts, the quality of the analyst–patient relationship sets off transference, for others transference (to some extent precooked by the patient through his life experiences prior to meeting the analyst) influences the quality of the relationship, as Bordi points out so well. In analytic field theory the two elements influence and create each other. Green (2005) says that analysis is a process in which advancing towards the object mobilizes all the transformations of the past relevant to the present situation. I would add that the qualities of the object jointly determine these transformations and above all that these transformations are not a question of process.

I realize that my work (and my concept of transference) lacks a linear structure, such as can be found in Meltzer (1967) in *The Psychoanalytical Process*, but I think that the work of the field (which can also be compared to respiratory or peristaltic movements) is perfectly rendered by images of motion: ebb and flow, undertow, wave following wave. There are continuous movements back and forth that make one think one is heading towards a conclusion but then a new movement starts, there is a new expansion in a sort of incessant process of constructing, deconstructing and reconstructing stories – and especially the apparatus to think stories.

Seen this way, the stories become nets that contain emotions, patterns that allow variously coloured threads to be woven into different webs.

The task I have given myself – or have been given – concerns my clinical practice. That's why I make such frequent reference to my previous work. I do this out of a need to show the progressive construction of an analytic identity, a work in progress.

Although there can be no doubt that I share the basic heritage of every analyst – the centrality of the patient's story, infancy, sexuality, the centrality of the patient's inner world and its objects – I regard it as more useful, more constructive and, potentially, more open to a dialectical approach, to emphasize the specific nature of my analytic kitchen, which has been progressively structured over many decades of full-time analytic work often with severely ill patients. This experience certainly also accounts for my interest in apparatuses for thinking, feeling and dreaming rather than content, although of course the former without the latter would make no sense.

To reiterate: in my way of working it is the patients themselves who continually retell, in different ways, their childhood or their family novel; they are like living elements that constantly bring forth new gestalts.

For me, this story is a fundamental deposit left by a third party, something like a left-luggage office in a railway station where the contents of the cases are periodically changed so as to reflect identities that are in a constant state of flux and open to the future.

I could have shown everything that is normally evinced in classical psychoanalysis – repression, the emergence of memories, remembering traumas, the reconstruction of childhood scenes, or the importance of implicit memories. However, I have preferred to point out some perhaps rarer plant life – plus the occasional original leaf.

For me, in my analytic kitchen, the patient's story is primarily the story of possible 'narrative derivatives', since my focus of interest is on 'the dream in the session and especially the tools that generate it'. In this respect I am not very far removed from Bion (1983) when he describes a patient who had told him about a heart operation: 'Whether the operation was really carried out or simply an incision made on the skin, I don't know. For all I know it may have been a psychological incision.' I can know what is narrated and even more what I witness and co-author.

Each patient that comes to my analytic restaurant is totally different and, in my opinion, is entitled to have his analysis unfold in his preferred narrative genre – past, present or future. What matters to me is how he works, the function/dysfunction of his and my mind together – whether he is speaking of himself as a child, his wife or *Star Trek*.

Why then, you may ask, do I not do this by reporting a full case study that would show what I mean by the 'precipitate of microtransformations' into 'stable macro-transformations' that take up residence in the patient's inner world – and later in his story – in continuous *après-coups*? Why do I not show the development over time of the ability to engage in waking dream thought (alpha function) or nocturnal dreams? Self-evidently there are reasons of confidentiality that prevent me from publishing the full story of an analysis. I have had to settle for short flashes which only the patient will be able to recognize.

For me the diversity of models has always been a source of curiosity, stimulation and growth. Comparing different ways of working and tracking down their underlying implicit models has been one of the most interesting tasks I have found myself doing in various situations.

It is true that there are radical differences in implicit models, in techniques and theories, but I also think there is a part of analysis that operates independently from the knowledge that patient and analyst possess, the part, namely, that depends on how the mind of that particular analyst 'mates' with the mind of that particular patient, on that particular day – with all the transformations they generate.

This is exactly the share that is always at work and that really is our greatest common denominator. No one has shown that one model treats patients better than another; perhaps all we can say with any confidence is that a particular analyst, no matter what his orientation, enjoys our trust.

One question still remains unanswered: What should I do with 'neuroses' or 'transference psychoses'? Should I make them into a mode of functioning that at some point will probably come to life at some place in the field (through what story, silence or dream I cannot know) – along with many other possible new worlds that are not pure repetition or re-enactment but represent an unexpected and luckily unpredictable opening-up of meaning? What else is it that drives us in our exciting job if not the desire to discover what exists beyond the Pillars of Hercules of the repetition compulsion? What is it in the parallel universes that expects the Starship Enterprise to continue its journey? Fortunately we don't know the answer!

Giving a name to what we do without knowing that we are doing it is, in my opinion, what research in psychoanalysis is about.

Having messed up my analytic kitchen, I now find myself having to reorder things. I still (albeit in a more conscious way) count transference among my most valuable tools – as long as it is used implicitly. Putting it at the forefront is like wanting to keep at a distance something that pulsates in the room in the present.

To me it is of little import where it comes from. Ogden (1994a) in an interview with Mitchell once said that meeting the other person is the only way to release the scream you cannot produce alone – as long as one is not stunned and overwhelmed by it.

Ultimately, transference is also the transference of a defect: the patient who transfers to us his scream, the patient who transfers to us his inconceivable pain, the patient who speaks coolly of ice-cream to Bion, transfers above all his 'non-ability' to alphabetize these mental states. He obliges us to do it for him, he triggers reveries, he obliges us to exercise containment and to expand the container. This leads Bion, permeable to the despair of the patient, to make the transformation into *I scream*. It leads us to transfer – this time from us to him – our ability to weave protosensorial and protoemotional states into images; it obliges us to pass on to him a method for daydreaming (development of the alpha function); it leads us to hand on to him threads with which to weave more stabilizing containers, broad and elastic; it forces us, as we dream for him, I repeat, to pass on to him the method, I repeat to myself, for feeling, thinking, dreaming.

A possible first image is that of a space (field) to which a collector brings letters or fragments of letters of the alphabet; in this receptive space there are craftsmen (elaborative and transformative functions) who work these fragments into letters and the letters into fragments of speech. Gradually as these fragments acquire meaning and weight, they settle by force of gravity in a place in this space (internal world) from where they are then continuously aspirated into another place in this space where the syllables, the sentences become stories, coloured fabrics (stories and story) that suddenly another collector takes outside that space to other spaces we know nothing about (the patient's external reality).

A second image speaks to us more explicitly of a field where fragments of incomplete meaning, sensoriality, beta elements, isolated alpha elements are processed, alphabetized by the oneiric, containable, meaning-weaving functions of the field, functions which while defective in the patient are then introjected by him or developed by taking them from the field itself. In this field we have two types of dream function – the tireless function of the cameraman (alpha function) and another that is more like the work of the director who dreams the alpha elements that occur during nocturnal sleep, both if we consider this latter function as an alpha meta-function and as a function of directing and editing performed by an apparatus for dreaming dreams.

After all, albeit in a different language, this is what Riolo (1998) said in his Introduction to Corrao's *Writings*: after making the point that 'there are symbolic systems designed to decipher and communicate meaning and symbolic systems designed to produce and transform meaning', he states that 'Corrao's idea was that psychoanalysis belonged to the latter; it was a system for generating new thoughts'.

In her analysis Valentina gave birth to monsters from unknown worlds while she waited for a parcel, monsters that I had imagined in my reverie about the *Invasion of the Body Snatchers*. Margot did something similar with the big box she gave me where the gauze acquired a meaning it did not have before we met.

I could at this point say something provocative about Dora's first dream. Perhaps Dora just wanted to say that she was trapped inside an emotional fire, that it was true that there were things she felt were valuable about the analytic work they had done (the jewellery to be saved), but to quote a Sicilian proverb, 'Fuiri è briogna ma è sarbamente i vita' (it may be shameful to run away but it saves your life). This already foreshadowed the idea that her path to salvation was to break off the analytic work through flight. Perhaps after all she was right: by taking flight she saved herself from an experience that would have been too emotionally intense to live through. And I believe that Freud was also the unconscious arsonist who ignited emotions in the patient that psychoanalysis had not yet sufficient fire-fighters or civil protection to deal with.

So I believe that it is always useful to take a look at what's cooking; it helps us to adjust the analytic food so as to make sure that the patient, to quote Bion, has sufficient grounds for coming back the next day (and not too badly burnt!). As befits any good restaurant – or at least any good enough restaurant.

Notes

1 I think that in some ways transference can be compared to the dowry brought by the bride. Although it was important, in the end everything depended on how the married couple functioned and what it co-generated. Moreover, the dowry is not static but bears constant fruit.
2 Albeit in a different context, Fausta Petrella (2005) told me that one of the first lobotomized patients had killed the surgeon who had carried out the operation.
3 Negative capability and selected fact.

9

Psychoanalytic exercises

This chapter is designed as a kind of workbook which starts from the assumption that the answers to the questions can be found in the first part of the book (and in my previous books).

I think this is useful because the analyst must be flexible; in order to understand, to communicate, to grow richer he should know not only his own language but also the language of others. My hope is that these exercises will stimulate the analyst's ability to think, to daydream and to play.

Needless to say, without a context (or even perhaps within a context) there can be no right answer. Let me repeat: these are only exercises 'on the bars', as it were, designed to help the analyst enter the scene better trained.

Exercise 1

Let us imagine a patient in analysis who at some point during a session says: 'Yesterday my computer was inundated with so many e-mails it broke down.'

Let us imagine that different analysts respond in the following different ways:

Analyst 1: 'Something similar happened when you were a child and your mother shouted at you in that unbearable way of hers that later caused you so many problems with your superiors, whose slightest remark paralizes you.'
Analyst 2: 'Yesterday maybe I said too many things to you and they clogged you up.'
Analyst 3: 'Spam is a problem.'
Analyst 4: 'Who sent you so many e-mails?'

179

Analyst 5: 'I imagine that you are very angry with the people who sent you all those e-mails.'

Analyst 6: 'Were there at least some interesting e-mails among them?'

(a) Try to explain what each analyst was thinking before he answered and what was his probable reference model.

(b) Add other possible answers, explaining the theoretical model implicit in the replies.

Exercise 2

What do you think is *the truth* in psychoanalysis? Historical truth? Narrative truth? Emotional truth?

Give examples to support your reply/replies.

Exercise 3

After a transference interpretation, at the Monday session a patient says, 'Today, the motorway was terrible, I was being tailgated by a lorry and I was terrified because it was so close behind me.'

Analyst 1: 'There is a part of you that in the absence of analysis persecutes you and you don't know how to escape this persecution.'

Analyst 2: 'Perhaps at the last session I interpreted too much and my words were the lorry.'

Analyst 3: 'This is a terrible experience, just like in the movie *Duel*.'

Analyst 4: '*This* is a terrible experience, just like in the movie *Duel*.'

Analyst 5: 'So I should drive more slowly!'

Analyst 6: 'Would it be impossible for you to drive faster?'

Analyst 7: 'The lorry loomed like your father checking that you had done all your homework in the evening.'

(a) Try to imagine how a patient (as you imagine him) would respond to each of these interpretations.

(b) Try to imagine how a patient nearing the end of analysis would respond to each interpretation.

(c) How would a severely paranoid patient respond?

(d) How would an obsessive patient respond?

(e) How would a phobic patient respond?

Exercise 4

If a patient said one of the following things:

- I am worried about SARS because my son is in China.
- Yesterday I saw a film on TV where the cowboys massacred the Indians.
- When I was little I was terrified by the doctor.
- My secretary is being persecuted by someone with a character disorder.
- I dreamt about a cat that was being attacked by a pit-bull.

Do all these formulations have the same communicative value? Why, or why not?

Do these formulations have the same communicative value as the previous example with the lorry? Yes or no? Why?

What drawings would a child make instead of these verbal formulations?

What games would he play which would correspond to this experience?

Exercise 5

'My wife, as you know, has been very depressed for a long time, which means she doesn't want to have sex with me, or at least I have to insist so much that I lose interest. So at one point during the Christmas holiday when Marisa made it clear she was willing, I didn't refuse. I started a relationship with her which, far from making me feel guilty, gives me energy, and even my relationship with my wife seems to be getting better.'

What interpretations could we come up with about what a patient is communicating by telling this story? What could we think? What could we say? What kind of patient could this be and at what stage of the analysis?

Exercise 6

'I came home full of enthusiasm and emotion and told my wife about my plans for a new book. Her reaction was to say that there was no point. I felt dejected and angry.'

'I started working on the computer. I even managed to drop my glasses and break them. All the progress I had made that afternoon went up in smoke because I had to buy some new glasses.'

What kinds of interpretations could be given here? What would a transference interpretation be like? And an interpretation in transference? And what about an interpretation centred on the functioning of the inner world? Is it a narrative? Is it saturated? Unsaturated? Historical–reconstructive?

Exercise 7

'On my way to the session I witnessed a scene that made me incredibly angry, so much so that I wanted to do something: a mother was cycling along and her little girl was running after her, panting and getting more and more out of breath. And her mother said: keep running so you'll lose some of that weight.'

The same questions as in the last exercise. One additional question: what dream might be told to express a similar emotional experience?

Exercise 8

After some cautious self–disclosure by the analyst the patient replies full of relief, saying that knowing what the analyst has revealed about himself really helps him a lot. Shortly afterwards, he talks about someone in a car who didn't give way at a stop sign and ran into him. As a result he banged his head on the ground, lost his memory and felt disorientated for a long time.

What does the patient seem to be saying? What kind of reply could be given to this communication?

Exercise 9

What is the difference between Strachey's classical concept of interpretation, a transference interpretation, an interpretation in transference and the interpretation of transference as understood by French psychoanalysts?

Give clinical examples.

Exercise 10

What is *après-coup*? In which model is its use particularly and consistently present?

Give an example.

Exercise 11

In what ways can the concept of projective identification be understood?

Give an example.

Exercise 12
What is enactment? Acting out? Acting in? A bastion?

Exercise 13
'In my dream I was chased up into my bedroom by insects and monsters. I was terrified.'

What might be the analyst's thoughts about this statement?

Suggest seven possible recorded interpretations.

Exercise 14
After the first summer break: 'As a child I was very fond of a boxer dog called Larry. He used to follow me around all the time. He liked me and I liked him. Then one day he disappeared and I've never heard of him since. Perhaps he got run over or was killed.'

What might be the analyst's thoughts about this statement?

Suggest seven possible verbalized interpretations.

Exercise 15
'I arrived late today because of the traffic and because the police have put up a number of roadblocks.'

What might be the analyst's thoughts about this statement?

Suggest seven possible verbalized interpretations.

Exercise 16
'Despite my many fears, including my fear of catching diseases such as hepatitis or tetanus, I have now decided to have my ears pierced.'

What might be the analyst's thoughts about this statement?

Suggest seven possible verbalized interpretations.

Exercise 17
'When I was a young girl my mother once told me to tell my dad to stop having sex with her, at least for a while.'

What might be the analyst's thoughts about this statement?

Suggest seven possible verbalized interpretations.

Exercise 18
'When I was little I was once in a room with a man I didn't know. I was very scared and didn't know what to do. Then everything went dark.'

What might be the analyst's thoughts about this statement?
Suggest seven possible recorded interpretations.

Exercise 19

A patient speaks of his violent and alcoholic brother whom he doesn't
want to have anything to do with, even though his mother wants
him to keep an eye on him. He adds that his brother refuses to take
no for an answer and can become dangerous if someone turns him
down.

He adds that he too finds it difficult to put up with refusals, and
when it happens he feels that has to cool down something that is
boiling.

What is the patient talking about?
What apparently is/are the problem/s?
Which interpretative strategy/strategies can you think of, and why?

Exercise 20

Which of the following communications could be an indication to
the analyst that he should be more interpretative and incisive – or
alternatively, less active?

• At the moment I have very little work to do and I am bored.
• The other day I saw a movie at the cinema, you know the one by
  Rossellini, *Stromboli*, where the volcano erupts.
• My friend Clara's analyst relates everything Clara says to herself,
  so Clara has learned what topics to avoid and what not to say.
• My husband doesn't make love to me for weeks at a time.
• My cat is really scared when the dog gets too close.

Exercise 21

In terms of the ♀ ♂ relationship what are the risks of over–active
and insistent interpretative activity?

Also in terms of the ♀ ♂ relationship what, on the other hand,
are the risks of the excessive development of ♀ in the absence of
significant interpretative activity (♂)?

Exercise 22

At the beginning of the week, the patient tells the analyst about her
mother who once left her behind at the supermarket and only realized what she had done some hours later. She arrived back at the

supermarket completely out of breath. Her daughter was still there but she was then questioned by the police.

How can we tell whether this incident is part of her family story, whether it is a statement in the 'here and now', whether it belongs to a reconstructive area or whether it is to be interpreted in the current transference? How could it be interpreted?

Exercise 23

After saying that her parents are very much against her analysis, a young patient recounts the following dream during the first session: 'I was in a car with the Cuban boy I was going out with and we started to kiss and hug because I wanted to. I wanted to be cuddled and he was so soft, so smooth. The only thing was that he wanted more and I didn't. Then eventually I agreed to strip naked and we were both naked and up close. Next to us there was a van with a bunch of guys. They were dancing and seemed very happy. And then he wanted to make love. He went behind the car and persuaded me to follow him. Just at that moment I realized that my aunt from Rome was there watching me. She said, "You can't do that as long as I'm here". And then somewhere else stood my parents, who were furious at me because I had left the house without telling them and then,' lowering her voice, 'there were other things I don't want to talk about. It was too horrible finding my aunt there, too embarrassing, it was like having a controller.'

Can this dream be interpreted as it is? Why? What could it mean?

Can associations be used – such as what the patient says before or after the dream? Why?

Can what comes into the analyst's mind be used as an association? Why?

Do we need to ask the patient actively for associations that lead to the latent text of the dream? Why?

Exercise 24

In many pathologies the problem is how to cope with archaic aspects of self, agglomerates of beta (or balfa) elements; I'll call them 'pit-bulls' to make the concept clear.

In phobias the pit-bull is put somewhere that becomes the area or the phobic object; all one needs to do is avoid it.

In obsessive syndromes the pit-bull is under constant control and is kept in a cage by using rituals.

In hypochondria the pit-bull is put into the corner where it is constantly kept under watch.

In people with character disorders it is violently evacuated.

How is the pit-bull managed in people suffering from:

(a) hysteria
(b) psychosomatic illnesses
(c) panic attacks?

Exercise 25

A patient says that he has bought a fantastic camera and goes on to recount an episode in which a photographer had come up to him and asked if he could photograph his cute little daughter for a clothes catalogue, giving as a reference the name and address of a fashion company. The man took a lot of photographs but then the patient became increasingly anxious that he might be a paedophile or a member of some criminal organization. He decided to remove his name from the telephone directory and even take it off his front door.

What is the patient probably talking about?

What could the analyst communicate to him, and in what style?

What kind of anxiety are we dealing here?

What kind of 'problems' might this patient have?

At what stage in the analysis might this happen?

Exercise 26

The Thursday evening session is ended by the analyst with a thoughtful, measured transference interpretation that is appropriate to the patient's anxiety with regard to separation from the analyst.

On Friday morning the patient looks at a wall of the room and asks, 'Has this picture always been there? . . . it's a typical psycho-analyst's picture.'

What kind of communication is the patient probably making?

How could the analyst intervene?

The next session (on Monday) begins with the patient saying that his personal trainer has told him to do some more bike work and to increase his speed, but has since left him alone.

What interpretations, comments, interventions could one make here? And why choose one as opposed to the other?

186

Exercise 27

A patient explains that he has a small company that does the sounds and the lighting for festive events. He wears a shirt with a shark that shows all its terrible teeth and underneath is written: 'There are no sharks in the Alps, don't worry.'

He then goes on to speak without stopping, producing new images, stories and short stories in a disturbed way that gives the impression that he is evacuating thoughts and images.

What do we think might be happening in the mind of the patient and in his relationship with the analyst?

Exercise 28

The analyst announces the cancellation of the last session of the week, and the day after this communication the patient dreams about a woman driving a 'white Fiat Uno', then about finding nowhere to park his car, and later about a woman who shoots him first in the arm and then in the heart. She has the eyes of a madwoman and reminds him of a next-door neighbour he used to be very afraid of.

How could this dream be interpreted? Or do we need the patient's associations to help us access the hidden meaning of the dream?

Exercise 29

A patient dreams of having had a dream: she had stomach cancer, but it was an external tumour covered with a sort of blue–green mould and with some kind of liquid oozing out of it.

The analyst feels disgust while she is recounting the dream. He hopes the patient won't come the next day and remembers a dream of his own he had the night before: there was something like a jar, a Pandora's box/jar he thinks in his dream, and despite the lid still being on the jar some spiders and other undefined horrible insects had managed to crawl out of it. The analyst goes down with flu the day after the session, missing a week of analysis.

What can we make of what happened?

On the basis of what theory?

Exercise 30

Analyst: Often you turn down my help.

Patient: Many people tell me that, even my parents. They say, you don't let anyone help you. The problem is what happens

187

when I show them my love, my suffering; they want to have a quiet time and not be disturbed.

Analyst: That confirms to me that you are afraid I am not available for you and not receptive to your emotions.

Patient: My husband is unbearable: he always wants to have sex with me from behind; he even wakes me up in the middle of the night to satisfy his needs without taking my pleasure into account at all.

Analyst: . . .

What probably happened in this sequence?
Why does sexuality put in an appearance?
What might the analyst be thinking?
How could he intervene?

Exercise 31

A young girl comes back from her summer holidays out of breath, saying that she ran all the way. She goes on to say that she wasn't afraid when her mother went away. Then she talks about a classmate who didn't do her holiday homework and hadn't even bought the book with the exercises, perhaps because she couldn't afford it.

She then speaks of a schoolmate – known as the 'big pig' – who has moved away.

Then she says that her sister messes up all their toys and then it is up to her to put them in order.

She ends the session with two drawings. The first depicts a girl in a box with lots of toys; the second, a steel bird with a steel tail and iron claws well hidden underneath a kind of pink swimsuit.

What should one think of these communications?

How could they be interpreted/commented on?

What would an analogous communication be like if it were made by a forty-year-old obsessive engineer after the first summer separation from analysis?

And what dreams might an engineer have instead of the drawings?

Exercise 32

A patient who works as a psychotherapist comes back from the summer holidays and starts talking about the cases he has been dealing with. He focuses in particular on a patient who is so emotionally tied to her husband and children that she has hysterics when they leave. Then he describes a woman patient whose husband has lost his job; when she heard the news, she felt as if the ground had given away beneath her feet. The husband is fragile and, what's more, he is given to trembling as if he had some kind of neurological disorder. He then talks about having spent the night before on call, during which he had been called out to a patient who had had an attack of acute abdominal pain for which there was no clinical evidence, and to a case of dysphagia, again without any organic evidence. He then talks about the peaceful holiday he spent with his girlfriend in Sicily and ends with a dream in which there was a pit-bull with a kind of split personality: it was brought to a show beribboned like a poodle but then it was also locked in a cage where it growled fiercely and nobody dared approach it.

What communication is the patient making?

How can one deal with this communication, which so closely resembles a matryoshka doll?

What does the dream seem to be saying?

How could the same 'story' be told by an eight-year-old phobic child who starts back at school (and analysis) again after the summer holidays?

Exercise 33

At an advanced stage of analysis with a psychotherapist who has been talking about a depressed patient he is not sure how to treat and to whom he does not know what to say, the analyst offers an interpretation in terms of the difficulties of coming into contact with a very distressed part of self with which he has not yet been able to establish any connection.

The patient responds by describing acts of cruelty to animals which he has witnessed. He gets progressively angrier at people who harm animals and who even make him feel the desire to kill these torturers.

He adds that he does not know how to cope with serious illnesses. Then he says he is not sure he wants to continue being a psychotherapist, he would like to stop having to deal with patients.

What might one think of this clinical sequence?

How could this be transcribed if everything were shifted two years back or two years forward in the same patient's analysis?

Why might the interval of time (two years earlier and two years later) be significant?

Exercise 34

A little girl comes back from her summer holidays and talks about going on a *ferrata* (an 'iron route', i.e. a path in the mountains fitted with metal ladders, etc.): she had had to come down a long ladder, using hooks, and she was afraid of falling. To get up her courage she started singing but her mother shouted at her to stop.

What communication is the girl making?

How could it be understood?

How would the same experience have been told by an adult?

Exercise 35

A boy who has the face of a little adult talks in the session of 'having to go along the same road and to visit all the usual places'. He speaks in a monotone and without a trace of empathy. He does a drawing in black and white where he says everything is normal. Then he says that he is anxious and can't sleep because he is already thinking about Christmas presents.

After an intervention by the analyst, he does a drawing full of coloured spots, then coloured circles, then mazes and finally flat grey lines; he says that 'everything is normal', 'but I'm bored'.

What communications are taking place?

What type of diagnosis could be made?

Exercise 36

A patient has the need to keep a significant emotional distance. He then talks about a new type of car where the hand brake comes on automatically in various situations detected by sensors.

How should we think of 'this handbrake'? As a 'useful' defence, something that for the time being is necessary for the patient? Or as an attachment to a bond, as dependence on the analyst?

Why?

How would this problem be expressed differently by a five-year-old child with a phobia of animals?

Or by a policeman with a phobia of guns?

Or by an engineer responsible for the sluice gates on a dam?

What game might a three-year-old child with a fear of fire play that would mean the same thing?

Exercise 37

At the moment he begins to give up his autistic defences, a patient has a dream: 'I came to a place I didn't know, there was a restaurant where the waitress took liberties, then there was a fence with horses grazing, and there were some frightening women with chainsaws.'

The analyst, partly by using what he 'feels' towards the patient, interprets that the patient is making a breakthrough in his emotional life, perhaps the waitress is the analyst himself who cannot be totally controlled. This means being able to live emotions peaceably in the same way as the horses kept in by the fence are peaceable; but it also involves the activation of emotions he feels dangerously attacked by, just as the women with chainsaws are dangerous.

After a brief silence, the patient says: 'It occurs to me that I had another dream: I went to a restaurant to eat with some friends and the food was good, then there were some dishes that were too stodgy and then suddenly out of the kitchen came some cooks carrying clubs who started hitting everyone on the head, just like those scenes where the police hit people at demonstrations.'

What comments could one make at this point?

Exercise 38

One day, a patient who suffers from panic attacks and who also has a phobia of knives says during the session: 'Yes, it's true, I love toma-toes, pizza, I could live on pizza alone, everything red, strawberries, cranberries, I like everything, the colour, the flavour, they're sweet.'

What fantasies can we have about this communication?

Exercise 39

A patient who has finished a long and, in his own estimation, very good analysis, asks for a new analysis. He has the impression he has put everything in place in his life. Nevertheless there is something he does not know how to express and that makes him feel bad.

Then he recounts a dream: he was in a beautiful house, the upper floors had been renovated, the paintings on the walls had been hung with skill and taste. Then he is terrified when all the paintings fall to the ground, as does a ceramic dish that shrieks.

He goes on to explain that as a child he was always afraid, he even remembers feeling terror when he was in his cot. He used to put soft toys in perfect order all around him, but he was afraid of what was under the bed, although he did not know what it might be: a wolf? the devil? At any rate, something terribly frightening.

The analyst, who had already heard these things several times, offers the interpretation that the patient was afraid of him, the analyst. But he felt that that was not it, there was something else under the bed . . . but he didn't know what it was.

What should we think of this story?

Could this same type of problem be told with a different plot?

If the patient were a vet, how might he narrate the same basic theme?

Exercise 40

Are male homosexual functioning (♂ ♂) and female homosexual functioning (♀ ♀) between minds necessarily related to biological sex?

In what sense do you mean what you said?

Exercise 41

Anna talks about her affectionate homosexual relationship with Martina; nothing is more wonderful than the evenings they spend together at the fireside pampering each other, maybe eating dessert. Then Anna says that her brother hates their parents intensely and she finds it almost impossible to establish any contact with him. She and Martina do voluntary work, especially helping deprived children.

She talks about being afraid of loneliness, because in actual fact her loneliness becomes animated with presences she cannot better define; likewise she is afraid of the dark.

Fear stops her from sitting her university exams.

She talks all the time in a soft voice, although occasionally she does flare up.

After this first meeting, what can we fantasize about this story?

Exercise 42

After several years of analysis Anna has started to live with Gigi, with whom she has a conflictual but dynamic relationship.

She has bought herself a big black dog and despite Gigi's disapproval she insists on attaching a big pink bow to its tail.

Now she speaks with a more confident, more secure voice even though she often has an engaging but rather fixed smile on her face.

What transformations have there been in Anna, what path can we imagine for her, what work still has to be done?

Exercise 43

An anorexic sees herself as fat and ugly because:

(a) She has a misperception?
(b) She has a distorted sense of reality?
(c) She has a delusional perception about her body?
(d) She sees with her mind's eye a self-image that has been reflected by her 'care-givers'?
(e) Her way of looking at herself is like a kind of ultrasound scan, which means she sees beyond appearances; she sees how she really is inside: full of anger, hatred or at least protoemotions that 'make her swell up and look ugly'?
(f) Why does bulimic behaviour often alternate with anorexia?

Exercise 44

Why does an anorexic wants to lose more weight?

(a) To achieve a perfect aesthetic/ascetic ideal of herself?
(b) To give an adequate response to the delusional perception she has of herself?
(c) To 'shrink' the Hulk she has inside by starving it; does she hope that by starving the pit-bull it will become a poodle?
(d) If (c) is true, then is bulimic behaviour paradoxical or does it correspond to a different strategy? And if so, what is that strategy?

Exercise 45

'When I look at myself in the mirror I think I am horrible both when I'm trying to lose weight – and then I still see myself as fat – and when I shake off my chains and eat to excess, even putting on twenty kilos in a very short time. I also feel uncomfortable at work; I call in sick, I run away and I only feel comfortable when travelling on an underground line I know is always packed with immigrants. There I can calm down.'

Even without any context, what reflections can we make about this communication from a young female patient with an eating disorder?

Exercise 46

A young boy arrives at the session (for the moment he comes twice a week until his parents can arrange for a third session) showing a small cut on his finger that is still bleeding.

Then he looks for some rope with which he tries to harness a kind of mountaineer-monster-robot so that it does not fall off the wall. However, despite the addition of the two pieces of sellotape, he says, 'today it looks like it's impossible to make it stick to the wall, it weighs too much'.

Towards the end of the session he jumps on the couch and says: 'And now for the leap of death!'

Then he constructs 'an ice road' made up of sheets of paper, adding: 'Let's hope the bridge doesn't collapse under the weight of the snow.'

What kind of basic theme does the child appear to be expressing?

How could the same theme be expressed by an adult patient suffering from phobias?

And what would happen if the patient were a middle-aged obsessive engineer?

Exercise 47

Marcello is a three-year-child whose mother had never been able to come to terms with the idea that he should be alone in the therapy room with his analyst.

After a long period during which she attends the sessions, she finally agrees to wait for the child outside the room.

The next day she phones to say that she cannot bring Marcello to the session because 'he had almost chopped his finger off while cutting a lemon in half with a knife and had ended up in the emergency department'.

What is Marcello's mother talking about?

Make at least five possible comments about the woman.

Could the same basic theme be expressed by an adult patient with a psychosomatic illness?

Or by a borderline adolescent?

Exercise 48

A patient is suffering from an obsessive disorder that induces him to perform repeated rituals when closing doors and windows because he is afraid that 'someone' might get into the house.

Sometimes he buys back issues of newspapers because he is afraid that he might have knocked down and killed 'someone' in the street.

He desperately checks his bank statement because he is afraid that 'someone' might get into his account and use up all his money.

Now he is more at ease with himself because his wife has had a tumour removed from her kidney and repeated ultrasound scans and scintigraphy have not shown up any malignant cells.

What does the patient seem to be talking about?

What other means of coping could the patient have, given the same level of anxiety?

In a situation where the anxiety increases, what kind of symptoms could he have?

How might the same type of problem be narrated by a three-year-old child? An eight-year-old? A sixteen-year-old adolescent?

And how would the psychopathological case histories differ?

Try to describe them.

Exercise 49

In cases of 'Stockholm syndrome' the victim of a kidnapping or abduction, usually a woman, falls 'in love' with the kidnapper. We can imagine that this is a way of coping with excessive persecution by taking the plunge and 'loving' the persecutor in order to 'appease' him.

If a young man feels after a psychotic break that 'the left side' has taken over from 'the right side' and goes on to have a dream in which the control room is taken over by bandits who have escaped from prison, what symptom might he develop? According to which lines of thought?

Exercise 50

A patient asks a lot of questions about the 'other people' who lie on the couch: 'Who are they?' 'Are they human beings or not?'

What is the patient probably talking about?

What answers could the analyst give?

How might a child in analysis ask the same question?

Exercise 51

A patient says she doesn't want to get pregnant because it would give her the sensation of having 'a stowaway on board'. The analyst interprets this by saying that the patient is afraid of developing emotions she wants to keep hidden and stowed away.

She speaks of a friend who is training to become a photographer who never manages to use the light meter properly and ends up wasting reels and reels of film.

What possibly happened?

Re-create another dialogue sequence with the same meaning.

Exercise 52

In the session a patient says that a child who is in psychotherapy with him peed in his room and he had a really hard time of it drying the carpet. As a result he wasn't very well disposed towards the next patient because he was so tired.

Which of the following hypotheses would you opt for?

(a) The patient is talking about the effort he has to make away from the analysis.
(b) The patient is talking about a real external event and demonstrating the skills he has acquired.
(c) The patient is talking about his emotional incontinence.
(d) The patient is talking about an emotional incontinence that has not been absorbed by the analyst.
(e) The patient is talking about the analyst's interpretative incontinence which has drenched him and prepared him badly for the next session of analysis.
(f) Others: explain.

On the basis of the hypothesis you have chosen, what interpretative formulation might you provide?

Exercise 53

Two analysts are analysing two sisters.

One of them is bombarded with phone calls from Sara during the summer holidays.

The other, before the resumption of the sessions, receives a call from Carla asking to be seen ahead of time. The analyst agrees to this request.

Carla speaks all the time about how unwell Sara has been, especially after she discovered that her father had blocked her bank account.

What is Carla talking about?

What action could Carla's analyst undertake?

What can one say about Carla's analyst violating the setting in this way?

Exercise 54

A patient talks about having contracted a sexually transmitted disease because her boyfriend did not use a condom. She is torn between leaving him and finding a way to protect herself on her own, although she doesn't know how – perhaps by refusing to have sexual intercourse with him, forcing him to use condoms or in other ways she hasn't yet thought of.

What could the patient be talking about?

(a) A real external event that distresses her.
(b) A lack of interpretative caution on the part of the analyst.
(c) The defence she will try to deploy to avoid being infected by the analyst.
(d) A suggestion that she implicitly gives the analyst about how to interpret.
(e) Emotions that are uncontrolled and proliferating inside her which are activated if contact is not protected.
(f) Being infected with her suffering and incontinent part.

What defences could she deploy if we think of the communication as an event in the current relationship?

Exercise 55

A patient returns from the weekend break and starts talking about his trip up into the snow-capped mountains where there was no signal for his mobile phone (the Italian word for signal in this context is *campo* = field). Because the phone kept on trying to find a signal and he thought that might damage it, he turned it off.

On his return he quarrelled with his girlfriend who had stayed in town; he was certain that she had forgotten him, proved by the fact that she had not bought the film for his camera that he had asked her to buy. He suspected that his girlfriend had not only forgotten the film but that she had also taken advantage of his absence to cheat on him.

He resolves to see how she will behave the coming weekend and if he continues to feel forgotten and cheated he will leave her before the upcoming Christmas holidays, when he was planning to go away with his three brothers.

This communication could be interpreted according to:

(a) a strong relational theory
(b) a field theory
(c) an interpretation/reconstruction.

Exercise 56

A patient begins the session by complaining that her husband had bought almost two kilos of mullet at the fishmonger's. It is true that her sister is staying with them together with her children, but she is frankly hacked off at the thought that she doesn't have big enough pots and pans to cook the fish and that in any case it will be a lot of work, even though the fish were excellent, fresh and beautifully coloured.

What in all probability is the patient talking about?

Her husband's unwanted sexual advances? Or the presence in the field of lively and colourful emotions that exceed her capacity to cope? About the session the day before (or the immediately preceding interpretation) when she felt she received more than she could 'cook' given the utensils she has? What could these tools be, based on the psychoanalytic theories you take as your model?

Try to imagine the rest of the session depending on the response of the analyst.

Try to write different sequences.

Exercise 57

A patient describes his wife as a 'contrarian'. How can we imagine the kind of relationship he describes? Try to imagine a hypothetical session in which he speaks of this. What genesis might this phenomenon have had? What does it reflect from the standpoint of the patient's psychic life and what from the point of view of the analytic work? What priority might the latter have?

Exercise 58

A patient has begun to become aware of her constant bickering with her husband: she says she feels as if she is constantly on the border between Israel and the Arab countries.

If one of them says 'it's round', it's a safe bet the other will say 'no, it's square'. If one wants fizzy mineral water, the other will want still

198

water. If one wants to go to the beach, the other will want to go to the mountains. This is what happens all the time, both with really important things and with minutiae.

Is she talking about her own double who is perpetually at odds with her?

Is she talking about a type of male homosexual mental functioning (σ σ) in which there is opposition but no receptive capacity? Is she talking about the disagreement she feels in the relationship with the analyst, namely where neither is willing to listen and accept the point of view of the other? Or what else is she talking about?

What defects can we imagine as being present in the current field? What historical hypotheses can we come up with to make sense of this disorder?

What metaphors could the analyst use to start 'working on' this problem? What could he say or what interpretation could he give the patient?

Try to write one or more sequences of sessions that correspond to some of these issues.

Exercise 59

Mutism in a child could be the other face of a feared incontinence.

Talking would be a possible modality between silence, stuttering and incontinence.

What other situations and psychosomatic expressions could have similar values?

Try to give clinical examples of a first meeting with a patient's parents and try to imagine a session where these are the underlying issues.

Exercise 60

An autistic clot could lead to thrombosis in the relationship (mutism) or a bleeding that is not containable in the relationship (evacuation).

Try and give other clinical examples and imagine other ways of managing or presenting autistic clots.

Bibliography

Arrigoni, M. P. and Barbieri, G. L. (1998) *Narrazione e Psicoanalisi*. Cortina, Milan.

Barale, F. (1999) 'Appendix'. In: Ferro, A. *La Psicoanalisi come Letteratura e Terapia*. Cortina, Milan.

Barale, F. and Ferro, A. (1992) 'Negative therapeutic reactions and microfractures in analytic communication'. In: Momigliano Nissim, L. and Robutti, A. (Eds) *Shared Experience: The Psychoanalytic Dialogue*. Karnac Books, London.

Barale, F. and Ferro, A. (1993) 'Sufrimiento mental en el analista y sueños de contratransferencia'. *Revista de Psicoanálisis de Madrid*, 17, 56–72. (First published in Italian in 1987.)

Baranger, M. (1992) 'La mente del analista de la escucha a l'interpretation'. *Revista de Psicoanalisis*, 49, 2.

Baranger, M. and Baranger, W. (1961–62) 'La situación analítica como campo dinámico'. *Revista Uruguaya de Psicoanálisis*, IV, 1.

Baruzzi, A. (1998) Preface to the Italian edition of *A Memoir of The Future 2*. Cortina, Milan.

Bezoari, M. and Ferro, A. (1990) 'Elementos de un modelo del campo analítico: los agregados funcionales'. *Revista de Psicoanálisis*, 5/6, 847–861.

Bezoari, M. and Ferro, A. (1991a) 'A oscilação significados afectos no trabalho da parelha analítica'. *Revista Brasileira de Psicoanálise*, 26, 3, 365–374.

Bezoari, M. and Ferro, A. (1991b) 'From a play between "parts" to transformations in the couple. Psychoanalysis in a bipersonal field'. In: Momigliano Nissim, L. and Robutti, A. (Eds) *Shared Experience: The Psychoanalytic Dialogue*. Karnac Books, London, 1992.

Bezoari, M. and Ferro, A. (1992a) 'El sueño dentro de una teoria del campo. Agregados funcionales y narraciones'. *Revista de Psicoanálisis*, 49, 5/6, 957–977.

Bezoari, M. and Ferro, A. (1992b) 'I personaggi della seduta come aggregati funzionali del campo analitico'. *Notiziario SPI*, Supplemento 2, 103–115, Borla, Rome.

Bezoari, M. and Ferro, A. (1994a) 'Listening, interpreting and psychic change in the analytic dialogue'. *International Forum of Psychoanalysis*, 3, 35–41. (First published in Italian in 1989.)

Bezoari, M. and Ferro, A. (1994b) 'Il posto del sogno all'interno di una teoria del campo analitico'. *Rivista di Psicoanalisi*, XL, 2, 251–272.

Bezoari, M. and Ferro, A. (1996) 'Mots, images, affects. L'aventure du sens dans la rencontre analytique'. *Revue Canadienne de Psychanalyse*, 4, 1, 49–73. (First published in Italian in 1990.)

Bion, W. R. (1962) *Learning from Experience*. Heinemann, London.

Bion, W. R. (1963) *Elements of Psycho-Analysis*. Heinemann, London.

Bion, W. R. (1965) *Transformations*. Heinemann, London.

Bion, W. R. (1966) 'Catastrophic change'. *Bulletin of The British Psychoanalytical Society*, 1966, No. 5.

Bion, W. R. (1970) *Attention and Interpretation*. Tavistock Publications, London.

Bion, W. R. (1974) *Bion's Brazilian Lectures 1*. Imago Editora, Rio de Janeiro.

Bion, W. R. (1975a) *Bion's Brazilian Lectures 2*. Imago Editora, Rio de Janeiro.

Bion, W. R. (1975b) *A Memoir of the Future. Book 1: The Dream*. Imago Editora, Rio de Janeiro.

Bion, W. R. (1977a) *A Memoir of the Future. Book 2: The Past Presented*. Imago Editora, Rio de Janeiro.

Bion, W. R. (1977b) *Two Papers: The Grid and Caesura*. Imago Editora, Rio de Janeiro.

Bion, W. R. (1978) *Four Discussions with W.R. Bion*. Clunie Press, Perthshire.

Bion, W. R. (1979) *A Memoir of the Future: 3. The Dawn of Oblivion*. Clunie Press, Perthshire.

Bion, W. R. (1980) *Bion in New York and São Paulo*. Clunie Press, Perthshire.

Bion, W. R. (1983) *Bion in Rome* [Italian seminars]. The Estate of W. R. Bion.

Bion, W. R. (1987) *Clinical Seminars and Four Papers*. Fleetwood Press, Abingdon.

Bion, W. R. (1992) *Cogitations*. Karnac Books, London.

Bion, W. R. (2005) *Tavistock Seminars*. Karnac Books, London.

Bion Talamo, P. (1987) 'Perché non possiamo dirci bioniani'. *Gruppo e Funzione Analitica*, 279.

Birksted-Breen, D. (2003) 'Time and the après-coup'. *International Journal of Psychoanalysis*, 84, 6, 1501–1515.

Bollas, C. (1999) *The Infinite Question*. Routledge, New York, Hove.

Bolognini, S. (2002) *L'Empatia Psicoanalitica*. Bollati Boringhieri, Turin.

Borges, J. L. (1941) 'The garden of forking paths'. In: *Ficciones*. Everyman, London, 1993.

Borgogno, F. (1994) 'Spoilt children'. *Richard e Piggle*, 2, 2, 135–152.

Botella, C. and Botella, S. (2002) *La Figurabilité Psichique*. Delachaux et Niestlé, Paris.

Corrao, F. (1986) 'Il concetto di campo come modello teorico'. *Gruppo e Funzione Analitica*, 7, 9.

Corrao, F. (1991) 'Trasformazioni narrative'. In: *Orme*, vol. 1. Cortina, Milan.

De Simone, G. (2004) *Le famiglie di Edipo*. Borla, Rome.

Di Chiara, G. (2003) *Curare con la psicoanalisi*. Cortina, Milan.

Diderot, D. (1796) *Jacques the Fatalist*. Collier, New York, 1962.

Eco, U. (1962) *The Open Work*. Harvard University Press, Cambridge, MA, 1989.

Eco, U. (1979) *The Role of the Reader*. Indiana University Press, Bloomington, IN.

Eco, U. (1990) *The Limits of Interpretations*. Indiana University Press, Bloomington, IN.

Eco, U. (1996) *Semiotica e filosofia del linguaggio: i concetti fondamentali della semiologia e la loro storia*. Einaudi, Turin.

Faimberg, H. (1988a) 'A l'écoute du télescopage des générations'. *Topique*, 42, 233–238.

Faimberg, H. (1988b) 'The telescoping of generations'. *Contemporary Psychoanalysis*, 24, 99.

Faimberg, H. (1996) 'Listening to listening'. *International Journal of Psychoanalysis*, 77, 4, 667.

Ferro, A. (1985) 'Psicoanalisi e favole'. *Rivista di Psicoanalisi*, XXXI, 2, 216–230.

Ferro, A. (1987) 'Il mondo alla rovescia. L'inversione del flusso delle identificazioni proiettive'. *Rivista di Psicoanalisi*, XXXIII, 1, 59–77.

Ferro, A. (1991a) 'From raging bull to Theseus: the long path of a transformation'. *International Journal of Psychoanalysis*, 72, 3, 417–425.

Ferro, A. (1991b) 'La mente del analista en su trabajo: problemas, riergos, necessitades'. *Revista de Psicoanálisis*, 5/6, 1159–1177.

Ferro, A. (1992) *The Bipersonal Field: Experiences in Child Analysis*. Routledge, London and New York, 1999.

Ferro, A. (1993a) 'Disegno, identificazione proiettiva e processi trasformativi'. *Rivista di Psicoanalisi*, XXXIX, 4, 667–680.

Ferro, A. (1993b) 'From hallucination to dream: from evacuation to the tolerability of pain in the analysis of a preadolescent'. *Psychoanalytic Review*, 80, 3, 389–404.

Ferro, A. (1993c) 'The impasse within a theory of the analytic field: possible vertices of observation'. *International Journal of Psychoanalysis*, 74, 5, 971–929.

Ferro, A. (1993d) 'Zwei Autoren auf der Suche nach Personen: Die Beziehung, das Feld, die Geschichte'. *Psyche*, 47, 10, 951–972.

Ferro, A. (1994a) 'Criterios sobre la analizabilidad y el final del análisis dentro una teoria del campo'. *Revista de Psicoanálisis*, 51, 3, 97–114.

Ferro, A. (1994b) 'Del campo e dei suoi eventi'. *Quaderni di Psicoterapia Infantile*, 30. Borla, Rome.

Ferro, A. (1994c) 'El dialogo analítico: mundos posibles y transformaciones en el campo analítico'. *Revista de Psicoanálisis*, 51, 4, 771–790.

Ferro, A. (1994d) 'Gruppalità interne di relazione e di campo nell'analisi duale'. *Gruppo e Funzione Analitica*, Quaderni, 1, Borla, Rome.

Ferro, A. (1994e) 'Mondi possibili e capacità negative dell'analista al lavoro'. Atti X Congresso Nazionale S.P.I., Rimini.

Ferro, A. (1996a) *In the Analyst's Consulting Room*. Psychology Press-Routledge Brunner, London and New York, 2002.

Ferro, A. (1996b) 'A sexualidade como gênero narrativo, ou dialeto, na sala de analise'. In: *Bion en São Paulo: Ressonancies*. Org. M. Olympia de A. F. França, pp. 175–184.

Ferro, A. (1996c) 'Carla's panic attacks: insight and transformations: what comes out of the cracks: monster or nascent thoughts?' *International Journal of Psychoanalysis*, 77, 997–1011.

Ferro, A. (1996d) 'Elógio da Fileira C: A Psicanálise como forma particular de Literatura'. In: *Silêncios e luzes: sobre a experiênza psíquica do vazio e da forma*. Org. L. C. Uchôa Junqueira Filho. Casa do Psicologo, São Paulo.

Ferro, A. (1996e) 'Los personajes del cuarto de análisis: qué realidad?' *Revista de Psicoanálisis de Madrid*, 23, 133–142.

Ferro, A. (1996f) 'Entrevista com Antonino Ferro'. *IDE*, 29, São Paulo, 1996.

Ferro, A. (1997) 'The unity of the analysis underlying the similarities and differences in the analysis of children and adolescents'. *Bulletin 50 European Psychoanalytical Federation*.

Ferro, A. (1999a) 'Contenitore inadeguato e violenza delle emozioni: dinosauri e tartarughe'. *Quaderni di Psicoterapia Infantile*, 39, Borla, Rome.

Ferro, A. (1999b) ' "Characters" and their precursors in depression: experiences and transformation in the course of therapy'. *Journal of Melanie Klein and Object Relations*, 17, 1, 119–133.

Ferro, A. (1999c) *Psychoanalysis as therapy and storytelling*. New Library/Routledge, London, 2006.

Ferro, A. (1999d) 'Camp terapèutic i transformacions emocionales'. *III Jornades del Department de Psichiatrie i Psicologia*. Barcelona. Fundacio Hospital. Sant Pere Clever.

Ferro, A. (1999e) 'Construction d'une histoire, dessin et jeu dans l'analyse d'enfants'. In: *Psychothérapie Psychanalytique de l'enfant et de sa famille*, sous la direction de Simone Decobert et François Sacco, ÉRÈS, 2000.

Ferro, A. (1999f) 'Discussion of Papers by Emde and Herzog' at the plenary session of the IPA Conference Santiago del Cile, July 1999 in 'Affect and development' by Nadine A. Levinson *International Journal of Psychoanalysis*, 81, 2, 313.

Ferro, A. (1999g) 'Interprétations, déconstructions, récits ou les raisons de Jacques'. In: *Inventer en Psychanalyse*. Dunod, Paris, 2002.

Ferro, A. (2000a) 'O respeito pela mente'. *IDE* 1, 2000, Sociedade Brasileira Psicoanàlise, São Paulo.

Ferro, A. (2000b) 'Temps de la reverie, temps de l'évacuation', *Enfance Psy*, 13, 129–136.

Ferro, A. (2000c) 'Comentarios sobre o artigo "Evidência" de Bion', *Revista de Psicanalise da Sociedade Psicanalitica de Porto Alegre*, VII, 2, 281–284.

Ferro, A. (2000d) *Psychanalystes en supervision*. Eres (2010).

Ferro, A. (2000e) 'Le jeu: personnages, récits, interpretations'. *Journal de la Psychanalyse de l'enfant*, 26, 139–160. (First published in Italian in 1998.)

Ferro, A. (2001a) 'La séparation entre le rêve et l' évacuation'. *Revue Française de Psychanalyse*, 2, 489–498.

Ferro, A. (2001b) 'Rêve de la veille et narration'. *Revue Française de Psychanalyse*, LXV, 285–297.

Ferro, A. (2001c) 'Entretien avec Antonino Ferro de Diana Messina Pizzuti'. *Cahiers de Psychologie Clinique* 16, 1, 209–223.

Ferro, A. (2001d) ' "Entrevista" realizada no XXIII Congresso Latino Americano de Psicanálise/2000 a Gramado. Entervistadora: Telma Barros'. In: *Picanálise em Revista*, Vol. 1, N1, Recife.

Ferro, A. (2001e) 'El sueno de la vigilia: Teoria y clinica'. *Revista Peruana Psicoanalisis*, 2, 31–38. (First published in Italian in 1998.)

Ferro, A. (2001f) 'Psicànalise e Narraçao'. *Alter*, xx, 1, 7–20.

Ferro, A. (2002a) 'Some implications of Bion's thought: the waking dream and narrative derivatives'. *International Journal of Psychoanalysis*, 83, 597–607.

Ferro, A. (2002b) 'Superego transformations through the analyst's capacity for reverie'. *Psychoanalytic Quarterly*, LXXI, 477–501.

Ferro, A. (2002c) 'Signaux en provenance du champ analytique et transformations émotionnelles'. In: Botella, C. *Penser les limites. Ecrits en l'honneur d'André Green*. Delachaux et Niestlé, Paris.

Ferro, A. (2002d) 'Narrative derivatives of alpha elements. Clinical implications'. (Paper IPA Congress, Santiago del Cile, 1999). *International Forum of Psychoanalysis*, 11, 184–187.

Ferro, A. (2002e) 'Psicoanalisis futuro'. *Revista de Psicoanálisis* 59, 2, 323–327.

Ferro, A. (2002f) 'Quelle réalité dans la séance analytique?' *Bulletin FEP*, 56, 89.

Ferro, A. (2002g) 'Sapeurs-pompiers: un appel pour Othello et Neron'. *Revue Française de Psychanalyse*, 5, 1545–1549.

Ferro, A. (2002h) *Seeds of Illness, Seeds of Recovery*. New Library/Routledge, London, 2004.

Ferro, A. (2003a) 'Marcella: from explosive sensoriality to the ability to think'. *Psychoanalytic Quarterly*, LXXII, 183–200.

Ferro, A. (2003b) 'Probleme der Theorie und Technik bei der Behandlung von Patienten im Entwicklungsalter'. *Kinderanalyse*, 2, 11, 155–181.

Ferro, A. (2003c) 'The analyst as individual, his self-analysis and gradients of functioning'. *Bulletin EPF*.

Ferro, A. (2003d) 'Commentary on Ilany Kogan's "On Being a Dead, Beloved Child" '. *Psychoanalytic Quarterly*, LXXII, 777–783.

Ferro, A. (2003e) Entrevista in *Sobre Psicanalise & Psicanalistas*. 1° Livro de Entrevistas da Revista de Psicanalise da SPPA (Sociedade Psicanalitica de Porto Alegre).

Ferro, A. (2003f) 'Faktoren der Heilung und die Beendigung der Analyse: Ein Modell der Psyche'. *Der Analytiker im psychoanalytischen Prozess*. Deutsche Psychoanalytische Vereinigung, Stuttgart.

Ferro, A. (2003g) 'La persona dell'analista e i suoi gradienti di funzionamento'. *Rivista di Psicoanalisi*, 49, 4, 799–805.

Ferro, A. (2003h) *Il lavoro clinico. Nuovi seminari di San Paolo e Riberao Preto*. Cortina, Milan.

Ferro, A. (2004a) 'Réalité des faits et réalité interne: des dérivés narratifs aux émotions premières'. In: Chouvier, B. and Rousillon, R. (Eds) *La Réalité Psychique*. Dunod, Paris, 2004.

Ferro, A. (2004b) 'Alfa+ e il dovere del medico: (parata e) risposta a Davide Lopez'. *Rivista di Psicoanalisi* 50, 1, 203–208.

Ferro, A. (2004c) 'Interpretations: signals from the analytic field and emotional transformations'. *International Forum of Psychoanalysis*, 13, 31–38.

Ferro, A. (2004d) 'Psicoanalisi e narrazione un modello della mente e della cura'. *Psiche*, 2, 23–33.

Ferro, A. (2004e) 'Fatores de cura e término da analise'. *Revista Brasileira de Psicoterapia*, 5, 3, 235–251.

Ferro, A. (2004f) 'L'étrange cas d'Hannibal Lecter et de son analiste Davy Crockett'. *Revue Française de Psychoanalyse*, 5, 1481–1492.

Ferro, A. (2004g) 'Asociaciones libres y pensamiento onirico de la vigilia'. *Revista de Psicoanálisis*, 61, 3, 769–780. (First published in Italian in 2002.)

Ferro, A. (2005a) ' "Commentary" on Field Theory by Madaleine Baranger and on The confrontation between generations as a dynamic field by Luis Kancyper'. In: Lewkowicz, S. and Flechner, S. (Eds) *Truth Reality and the Psychoanalyst*. IPL, London.

Ferro, A. (2005b) 'Introduzione a "Pensare per Immagini" '. In: Ferruta, A. (Ed.) *Monografia Rivista di Psicoanalisi*. Borla, Rome.

Ferro, A. (2005c) 'Which reality in the psychoanalytic session?' *Psychoanalytic Quarterly*, LXXIV, 421–442.

Ferro, A. (2005d) 'Reflexions à propos de l'interpretation'. *Psychanalyse en Europe-Bulletin FEP*, 59, 44–46.

Ferro, A. (2005e) 'The analyst at work: four sessions with Lisa'. *International Journal of Psychoanalysis*, 86, 1247–1256.

Ferro, A. (2005f) 'Pensé onirique, narration et champ dans le travail psychanalytique'. *Journal de la Psychoanalyse de L'enfant*, 37, 107–137.

Ferro, A. (2005g) 'Bion: theoretical and clinical observations'. *International Journal of Psychoanalysis*, 86, 1535–1542.

Ferro, A. (2005h) 'Faktoren der Heilung und die Beendigung der Analyse'. *Psychoanalyse im Widerspruch*, 34, 77–94.

Ferro, A. (2005i) 'Narcisismo e Trauma: a atualidade e a historia'. *Revista da Sociedade Brasileira de Psicanalise de Porto Alegre*, 7, 2, 347–368.

Ferro, A. (2005j) 'Assim é se lhe parece, ou dois autores em busca de roteiros e cenografias: transformações e interpretações'. *Revista de Psicanálise da SPPA*, 12, 3, 487–514.

Ferro, A. (2006a) *Mind Works. Technique and Creativity in Psychoanalysis.* Routledge/New Library, London and New York, 2009.

Ferro, A. (2006b) Que tipo de sexualidade nos diz respeito en quanto analistas? Una ipotese radical. In: Lewkowicz, S. et al. (Eds) *Psicanalise e Sexualidade.* Casa do Psicologo, Sao Paulo.

Ferro, A. (2006c) Como escribir un trabajo psicoanalitico: una receta psico-analitica. *Revista Cilena de Psicoanalisis*, 22, 2, 194–195.

Ferro, A. (2006d) 'Contratransferência e os personagens na sala de análise'. In: Zaslavsky, J. and dos Santos, M.J.P. (Eds) *Contratransferência: Teoria e Prática Clínica.* Editora Artmed, Sao Paulo.

Ferro, A. and Basile, R. (2004) 'The psychoanalyst as individual: self-analysis and gradients of functioning'. *Psychoanalytic Quarterly*, 73, 3, 659–682.

Ferro, A. and Basile, R. (2006) 'Unity of analysis: similarities and differences in the analysis of children and grown-ups'. *Psychoanalytical Quarterly*, 75, 2, 477–500.

Ferro, A. and Meregnani, A. (1994) 'Listening and transformative functions in the psychoanalytical dialogue'. *Bulletin Féderation Européenne de Psychanalyse*, 42, 21–29.

Ferro, A. and Meregnani, A. (1998) 'The inversion of flow of projective identi-fication in the analyst at work'. *Australian Journal of Psychotherapy*, 16, 94–112.

Ferro, A., Pasquali, G., Tognoli, L. and Viola, M. (1986a) 'L'uso del simbo-lismo nel setting e il processo di simbolizzazione nella relazione analitica'. *Rivista di Psicoanalisi*, XXXII, 4, 539–553.

Ferro, A., Pasquali, G., Tognoli, L. and Viola, M. (1986b) 'Note sul processo di simbolizzazione nel pensiero psicoanalitico'. *Rivista di Psicoanalisi*, XXXII, 4, 521–538.

Fonagy, P. (2003) 'Rejoinder to Harold Blum'. *International Journal of Psychoanalysis*, 84, 3, 103.

Freud, S. (1914) 'Erinnern, Wiederholen und Durcharbeiten'. *GW* 10: 126.

Gabbard, G. O. and Lester, E. P. (1995) *Boundaries and Boundary Violation in Psychoanalysis*. Basic Books, New York.

Gaburri, E. (1987) 'Narrazione e interpretazione'. In: Morpugo, E. and Egidi, V. (Eds) *Psicoanalisi e narrazione*. Il Lavoro Editoriale, Ancona.

Gaburri, E. (Ed.) (1997) *Emozione ed interpretazione*. Bollati Boringhieri, Turin.

Gaburri, E. and Ferro, A. (1988) 'Gli sviluppi kleiniani e Bion'. In: Semi, A. (Ed.) *Trattato di psicoanalisi*, vol. 1. Raffaello Cortina, Milan.

Gibeault, A. (1991) 'Intérpretation et transfert'. In *Psychanalyse en Europe. Bulletin FEP*, 36.

Ginzburg, A. (2006) 'Gli isomorfismi, una strategia inconscia per ricordare, ripetere, rielaborare'. Paper presented at SPI-APA, Bologna.

Green, A. (1993) *Le travail du negatif*. PUF, Paris.

Green, A. (2005) *Jouer avec Winnicott*. PUF, Paris.

Greimas, A. J. (1966) *Structural Semantics*. Bahri Publications, New Delhi.

Greimas, A. J. (1970) *On Meaning: Selected Writings in Semiotic Theory*. Tr. P. J. Perron and F. H. Collins. Frances Pinter, London, 1987.

Grinberg, L. (1981) *Psicoanalisis. Aspectos Teoricos y Clinicos*. Paidos, Buenos Aires.

Grotstein, J. (2006) Personal communication.

Grotstein, J. (2007) *A Beam of Intense Darkness. Wilfred Bion's Legacy to Psychoanalysis*. Karnac Books, London.

Guignard, F. (1997a) *Epitre à l'objet*. PUF, Paris.

Guignard, F. (1997b) 'L'interprétation des configurations oedipiennes en analyse d'enfants'. In *Psychanalyse en Europe. Bulletin FEP*, 50.

Guignard, F. (1996) *Au vif de l'infantil*. Delachaux et Niestlé, Lausanne.

Guignard, F. (2004) Personal communication.

Guignard, F. (2006) Personal communication.

Hamon, P. (1972) 'Pour un statut sémiologique du personnage'. In: Barthes, R., Kayser, W., Booth, W. C. and Hamon, P., *Poétique du récit*. Editions du Seuil, Paris 1977, pp. 115–180.

Hautmann, G. (1996) 'Pellicola di pensiero: sensorialità, emozione, gruppalità, relazione nella veglia e nel sonno'. Tr. It. In: *Psicoanalisi e metodo*, vol. 1. Borla, Rome.

Imbasciati, A. (1994) *Fondamenti psicoanalitici della psicologia clinica*. UTET, Turin.

Jacobs, T. (1999) 'On the question of self-disclosure by the analyst: error or advance in technique'. *Psychoanalytic Quarterly*, 63, 2, 159–172.

Kaes, R., Faimberg, H., Enriquez, M. and Baranes, J. J. (1993) *Trasmissione della vita psichica tra generazioni*, Tr. It. Borla, Rome, 1995.

Kancyper, L. (1997) *Il confronto generazionale*. Tr. It. Franco Angeli, Milan, 2000.

Klein, M. (1946) 'Notes on some schizoid mechanisms'. *International Journal of Psychoanalysis*, 27, 99–110.

Klein, M. (1948) 'A contribution to the theory of anxiety and guilt'. *International Journal of Psychoanalysis*, 29, 113–123.

Klein, M. (1952) 'The origins of transference'. *International Journal of Psychoanalysis*, 33: 433–438.

Lebine, H., Jacobs, D. and Rubin, L. (Eds) (1998) *Psychoanalysis and the Nuclear Threat*. Analytic Press, Hillsdale, NJ.

Lewkowicz, S. and Flechner, S. (Eds) (2005) *Truth, Reality and the Psychoanalyst*. IPI, London.

Luzes, P. (2001) Personal communication.

Magris, C. (1982) *Itaca e oltre*. Garzanti, Milan.

Mancia, M. (1994) *Dall'Edipo al sogno*. Raffaello Cortina, Milan.

Mancia, M. (2005) 'Memoria implicita e inconscio precoce non rimosso: loro ruolo nel processo terapeutico'. Centro Milanese di Psicoanalisi, 20 October.

Manguel, G. (1986) *Une histoire de la lecture*. Actes du Sud, Paris, 1998.

Marrone, G. (1986) *Sei autori in cerca di personaggio*. Centro Scientifico Torinese, Turin.

Meltzer, D. (1967) *The Psychoanalytical Process*. Clunie Press, Perthshire, 1970.

Meltzer, D. (1974) 'Adhesive identification'. *Contemporary Psycho-Analysis*, 11, 289–310.

Meltzer, D. (1984) *Dream Life: A Re-Examination of the Psycho-Analytical Theory and Technique*, Clunie Press, Perthshire.

Meltzer, D. (1992) *The Claustrum: An Investigation of Claustrophobic Phenomena*. Clunie Press, Perthshire.

Meltzer, D. (1996) 'Relation between anal masturbation and projective identification'. *International Journal of Psychoanalysis*, 47, 2, 3.

Meotti, A. (1987) 'Appunti su funzione alfa, dolore sensoriale, dolore mentale, pensiero'. In: Neri, C., Correale, A. and Fadda, P. (Eds) *Letture bioniane*. Borla, Rome.

Muschio, C. (2005) *La cantina di Isabella*. Borla, Rome.

Neri, C. (1998) *Group*. Jessica Kingsley Publishers, London and Philadelphia.

Neri, C., Correale, A. and Fadda, P. (2006) *Lire Bion*. Ramonville Saint-Agne, Érès.

Nissim, L. (1984) *Sharing Experience*. Karnac Books, London.

Ogden, T. (1979) 'On projective identification'. *International Journal of Psychoanalysis*, 60, 357–373.

Ogden, T. (1986) *The Matrix of the Mind: Object Relations and the Psychoanalytic Dialogue*, Jason Aronson, London.

Ogden, T. H. (1994a) *Subjects of Analysis*. Jason Aronson Inc., Northvale, NJ.

Ogden, T. H. (1994b) 'The analytic third: working with intersubjective clinical facts'. *International Journal of Psychoanalysis*, 75, 3–19.

Ogden, T. (2006) 'Holding e contenimento. Essere e sognare'. In: *L'Annata Psicoanalitica Internazionale*, 2, 153–169.

O'Shaughnessy, E. (1999) 'Relating to the superego'. *International Journal of Psychoanalysis*, 80, 861.

O'Shaughnessy, E. (2005) 'Who's Bion?'. *International Journal of Psychoanalysis*, 86, 1523–1528.

Paniagua, C. (2002) 'Un caso di fine analisi'. In: Ferro, A. (Ed.) *Psicoanalisi e Pluralismo delle lingue*. Bollati Boringhieri, Turin.

Pavell, T. J. (1976) 'Possible worlds in literary semantics'. *Journal of Aesthetics and Art Criticism*, 34, 2, 165.

Petofi, J. S. (1975) *Vers une théorie partielle du texte*. Buske, Hamburg.

Petrella, F. (1988) 'Il modello freudiano'. In: Semi, A. A. (Ed.) *Trattato di psicoanalisi, vol. 1: Teoria e tecnica*. Raffaello Cortina, Milan.

Petrella, F. (1993) *Turbamenti affettivi e alterazioni dell'esperienza*. Raffaello Cortina, Milan.

Petrella, F. (2005) Personal communication.

Platinga, A. (1974) *The Nature of Necessity*. Oxford University Press, London.

Propp, V. (1928) *Morphology of the Folktale*. Research Center of Indiana University, Bloomington, IN.

Quinodoz, D. (2003) *Le parole che toccano*. Tr. It. Borla, Rome, 2004.

Quinodoz, J. M. (2003) *I sogni che voltano pagina*. Tr. It. Borla, Rome, 2001.

Renik, O. (1997) 'La soggettività e l'obiettività dell'analista'. *Quaderni di Psicoterapia Infantile*, 39, 109.

Renik, O. (1998) 'The analyst's subjectivity and the analyst's objectivity'. *International Journal of Psychoanalysis*, 79, 487–498.

Renik, O. (1999) 'Play one's card face up in analysis: An approach to the problem of self-disclosure'. *Psychoanalytic Quarterly*, 68, 4, 521–539.

Riolo, F. (1989) 'Teoria delle trasformazioni. Tre seminari su Bion'. *Gruppo e Funzione Analitica*, 2, 7.

Riolo, F. (1998) 'Introduction'. In: Corrao, F. *Orme*. Cortina, Milan.

Rocha Barros, E. (1994) 'A interpreçao: seus presupostos teoricos'. *Rivista de Psicanàlise SPPA*, 1, 3, 57–72.

Rocha Barros, E. (2000) 'Affect and pictographic image: The constitution of meaning in mental life'. *International Journal of Psychoanalysis*, 81, 1087.

Ryan, M. L. (2001) *Narrative as Virtual Reality*. Johns Hopkins University Press, Baltimore.

Sandler, J. (1976) 'Countertransference and role responsiveness'. *International Review of Psychoanalysis*, 3, 43–47.

Schachter, J. (2002) *Transference*. Analytic Press, Hillsdale, NJ.

Semi, A. A. (2003) *Sogno e Storie*. National Congress of the Italian Psychoanalytic Society, Rome.

Smith, H. F. (2000) 'Countertransference, conflictual listening and the analytic object relationship'. *Journal of American Psychoanalytic Association*, 48, 95–128.

Todorov, T. (1971) *Poetica della prosa*. Tr. It. Edizioni Teoria, Rome–Naples, 1989.

Tolstoy, L. (1884) *Avanti popolo*. Tr. It. Edizioni Stampalternativa, Viterbo, 2005.

Van Dijk, T. A. (1976) 'Pragmatics and poetics'. In: *Pragmatics of Language and Literature*. North Holland, Amsterdam.

Viderman, S. (1979) 'The analytic space: meaning and problems'. *Psychoanalytic Quarterly*, 48, 257.

Widlocher, D. (1996) *Les nouvelles cartes de la psychanalyse*. Odile Jacob, Paris. (Tr. It. Borla, Rome, 2004.)

Williams, P. (2001) 'Some difficulties in the analysis of a withdrawn patient'. *International Journal of Psychoanalysis*, 82, 727–746.

Winnicott, D. W. (1971) *Playing and Reality*. Tavistock Publications, London.

Index

211